CAMBRIDGE LIBRARY COLLECTION

Books of enduring scholarly value

Education

This series focuses on educational theory and practice, particularly in the context of eighteenth-and nineteenth-century Europe and its colonies, and America. During this period, the questions of who should be educated, to what age, to what standard and using what curriculum, were widely debated. The reform of schools and universities, the drive towards improving women's education, and the movement for free (or at least low-cost) schools for the poor were all major concerns both for governments and for society at large. The books selected for reissue in this series discuss key issues of their time, including the 'appropriate' levels of instruction for the children of the working classes, the emergence of adult education movements, and proposals for the higher education of women. They also cover topics that still resonate today, such as the nature of education, the role of universities in the diffusion of knowledge, and the involvement of religious groups in establishing and running schools.

Intellectual Education and Its Influence on the Character and Happiness of Women

The Shirreff sisters, Emily (1814–97) and Maria (later Grey; 1816–1906) were pioneers in the field of education for girls in the wider context of women's rights. They jointly wrote the influential Thoughts on Self-Culture, Addressed to Women (1850), and Emily was briefly the principal of the college at Hitchin which became Girton College, Cambridge. The sisters founded the Girls' Public Day School Company in 1872; by 1905 it had opened 37 girls' schools across Britain. This 1862 second edition of Emily's book on intellectual education contains no alterations from the original of 1858. It considers the theory and purpose of education, and the particular issues of its application to girls, before suggesting appropriate curricula (including advice on the care of health and morals) for each age group from seven to eighteen, with a final chapter on life after the classroom and 'some peculiarities of woman's social position'.

Cambridge University Press has long been a pioneer in the reissuing of out-of-print titles from its own backlist, producing digital reprints of books that are still sought after by scholars and students but could not be reprinted economically using traditional technology. The Cambridge Library Collection extends this activity to a wider range of books which are still of importance to researchers and professionals, either for the source material they contain, or as landmarks in the history of their academic discipline.

Drawing from the world-renowned collections in the Cambridge University Library and other partner libraries, and guided by the advice of experts in each subject area, Cambridge University Press is using state-of-the-art scanning machines in its own Printing House to capture the content of each book selected for inclusion. The files are processed to give a consistently clear, crisp image, and the books finished to the high quality standard for which the Press is recognised around the world. The latest print-on-demand technology ensures that the books will remain available indefinitely, and that orders for single or multiple copies can quickly be supplied.

The Cambridge Library Collection brings back to life books of enduring scholarly value (including out-of-copyright works originally issued by other publishers) across a wide range of disciplines in the humanities and social sciences and in science and technology.

Intellectual Education and Its Influence on the Character and Happiness of Women

EMILY SHIRREFF

CAMBRIDGE
UNIVERSITY PRESS

CAMBRIDGE
UNIVERSITY PRESS

University Printing House, Cambridge, CB2 8BS, United Kingdom

Cambridge University Press is part of the University of Cambridge.
It furthers the University's mission by disseminating knowledge in the pursuit of
education, learning and research at the highest international levels of excellence.

www.cambridge.org
Information on this title: www.cambridge.org/9781108084697

© in this compilation Cambridge University Press 2017

This edition first published 1862
This digitally printed version 2017

ISBN 978-1-108-08469-7 Paperback

INTELLECTUAL EDUCATION

AND

ITS INFLUENCE ON THE CHARACTER AND HAPPINESS OF WOMEN.

BY

EMILY SHIRREFF,

ONE OF THE AUTHORS OF "THOUGHTS ON SELF-CULTURE."

A NEW EDITION.

LONDON:

SMITH, ELDER AND CO., 65, CORNHILL.

1862.

PREFACE TO THE SECOND EDITION.

This Second Edition, containing no alterations, would scarcely need the pomp of a Preface, were it not that I gladly take this opportunity of noticing an objection frequently brought against the first, and which, if left unanswered, might seriously affect its chance of being useful to those who perhaps most need its assistance. This objection is, that I require too much, and that my plan of study is an impracticable one. Now, in the first place, with regard to quantity, my demands, both as to time and number of subjects, fall decidedly short of what is practised in the present day in the most approved systems of public education for girls; yet it will surely be allowed that private teaching, when good, ought to accomplish more than class teaching. But waiving this comparison, I would, in the second place, remind the objectors, that any plan of study laid down in a book must be unfit, in some of its details for a large number of those who may attempt to follow it. Too hard for some, it will be too easy for others; yet is there no other way of illustrating a method and giving a clue to its application. All, therefore, that can fairly be demanded of a written system is that it should be *elastic*, that is, apt to be applied to a variety of cases. That such was my purpose, carefully kept in view while unfolding my plan of study, must, I think, be allowed; since not only is it distinctly stated more than once, but I have myself endeavoured to show in what manner modifications might be introduced to suit peculiar dispositions or circumstances. It must also be evident to every candid reader that the *method* of study, not the number of books, is the essential point on which I dwell throughout; and that, in my view, the good or ill success of any education is not to be tested by the variety of acquirement, but by its efficiency in giving to the young creature the full use of its moral and intellectual faculties, wherewith to meet the struggles and difficulties of life. Let those who object to my plan of study accomplish this essential purpose by means of an easier one, and gladly will I give up mine to their criticism. Another way in which people exaggerate the difficulty of what I have proposed is by forgetting that a system is *a whole;* and that, while I believe girls who from twelve years old have been taught according to a given method, will be able at sixteen to read such or such books, I am far indeed from asserting that girls who have been brought up till that age in the prevalent absence of any habits of thought or real study, would be able to read a page of the same books with profit. And this brings me to another objection which I cannot pass over, namely, that my method requires teachers of a stamp not easy to find. This reproach, at least, I am content to endure; for my book will not have been written in vain if it tends to give some additional proof of the necessity for a higher mental standard in those who undertake the task of education ; if it helps to impress on the minds of parents that teaching even, and, far more, the power of forming mind and character, are not things to be expected from every shallow-brained girl who has learnt music and modern languages, instead of acquiring any other mechanical means of earning her bread. Whenever well-instructed thoughtful women shall be found to teach, I believe that what I desire to have taught will be seen not to be above average abilities. At any rate, teachers of that class will know how and when the course should be varied ; for they will have that power which the undisciplined mind never possesses—the power of grasping a principle, and of perceiving its applications and consequences.

London, March, 1862.

TABLE OF CONTENTS.

CHAPTER I.

GENERAL VIEWS.

CHAPTER II.

APPLICATION OF GENERAL PRINCIPLES TO FEMALE EDUCATION.

Section 1.

CHAPTER IV.

EARLY TEACHING.

CHAPTER V.

CHAPTER VI.

CHAPTER VII.

STUDIES AND GENERAL MANAGEMENT FROM SIXTEEN YEARS OF AGE TO EIGHTEEN.

Section 1.

CHAPTER VIII.

SOME PECULIARITIES OF WOMAN'S SOCIAL POSITION.

INTELLECTUAL EDUCATION.

CHAPTER I.

GENERAL VIEWS.

FEW subjects have attracted more attention in the present day than that of education, and on few subjects also has public opinion undergone more change within a comparatively short period. The old prejudices which so long opposed it have been abandoned one by one, and we seem in more danger of looking upon classes and class-books as the panacea for all national evils, than of disputing the universal necessity of education. Discussion now turns on a more perplexed and complicated question, namely, *what* shall the education be? And there is but one way of deciding that point, which is by first establishing what is the ultimate purpose of education. To judge from debates in Parliament, discussions on competitive examinations, plans for popular instruction, &c., we are far enough from having come generally to any clear views on that point.

It is not my purpose to enter into those wide and intricate questions of national education and the results of school and college training, but the tone of opinion prevalent concerning them affects also female education in every class. The same errors which there give rise to such interminable disputes clog our progress also, and make mental cultivation among women a question of fashion or individual taste.*

---

* The opinions advocated in the present work, and especially the general principles of education which are considered in this and the following chapter, have already been set forth and explained in their reference to woman's life and influence in a former work—*Thoughts on Self-Culture, addressed to Women*, by MARIA GREY and EMILY SHIRREFF. I trust, however, that the different scope and purpose of my present undertaking may cause a partial return over the same ground, and save me from the charge of mere repetition. We then addressed ourselves to young girls, with a view of assisting them in their attempts at self-improvement; I now address mothers wishing to undertake the education of their daughters, and often too young and inexperienced, and too carelessly educated themselves, to know the full extent of the task before them. But in both works alike it was necessary to start from those same principles which lie at the foundation of all education deserving of the name.

1

The source of these errors I believe to be the habit of looking upon intellectual education as simply the means of imparting knowledge, without inquiring whether it has not also a work to perform in disciplining the mind, in impressing on it those habits and tendencies which in youth the half-developed nature is docile to receive, and which give to the man the full command of his faculties for whatever future labour he may undertake. Perhaps a glance at some points in the history of intellectual education in modern times may enable us to perceive how this view was obscured even while more and more attention was given to the subject generally.

What were the views of education held by those great men who, in the first dawn of modern civilization, established the system of university studies, it is difficult now to determine. The question was very simple then compared to what it has become since. During many ages learning consisted solely in the knowledge of what the Greeks and Latins had done before us, and of the theology of the Fathers. There could be no doubt, then, that this information was indispensable to every man pretending to education. But as time went on the boundaries of knowledge enlarged more and more. Modern languages and literatures sprang up by the side of those ancient languages to which men had so long devoted all their energies as to the sole depositaries of science and philosophy. Physical science began to rear its giant growth, and drew off the minds of multitudes from the old paths of scholastic learning. The relations of society became more numerous and complicated. New interests, distant undertakings, and far-reaching commerce, gave an extension to political science and jurisprudence which rendered necessary an amount of information undreamed of in earlier times; while the accumulation of wealth, the immense increase of population, the spread of luxury, made life a fierce competition to all who could not afford idleness, and men felt more and more that their success must depend on the activity of their brains and on the available resources of their knowledge.

One consequence of these great changes was a disposition to examine the old uniform system of education, and to ask whether it could still be considered fit for times of progress. And here the error began under whose evil influence we are still labouring—error, not in proposing the question, but in the method of considering it. The public mind, newly awakened to the value of knowledge, cared little about *principles of education*. The inquiry into the value of the established systems was solely directed to the obvious results of book knowledge attained at a given age; and that was manifestly inadequate to the exigencies of modern life.

In vain did men well versed in the subject dwell upon the proper office of education in drawing forth the full capabilities of the human creature, rather than in fitting him for some peculiar calling; the so-called practical man wanted fruit in seed-time, the necessities of life gave plausibility to the outcry, and popular clamour seemed to be fighting the battle of knowledge against schools and universities. From the contempt for principles, want of purpose and method in the details naturally followed. With one set of persons physical science was the great object, with another modern languages were all important; one class objected to the study of mathematics, another thought the classical languages useless; nor, in the absence of any presiding idea, is it possible that this confusion should cease. Dr. Donaldson justly remarks that ' the causes of all the unprofitable discussions which have arisen respecting the utility of particular branches of study are to be sought in the vague and erroneous manner in which we use the terms education, information, knowledge. We are in the habit of speaking of mere information as if it were exact knowledge, and we still more frequently allow special or professional knowledge to assume the honours which are due to general education.' Further on he continues, ' We must distinguish between education, properly so called, and professional training. The former is designed for the cultivation of the intellect and the development of the reasoning faculties; the latter is intended to adapt a man for some particular calling, which the laws of society and the principle of the division of labour have assigned to him as an individual member of the body politic. Now the training of the individual for this particular purpose is not an education of man as such. . . . . It was for this reason that the clear-headed Greeks denied the name of education (παιδεία) to that which is learned, not for its own sake, but for the sake of some extrinsic gain, or for the sake of some work, and distinguished formally between those studies which they called liberal or worthy of a free man, and those which are merely mechanical or professional. In the same way Cicero speaks of education properly so called, which he names humanity (humanitas), because its object is to give a full development to those reasoning faculties which are the proper and distinctive attributes of man as such. (See Cicero Pro Archia Poeta, i. De Oratore, i. 9. Aul. Gellius, xiii. 16.) . . . . The test of a good education is the degree of mental culture it imparts; for education, so far as it is scientific, is the discipline of the mind.'*

---

* Dr. Donaldson's *New Cratylus*. Introduction, p. 6. 2nd Edition.

It is not that a formal preference has always been given to the professional over the liberal education, but the extreme anxiety for *useful*, in other words, for directly practical knowledge with reference to the mode of life to which individuals were destined, sufficiently indicates that the distinct objects of the two educations have been confounded in the public mind. And it is this error which has vitiated our views of popular education, and of the education of women, and introduced disorder into both. Fortunately, however, this very confusion leads to the detection of the error, for by showing us a false theory pushed to its consequences it enables us to ascertain its weak points.

So long as the education of boys belonging to the upper and middle classes of society was alone under consideration, the mistaken method of viewing the subject might easily pass unobserved by all who were not accustomed to look somewhat deeply into these questions, and for this reason, that knowledge which was erroneously made the test of their education was really of great practical importance to them. Though we ought to be content that the boy should know little if he have acquired the power of learning much, yet the learning sooner or later cannot be dispensed with. It is required by the whole business of life, and we cannot wonder, when so high a market value attaches to knowledge, that it should be forgotten that education has other duties than to impart it. But when the subject began to be considered with reference to a wider range of persons, the omission became evident. When women, for instance, began to seek education, and when that of the people became a political necessity, the question incessantly repeated was, ' What can be the use of such or such knowledge to them? what will they want with this or that for their domestic avocations, or their lives of constant labour?' To this question there was no answer, according to the ordinary views, and consequently the limits of popular education are yearly discussed, with every variety of opinion concerning the immediate practical value of what is taught, while women's education fluctuates without any principle at all, according to the fashion of the day.

The reason is evident. Knowledge *has no* practical value, using those words in the sense commonly attached to them, of *money value*, to women, or to men tied down to manual labour. To the latter, indeed, it may afford a hope of escaping from such labour to a higher sphere of employment; but to women it holds out no worldly inducement whatever. So long, therefore, as education is tested by the amount of knowledge acquired at a certain age, and needed for certain immediate purposes, female education may be tolerated as a harmless fashion, but it has no real purpose or importance.

But if, when those great questions of school and university teaching were first mooted, another method had been followed; if, instead of asking simply, 'What is taught—how much knowledge does this system impart?' the question had been, 'Why is it taught?—to what does it fashion the young minds subjected to its influence?'—the result would, I conceive, have been very different. The old system might or might not have been condemned; but assuredly some definite principles would have been laid down for the new.

Now, the fundamental truth to start from appears to me to be this—that education, apart from all secondary objects (that is, all objects which have reference to peculiar circumstances or positions), has one and the same purpose for every human being; and this purpose is the systematic and harmonious development of his whole moral and intellectual nature. It follows that the elementary principles must be the same for all. The *means* necessarily vary according to circumstances, position, and the spirit of the times. The exigencies of life may force us to leave the work incomplete; but the foundation must be the same, the aim alike in every case. The human creature, whether man or woman, a peasant or a prince, is born with the germ of certain faculties—capable in some degree of moral feeling, of responsibility, of forethought, of reason, of judgment—and it is the business of education to train those faculties for use. We know no other way of doing this than by exercising them in the guidance of conduct and the acquisition of knowledge, thus facilitating their action by the power of habit. It is a wholly separate—I might almost say an irrelevant—question, how far the knowledge acquired in the course of educational study will be available hereafter. That *cui-bono* cry, which an eminent man of the present day has denounced as the bane of the philosopher who seeks knowledge for its own sake, is the true touchstone by which we may discern whether the fundamental principles of education are understood or not.

It is, then, because those principles have been neglected in the eagerness for profitable knowledge, that we are still halting between different systems of school and university teaching; and that, neither for women nor for the working-classes, is it possible to establish any system at all. There is a strong feeling that the poor ought to be educated, but why, and how far, remains yet to be settled. If we argue upon grounds of mere worldly utility, we never can get rid of petty squabbles as to the amount of arithmetic, grammar, or history, which may or may not turn out to be profitable to them; and it must ever remain an open question whether industrial schools are not better than those of a more intellectual character. But if we take our stand upon the ground that the human being remains a mutilated creature if the capacities of his mind are left dormant, or if, when awakened by circumstances, he has no command over them, then it becomes at once apparent that every study which tends to exercise those powers is useful in the highest sense of the word, and that the only limitations to this mental discipline and to the knowledge which it is good for all human beings to acquire are those imposed by time and means. The education of women has no firm standing on any other grounds. Fashion and custom may make certain acquirements *desirable*, but the *necessity and consequent duty* of education lies in that broad principle alone. The same of course holds good for men of the higher classes also; but it is more easily lost sight of, owing to the practical necessity in this case of acquiring knowledge, so that the *cui-bono* cry gets at least a plausible and intelligible answer.

Men having thus put out of sight what we may call the true human purpose of education, two great evils followed. First: *The necessary connexion between moral and intellectual cultivation has been forgotten, or lost sight of*, and the development therefore has been one-sided. Secondly: The external, or money-value, of knowledge increasing day by day, its intrinsic worth and beauty has been obscured, and thus *the love of truth has kept no pace with the progress of knowledge.*

The systematic and harmonious development of the moral and intellectual nature is, as I have stated above, the business of education; but where this truth is unrecognized, or forgotten, the want of a definite purpose entails want of system and harmony. Accordingly, nothing is more remarkable than the absence of harmony or completeness in modern education. The defect is conspicuous alike in that of both sexes; but the mal-proportions differ, and indeed are generally reversed. Intellectual training, for instance, which is acknowledged to be necessary for boys, engrosses the larger share of attention in their education, while their moral development is almost unheeded, left to 'the reproof of chance' and the influence of circumstances. On the other hand, with girls, intellectual cultivation having no distinct purpose, is regulated by caprice or the fashion of the day; but their moral training is conscientiously cared for, and being often admirable in intention, at least, it produces as much fruit as can be expected when it is coupled with narrow views and undisciplined intellects. In both cases the defect is the same—namely, ignorance or forgetfulness of the necessary action and reaction upon each other of intellectual and moral culture, producing an unnatural divorce between the life of the intellect and the life of action and feeling. The origin of the defect is also the same in both cases. So long as it is supposed that we can, with impunity, choose between our intellectual and moral faculties, and neglect that form of culture which seems least essential to our worldly position and objects, education must remain a mere question of ambition, of fashion, or of policy, into which principle cannot enter. The course that has been pursued is perfectly consistent with this view.

It is because the subject is less encumbered with extraneous considerations when the working-classes are in question, that it is useful to study it in that aspect. We are forced there to go to the foundation of the matter, or give it up altogether. Neither fashion nor ambition comes in to obscure it, and it then becomes apparent that every argument which is brought against *over-educating* (as it is termed) the classes destined to manual labour tells equally against giving knowledge to women; the two things must be defended upon the same principles, and it is from the tone of the defence that we are made to perceive that the principles are misapprehended. Examine any of the many debates on national education, and what do we find? Long discussions about the use boys or girls will be able to make of this or that piece of knowledge; what they will want with geography while working in a factory; how grammar will help them to plough or make shoes, &c. Are not questions of the same kind raised with regard to giving women any knowledge beyond the circle mere routine has sanctioned? The notion that cultivated intelligence will affect character and the general tone of mind, and therefore the capacity for whatever task the future may bring, is equally left out of sight in both cases.

Moral culture is indeed nominally acknowledged to be necessary for all; but as it is at the same time generally considered to be synonymous with religious teaching, it is either neglected in school education as belonging to the province of the religious teacher of each sect, or else the religious teaching, in which it is supposed to be included, is made the groundwork of the whole system: in either case it is separated from intellectual discipline. The effect of this mode of viewing morals and religion has been to diminish their influence on the minds of men who are engrossed with practical interests; the effect on women, as on the working-classes, has been to lessen the value for mental culture, to make it appear at least a thing apart from all the real duties of the spiritual being. And thus, in proportion as moral education was considered alone important, it lost vigour and consistency.

In early childhood, moral training is almost entirely a matter of feeling and association. It depends on the home influences, whatever they may be, and is therefore the conscious or unconscious work of the parents, and especially of the mother, long before one word of precept or of dogma can be understood. Later, when it becomes also a matter for the understanding, it depends much upon the degree of cultivation which that understanding has received. The same dogmas and the same precepts are taught to all; their reception, and the fruit they will bear, must vary in each individual according to his power of understanding them, of seeing their full scope, of scanning their remote bearings, and of applying their general principles to the particular circumstances of his own case. The mere desire to do right, to live morally and religiously, though it may acquit the individual conscience, will not supply the place of sound judgment in discerning real good from specious evil, of foresight, or of reflection, on which depends our power of learning wisdom from experience. Whoever studies the life of the labouring classes, can hardly fail to acknowledge that their sufferings and their vices are in a very great measure owing to their ignorance and want of forethought. Here, then, we see the necessity of mental discipline, which opens up the resources of knowledge, and gives to the mind the habit of looking to something beyond the necessities of the present hour.

And whoever will in like manner examine the lives of women, will see that most of their faults and their follies, and much of the suffering they endure, as well as of the evils that result to society, spring from the same source—namely, from the ignorance which leaves them a prey to frivolity or *ennui;* to the mental feebleness which prevents their appreciating their position, with its duties, advantages, and difficulties; and which exposes them to become the victims of enthusiasts, quacks, or hypocrites, under various garbs. The remedy is the same in both cases— knowledge and mental discipline, which will give new vigour to the moral nature.

The moral cultivation of women is due almost exclusively to religious feeling; philosophically they are in general as indifferent to moral as to metaphysical speculation. If the Scriptures were really studied, a far wider system might be gathered from their teaching. Worldly knowledge and the saddest worldly wisdom have been recorded in many of its pages ; while the expansive nature of the spiritual principles of the New Testament is one of the characteristic points which most peculiarly marks its superiority over all other religious systems. But these things are not discerned by those who are guided by feeling only, nor by those whose 'impious diffidence,' as Bacon calls it, makes them think they do honour to the Scriptures by refusing the aid of other knowledge to interpret them. To the majority of minds the morals of religion are essentially narrow, seldom rising from individual to social considerations, or they are confined at best within a circle which is far from commensurate with the many duties and multiplied relations of life. The utmost individual purity and uprightness, aided by the truest religious feeling, will not save us from doing mischief amid the complicated conditions of our social existence—from exercising a wrong influence, or failing to exercise a right one—unless the mind, purified by religion, has been strengthened by the exercise of thought and judgment, and has acquired by patient labour and study the means of judging rightly. This fact would seem too obvious to need discussion, if the division still maintained in education between moral and religious training on the one hand, and intellectual exercise on the other, did not prove that the former is still expected to be a sufficient preparation for life, for all who do not require to use their intellect for some direct purpose of worldly advancement. It will be admitted that truly excellent persons are ill-judging and narrow-minded, and therefore liable to do all the mischief to society that follows from ignorance and prejudice; but it is not yet generally acknowledged that the only remedy is the early discipline of the intellect—the early formation of those habits of mind by which we become accustomed to compare, to reason, to judge, to act upon system. This discipline can in ordinary life be carried on only by means of carefully-directed studies. The actual subject studied may have little or no bearing on the actual life of the individual; but the mental toil is strengthening the mind for whatever it may find hereafter to do. It is breaking in the faculties to habits which are essential to all future operations, whether practical or intellectual.*

---

* Tout est lié dans les dispositions morales et dans les habitudes de l'homme. Un travail qui met de l'ordre dans les idées prépare à l'ordre dans la conduite. L'exercice de l'attention la fortifie, et par elle le jugement et la mémoire, les deux facultés les plus essentielles dans les affaires de la vie.—*Bibliothèque Universelle.* Quoted by Mrs. Marcet, in *Conversations on Political Economy,* p. 147. 7th Edition.

Had this connexion between moral and intellectual culture been generally remembered, they would have stood or fallen together. But when moral training is regarded as synonymous with religion, and religion with theology, all that mental discipline which would have braced the moral system, which would have given breadth and clearness of views and strength of conviction, is left out. Whenever such discipline shall be generally held to be necessary in this respect—when it shall be clearly and generally perceived that judgment, prudence, and systematic action, the things we value most in daily life, result from it—and when higher views of morals and religion shall have proved that it is a duty as well as a privilege to every creature born to the inheritance of immortality to cultivate all the powers God has given, and to cherish the love of truth in every form; whenever these things shall be acknowledged, then, and not till then, there will be an end of all disputes, and confusions, and difficulties which still encumber the education of all who do not need to use their intelligence for some end of profit or of ambition. Differences of opinion will always remain about the means and the details, but concerning the general method and purpose of the whole there will be none. Circumstances will confine the education of the majority within very narrow limits, but contentions about an arbitrary limit in any case will be set at rest for ever.

The second evil which I mentioned as resulting from the misconception of the true purpose of education, was that the money-value of knowledge had usurped the first place, and put out of sight its true worth and claims to be sought and loved for its own sake. Female education affords a lamentable illustration of this fact. Women have no worldly use for knowledge; accordingly it has been thought superfluous to give them any. The prejudice that made it seem unfeminine has passed away in great measure; but that we owe the change to fashion more than to principle may be seen by the course pursued in education. Even now, if women really loving knowledge are led to seek it in any unusual channels, they have often more difficulty in giving a plausible aspect to their conduct than had they been led away by the most frivolous folly. I think it must be acknowledged, for instance, that a woman would find it harder to explain her motives, and to procure a patient hearing for them, if she wished to spend fifty pounds in making a geological tour, than if she proposed to throw away twice or three times that sum in attending a series of fêtes at Paris or Vienna.

In justification of women, however, we must be allowed to remark, that the low appreciation of the value of knowledge is by no means a mere female error. It does not originate with women; they have only acted upon the principle which they have seen governing the world. Men who are not *forced* to acquire knowledge too generally spend their leisure quite as frivolously, and far more blameably, than women. The follies of the latter are on a small scale, and treated with a laugh as they deserve; but the follies of the former are on a magnificent scale, and we do not venture to laugh at what breaks down the fortunes of families and interrupts the business of nations. Women are without any external motive to intellectual exertion, but no man is without the stimulus of honourable ambition, if he is capable of feeling it. Those who throw away their lives in sporting, in yachting, or in any other form of idle pleasure, do it in contempt of advantages which rarely, or never, are placed within the reach of women. They have had the same education which has ripened the finest intellects in the country, and they cherish ignorance; they have a noble sphere of action, whether for private or public usefulness, and they prefer to grovel in idleness; no conventional barriers restrain their pursuit of knowledge; libraries, public institutions, the society of the learned, the whole range of the world, is open to them; and they prefer a kennel, or a race-course, or haunts more ignoble still, where they may parade their degradation in every capital throughout Europe.

There is great unfairness in comparing the use women make of their time and faculties with that of the great working body of men. Their circumstances are too different to allow of any parallel. Women can fairly be compared in these respects to men of leisure only; and many as are the bright exceptions among them to the miserable folly alluded to above, and great as the service is which such men have done to their country and to mankind by noble labour in many fields, it is but just to remember how many motives appeal to them which do not exist for women. Though exempt from necessary toil, some find pleasure in an active career; some love its mere importance; others value the power; some covet mere distinction; some few behold 'Fame's starry crown,' and though it shines over their grave alone, they are content to strive for it, if while they perish they leave the mark of their genius upon their generation. And so, spurred on by motives great and small, men strive, and labour, and hope. But not so with us. Our striving must be in silent obscurity; our labour compensated by no public triumph; our hope rest on no worldly reward. We may watch with interest and sympathy the career of active and ambitious men, but those whom we must strive to imitate are the loftier spirits who have toiled for Truth alone; who, when they have given forth the fruit of their labour to benefit their fellow-creatures, have forgotten the glory in the earnestness of their pursuit—men who have felt that in the discovery of truth was an intensity of enjoyment beyond any reward their labour could bring.   These are the masters and teachers whose example may be of use to woman in her humble sphere, excluded as she is by the conditions of her lot from the paths they disdain to follow; teaching her, like them, to rise above the views that make those paths most alluring to the vulgar herd.

Indifference to knowledge, except as a marketable commodity, naturally makes leisure appear synonymous with idleness.   The absence of a compulsory task to perform makes it appear that there is *nothing to do.* From this confusion, so indicative of a low state of public feeling on the subject, springs an overweening value for professional occupations, not only with those who look to the profit alone, but with those who justly look upon the existence of a large *idle* class as a pest to society.

The work of the world must be done, the vast and complicated machinery we call society must be kept in action; and we do right to honour those who toil usefully and uprightly at this task, and still more those who bring high purpose and keen intellect to the labour.   The error begins when we honour this toil above that of the studious searcher after knowledge; when we think that the career to which a man is bound by hopes of gain or ambition ranks higher than that of him who is content to 'scorn delights and live laborious days,' without any other hope than that of getting some nearer glimpse of truth, to whom the world's noisy interests are as nothing, because he is dwelling in the contemplation of Eternal order and beauty.   When I say the course of such a man is looked down upon with contemptuous or quiet pity, while that of the other is applauded and envied, we only give a melancholy proof of how far the worship of Mammon has dimmed our spiritual perceptions, how the cravings of the body have silenced the 'still small voice' that speaks from God's wide creation to His noblest work—the soul of man; how utterly the music of the spheres is lost to us amidst the noisy babblings of the market-place.

What are the motives that lead men into professions?   In general the necessity of working for a subsistence, or at best the desire of increasing a small independent income.   Some professions lead to distinction in public life, and these are sought with less regard to money; there is also a strange feeling that a man 'has nothing to do' unless he is professionally employed, and thus men who might live independently go to increase the throng and competition in every path of public life, merely because they dare not trust themselves with the disposal of their own time; while others are made to feel that unless landed property gives them a distinct and recognized occupation, or at any rate an acknowledged exemption from any other, society will look down upon them as useless drones if they are content with following their own pursuits, and spreading the influence of refined habits and tastes, and the tone of a cultivated mind, through a private circle. The same views make parents prefer tying down the heir to their wealth to any professional drudgery sooner than expose him to the perils of leisure, unless political life opens a wide field to his ambition. I do not wish to undervalue this system; it works in many respects most beneficially for society; and when we compare England with other countries where men do not go into any professions but the military, unless driven by absolute poverty, we may well rejoice that such a custom should prevail among us, at least till a different tone of education has taught men that life is not a holiday, though it be not spent at school. But while we recognize the uses of the system, let us not praise it for more than it is worth; jails are necessary to the welfare of society, but let us not wreath the treadmill with laurels, nor forget that the noblest minds are those which need no outward restraint, no spur to exertion, no golden chain to bind them to a course of social duty and usefulness.

It is a sad thing to reflect how many men fit for better things are driven by real necessity into professions, and instead of taking rank among the enlighteners of mankind, 'fall into that gulf in which many of the world's greatest geniuses lie buried—professional eminence.' * But sadder still is it to see that those to whom all the noble unremunerated labour of the world ought to fall can find nothing to do to save them from mischief but to compete with others for rewards of which they should be independent.

It is the remark of a man actively engaged himself in professional labour, that 'the happiest men in existence, *sua si bona nôrint*, are persons engaged in literature or science as an employment.'† 'The active operations of the intellect do not,' says the same writer, 'depend for success, or gratification upon success, in the pursuit of their object; their labours are

---

* BURTON : *Life of Hume*, vol. i. p. 28.
† *Elements of the Pathology of the Human Mind.* By Dr. THOMAS MAYO, p. 42.

their reward.' And the most privileged of men are those who have
leisure for such happiness and faculty to feel it. Inevitable as all the toil
of the world undoubtedly is, how can it fail to strike every reflecting
mind that the labour is for the *means of living* only. We must have food,
and shelter, and clothing, and live as others our equals live; and we must
be protected from the vicious and saved from the folly of the ignorant;
and as the task becomes harder and harder in the fierce competition of
increasing numbers, intellect must combine means hitherto unthought of,
extort from Nature her hidden secrets, and bend the elements themselves
to aid the industry of man. But still the greatest part of this vast and
magnificent labour is to satisfy the wants of our bodily life only; it is
the preparation of the means of living as much as the Indian hunter's toil
when he has brought down his game, and lighted the fire under his forest-
hut. And when does the real life begin? To each one of us real life is in
those hours, be they few or many, when we are free to give ourselves up
to the enjoyment of our affections, or when we 'commune with God and
are still,' reading His laws impressed on the universe, and on our own
spiritual being; when, though we may not 'shuffle off this mortal coil,'
we lay aside for a time its poor wants and cares, its passions and desires,
and have leisure to feel the craving after truth, the perception of the
beautiful, the love of the purely good and great, which give our souls an
earnest of immortality.

It is true that He who gave us these glorious aspirations gave also the
bodily wants and delights, and appointed the necessity of labour as the
school without which few would train their nobler powers; but all that
looks to earthly life is stamped as perishable. 'Passing away' is the one
unvarying character in a world of change; while, on the contrary, those
higher aspirations are changeless and undying, never satiated, growing by
the contemplations they feed on, they point to a life beyond, with a conviction to many minds above the force of proof.

Thought and affection: these are life. The more we have leisure and
power to cherish them, the more during our span of years we may be
said really to live, instead of lingering among the preparations for life.
How, then, can we venture to think lightly of the leisure which is not
tied down to a money-seeking labour—*leisure to live?* Some professions
call forth a great deal of thought and speculation, or force a considerable
amount of knowledge, valuable in itself, and in the pursuit of which the
highest faculties are exercised. In proportion as it is so, professional
labour approaches to the dignity of independent philosophic pursuits; for

there is nothing in receiving payment for toil which can lessen the worth of the latter; the sordid view is that which considers its worth stamped by the payment. If we own how few are worthy of leisure, then we value the forced occupations on the right grounds—namely, as saving men, in one sense, from themselves—in rescuing ordinary minds from the many chances of deterioration that would attend their being left to self-regulation. All men are not fit to be 'a law unto themselves;' and so with pursuits—all men are not capable of loving knowledge for its own sake, and of making continual exertion without the hope of some positive and tangible reward. And it is well for society that such differences should exist; the only important point in considering them is to assign to them their proper rank.

In education, especially, any mistake on this point introduces great confusion, and from such confusion we have hitherto suffered. For if professional pursuits are in themselves intrinsically the most valuable, according to the rewards they lead to, then professional education is the most important part of the training of the man ; and those are right who reject the ancient notion of a *liberal* education which aimed at putting the man in possession of his faculties, trained for any purpose to which he might choose to apply them, in favour of the education which teaches certain branches of learning, with a view to their practical use in the calling to which he intends to devote himself. According to this view, the lower classes require none but the slightest tincture of education, for even reading and writing often rise beyond their wants; men of property require little education, unless they are ambitious of distinction in public life ; and women need as little, or even less, for the care of children, their one positive occupation, besides household matters, requires little knowledge.

But when we take the opposite view, and look rather at the human creature than at his actual business in the world; when we see that the great value of professional occupation to the majority of minds is to save them from the responsibility of that leisure they are not fit to make a worthy use of, then education appears in a new light; then we value most that which fits the man to regulate his own life ; we look to the human being with all his rich endowments, and that gift of time to dispose of, rather than to *society's workman*, ever toiling at a task, and not knowing what to do with his own life when compulsion ceases. A necessary inference from this view also is, that those who inevitably possess leisure require, not less, but more education, and of a higher and more severe cast than those who will be kept at school, in some measure, all their lives by the enforced labour of a profession.

Now those to whom this precious but perilous possession inevitably falls are the comparatively small number of men of fortune, and the whole mass of women of the upper and middle classes; for even in the latter, unless where the cares of a large family engross every hour, there is a fearful amount of leisure which too often leaves their uncultivated minds a prey to *ennui*, or to gossip and folly. If education do not infuse into persons so situated, whatever their means or position, that high tone of thought and those mental habits which lead to worthy pursuits without the spur of necessity, it is evident that they must sink far below the average of those who are forced to toil for a distinct purpose. And not only will this individual deterioration be the result of misused leisure, but their collective social influence will be bad instead of good. It will go to increase frivolity, and to strengthen false views both of life and of the value of knowledge.

In this country, where the struggle for existence is so fierce, where every weapon of successful competition is so valuable, men need perpetually to be reminded that the human intellect, and the knowledge it is able to aspire to and to grasp, are of more worth in themselves than all the worldly purposes for which they are put to daily vulgar use. And how shall they be reminded of this except by the example of those who, owing to gifts of fortune or natural condition, are able to stand aloof from the contest.

Dr. Mayo, after the passage before quoted on the happiness that may be found in intellectual exertion, laments that this source of happiness should be so rarely appreciated. 'The reason of this,' he says, 'is probably to be found in the extensive tendency of those who conduct the education of our youth to encourage ambition as the principal motive for those exertions. How can that boy learn to value the luxuries of science or literature who is only taught to appreciate them as a means of gaining applause?' *

Thus Dr. Whewell also, in his remarks on university education, laments the absence of any right spirit on these points. 'It might appear,' he says, 'as if our countrymen were too practical to love knowledge and speculation for its own sake, and to bestow time and systematic thought upon it, except it lead to something of profit or distinction.'

---

* *Elements of the Pathology of the Human Mind*, p. 42.

Further on he says,—'It is certain that the great body of young Englishmen, during their residence at the universities, will never, till their characters and dispositions have undergone a material change, derive any great portion of their education from their voluntary attendance on the public lectures of the university. They bring to the university *no tastes, no ambition, no preparation* which lead them to follow the speculations thus placed before them.'* And who must we blame for this sluggishness of intellect that ever needs a spur or a bribe to make it reach forth its strength? Who but those who in favoured positions have by their low example strengthened the belief that the practical, the so-called useful in the materialistic sense of that much abused word, was the highest thing man should aim at? If youths come to college so destitute of high aspirations and generous ambition, who are we to accuse? In general, the whole tone of society; and in each individual case, the parents. The father, too much immersed in business to have leisure for thought, or too much engrossed with pleasure or given up to mere indolence to be capable of thought; and the mother, with whom, whatever the father's position, rests the spiritual training of her child, that is, all of education which belongs to sentiment and motive, and must be *inspired* not taught.

But how should mothers inspire their sons with earnest love of knowledge—in other words, with the aspiration towards all that is true and beautiful—if they have never felt what they are called upon to impart? if they have never been roused from the torpor of a vacant unthinking existence to feel the grandeur and the worth of those pursuits which awaken the sense of the Godlike in man's intellect, so magnificent in its reach, so glorious in its triumphs? It is not great knowledge nor extensive powers that are required to be able to feel this. It is sufficient to be free from littleness—to have that nice sense of the proportions and due relations of things which belong to a well balanced mind—which enables it to feel the grandeur and beauty of what its understanding cannot fathom, and saves it from that common error of little minds, mistaking their own garden for the universe.

In a former work † I have taken my part in striving to enforce these views upon women, and to point out how, in this as in many other instances, they are the natural guardians of man's highest interests. Every tender thought, every lofty emotion, every generous sentiment

* WHEWELL on *University Education*, pp. 67 and 69.
† *Thoughts on Self-Culture*, chap. xii. Second edition. London: J. Petheram, 94, High Holborn.

2

that men may be in danger of forgetting in the clash and tumult of the world, should be shrined in the hearts of women, and thence go forth to purify and sustain and resist the lowering tendencies of active life. And against none is this aid more required than against the perversion of knowledge to be the mere servant of Mammon. Men will always love and value it sufficiently under that aspect; that which adds daily to our comforts and profits and pleasure will not fail to be honoured, but we may hope to see it reverenced in a higher spirit when that reverence shall become part of the home-creed of childhood—part of that spiritual nurture which the child receives from her who moulds his feelings and associations by the influence of hourly example and boundless love.

While men take the mere ambitious view of education, and women value certain acquirements for the sake of fashion only, a fearful amount of frivolity may co-exist with a great deal of information and intelligence ; but this will hardly be the case when women shall be so educated as to feel the true worth of knowledge, the true value of a serene region of earnest interest and delight in the midst of all the misleading and lowering influences of the world, and to uphold this feeling in society. Compared with two generations ago, there is in the present day an immense increase of information, and therefore, perhaps, a generally quicker intelligence and power of apprehension. Minds accustomed to know even the roughest outline of a variety of subjects, and to understand a great variety of terms, will more readily seize new knowledge when presented to them than minds more limited in their experience. But is there, with this increased information, any corresponding decrease of frivolity among us ? I fear not. The greater range of amusements, and the easier rate at which they may be enjoyed, rather tend perhaps to foster a frivolous tone; or, at least, that love of pleasure and distaste for quiet home-enjoyment which belong to the frivolous. People may follow the crowd to a lecture-room as to an assembly, and may know and use correctly many scientific terms where formerly they would never have attended to such subjects at all. But if they have only followed the crowd, and such is the case too often, there is no reason to expect that they should be less frivolous than before. It is not the occupation of an hour, but the intention of the mind, that influences character ; and, till we read or attend lectures—not for fashion's sake, nor for talk, nor to appear instructed, nor to get rid of time, but with a simple and earnest desire to *know*—not till then will the practice affect the tone of thought or daily habits. We may safely assert, that if real value for mental pursuits were at all proportionate to the spread of mere information, the life now led by a large proportion of the wealthy classes of society would become an impossibility. There would be no occasion to denounce or laugh at it; the system itself must fall before the wide and earnest views of life which would then govern the majority of educated minds. To those who, either removed themselves from that life of pleasure-seeking and frivolous excitement, or, pausing now and then as its course slackens or the heart wearies with its emptiness, have leisure to contemplate its social and domestic effects, it needs no argument to prove how great would be the benefit of such a change. Equal benefit would result to the listless lives of women who cannot afford, or by position or habits do not incline to join, the race of amusement; since the earnest pursuit which would sober the pleasure-seekers would become a fresh source of vitality to those who have neither pleasure nor business to rouse them.

I shall have occasion later to enter more fully into this part of the subject, for the suffering of women from the want of animating pursuit is of too serious importance not to be carefully considered in their education; here I have only touched upon it as one of the many reasons which make it needful that in educating girls we should aim not at this or that form of acquirement, but at making love of knowledge for its own sake the very spring of their intellectual life, and giving habits of mental exertion which shall help to counteract the many dangers of leisure and the narrowing tendencies of small cares and occupations amidst which women must unavoidably live.

The very fact that women have no professions to exercise their abilities, or make them feel the need of knowledge, which has been the plea for giving them little or no solid mental cultivation, is then in truth, as I said above, the reason why they need a higher and more severe tone of education; since, unless we would allow their faculties to be wasted both to themselves and society, they must be educated to feel from within what comes to the more active portion of mankind from without. They must be educated to feel the constant necessity of self-improvement and their responsibility as members of society, although not sharing in its active labours. It is not indeed difficult to show how many of woman's home duties, both as wife and mother, would be far better discharged by more cultivated minds, and how far her sphere of enjoyment and influence is increased by extending to man's intellectual life the power of sympathy she exercises so strongly within the range of feelings and affections; but it is not sufficient to rest the plea for female education even on such

2—2

grounds as these. In educating a young girl we must feel that her future is too uncertain, too much beyond her own control, to venture to train her altogether for a position that may never be hers. The only safe course is to hold up individual perfectness, as far as such a term may be used, as the aim of education; in other words, the harmonious development of all her powers as her own individual right and duty; to train her, in short, as God's creature, not as man's subordinate. The subordination itself, so far as it is God's law, will be all the more clearly perceived and understood the more the mind is rendered capable of studying and comprehending other general laws of nature; for it were truly a dangerous satire upon man's supremacy to allow that it expects to be acknowledged only so long as women are feeble-minded and ignorant.

CHAPTER II.

APPLICATION OF GENERAL PRINCIPLES TO FEMALE EDUCATION.

§ 1.—In the last chapter I have attempted to examine some of the causes which have led to mistaken views of education generally; to errors which have assumed different forms as exhibited in the education of men and women of the upper and lower classes of society, but which, springing from the same origin, can be corrected only by the same return to fundamental principles.

Two errors appeared to lay at the root of the many mistakes and confusions into which the world has fallen upon this subject. *First:* the severance of intellectual from moral and religious culture, not perceiving the necessary bearing of the former on the latter, from which error sprang the neglect of mental cultivation by those who did not need it for some worldly purpose, and the too frequent neglect of moral discipline by the intellectually active. *Secondly:* that mental cultivation and the pursuit of knowledge being thus considered as mere instruments of worldly advancement, their real value has been slighted; they have been taken up for fashion's sake, or as a means of getting rid of time; practical and professional pursuits have risen to undue estimation, while those who had it most in their power to set a high example and to influence society, have favoured frivolity by misusing leisure. Thus, while the feeling that compulsory money-getting operations are the only real

business of life is encouraged, it follows that those who are exempt from
such compulsions may be idle and uninstructed if they please.

As we examined the subject more closely it became evident that
women are the principal sufferers from this grievous misapprehension of
the real worth and use of the human intellect; since, if consistently acted
upon, it would confine them entirely to the sphere of household occupations, which, in the majority of cases among the classes exempt from
manual labour, would not be sufficient to fill up their time or save them
from the familiar demon of the idle—*ennui*. We must now consider more
fully how these views bear on female education, and what, according to
sounder principles, ought to be the course of the latter.

One mischievous result of the neglect of mental discipline, when not
required for worldly ends, is that female education, which, as a general
rule, can have no such ends in view, has been regarded as a comparatively
light and easy matter. Men of intellect and high worth have been placed
at the head of public schools and colleges. The subject of education and
of tuition itself, with reference to boys, has always been considered worthy
to occupy the best minds; but female education has been almost univer-
sally abandoned to any who join sufficient boldness to their ignorance to
undertake a task on which they have never perhaps spent one month of
serious study. The half-educated mother, more engrossed, probably,
with the nursery than the school-room—the ill-educated governess, whose
instruction in essential things seldom, perhaps, equals that which a well-
ordered national school now professes to give—such have been the teachers
and directors of this so-called education. We cannot wonder that want
of system in the whole has been no less conspicuous than futility in the
details.

It is not easy to educate boys, yet it is a less arduous task than
educating girls, for it is less encumbered with social difficulties, with
inconsistencies, and contradictions. Parents may say to their sons, ' Seek
truth and maintain it; know evil and shun it; be conscious of rectitude,
and brave the world's dread laugh; feel your own strength, struggle,
aspire, and dare the battle with difficulties and dangers and temptations.'
And if a high and generous spirit has been fostered in the young mind, it
will rise the higher the more fiercely the contest presents itself. But no
such simple course is open to parents with their daughters. They may
form a resolute character, but they must enforce diffidence in conduct
and opinion; they may inspire generous and lofty aims, but they must
beware of kindling ambition; they may train the energy that overcomes

difficulties, but they must teach the bold spirit and strong will that generally accompany energy to be content with submission. They may teach love of truth and scorn of the world's baseness and folly, but they must inculcate deference to the world's opinion; they may earnestly strive to train the spiritual nature to that full development of all its powers which is its indefeasible right, but they must fit the woman for a career of dependence, of narrow aims and repressed action. When such a task is pronounced easy, we are justified in believing that those who so call it, or act as if it were so, are simply incapable of appreciating its difficulties.

Unfortunately, however, incompetent as mothers may be to conquer, or even to feel, such difficulties, the task cannot be taken out of their hands. So long as girls are brought up at home (and the reasons are manifold against any other system), the mother may delegate to another the labour of giving lessons, but hers must be the presiding spirit of an education carried on under her own eyes and subject to her constant interference. Should any mother answer to this, that she makes it a point of not interfering with the governess, I can only say that, in my opinion, she labours under a delusion. She may not *intentionally* interfere, she may be utterly ignorant of what passes in the school-room, but how can she prevent that indolent quiescence itself from interfering to influence her child's moral perceptions and views of duty, her associations of affection, and reverence, and gratitude? How can anything that the mother does, or leaves undone, be without its influence on the young creature who began conscious moral existence by worshipping *her* as the living image of goodness and wisdom, and is gradually learning to *judge* her as she begins to look round, to observe and to reflect? Many an error would be avoided by both parents if they would bear in mind that every part of their conduct which comes within their child's observation is part of that child's education. They create the moral atmosphere in which their children live; how vain, then, must it be to suppose that seclusion for a certain number of hours in a school-room can withdraw them from that all-pervading influence. Hardly do years mostly spent at school and college counteract home associations, for it is very common to find that the man in his public or professional capacity is what his public education has made him, while in his private and home life, in all that touches the inner springs of character and feeling, he is governed by the influence of his early home.

These facts, which place the responsibilities of mothers in such a strong light, are perhaps alarming to some minds. They may feel their own ignorance, and shrink from the vast labour that is expected of them. Yet, if mothers reflect enough upon the subject to feel this diffidence while their children are still young, let them not despair; the feeling, if earnest, will lead to improvement, and they have yet time enough before the duties of education become either arduous or complicated. From the manner in which all the burdens that children entail—expense, education, &c.—are sometimes spoken of, one might be tempted to imagine that the young creatures sprang up like mushrooms under the parental roof, and that their claims came as a sudden unlooked-for demand upon their parents' purse and energies. But when we consider the true state of the case, we find that time is not wanting to prepare for claims which are years in assuming any formidable shape. It is true that, to some people, every demand is sudden. There is in their minds no capacity for preparation. They must know, for instance, that every year expenses for their children increase, and will increase in yet greater proportion as they grow older ; still they continue to live every year up to their incomes, and are overwhelmed at last by claims which they should have been preparing during ten years to meet. So with the difficulties of education ; a young mother feels herself unfit to cope with them ; she acknowledges her deficiency, yet, during the eight or ten years which elapse before the serious business of teaching need begin, she continues the same course of trivial occupation which must inevitably and most effectually increase her unfitness.

But if, during all those years, she had given three, or even two, hours every day to the earnest study of those subjects which would best discipline and fit her own mind to educate her children, or to superintend their education, can we doubt that, with moderate average abilities, she would have made herself more fit for the office than are ninety-nine out of every hundred of the teachers who undertake it at present? It is true that the moral training of children allows of no such delay ; but although she may make mistakes in that, she may be sure that the earnestness of her own pursuits, the more intelligent observation which she would direct to indications of character, and the daily enlargement of her own mind, would all tell most beneficially upon her management of young children.

The excuse of want of time for study is one which any observer of the ordinary routine of feminine occupations must be reluctant to admit. Doubtless nursery-cares, illness, drudgery of various kinds, which small means may render necessary, act as serious interruptions. In most cases, however, the hindrance is much greater than it need be, owing to want of method, and of a due appreciation of the relative value of different claims, so that fifty trivial matters are allowed to assume the rank of necessaries which a more systematic view of duty would at once set aside. Allowing, then, for all that is really essential, few, I repeat, are those in the class of gentlewomen who might not devote two hours in the day to the labour of preparing for the most important duty of a woman's life. Even when mothers are wishing to do their best by teaching their children, how many an hour passed in giving lessons of music, or history, or grammar, to little creatures under ten years old, might be more profitably spent in play by the child and in serious study by the mother! What comparison can there be between such lessons and the labour which is to fit the mother for undertaking the duties of education later, to enable her to form character, and habits, and opinions, which will influence her children, perhaps, for life? Truly, while the anxious mother is educating herself, she may afford to be indifferent to those who will scoff because, in the meantime, her babies know less than other babies next door.

Earnest reading and study for this purpose should be considered in the same light as a professional occupation. Unfortunately, from never having known the rigidity of compulsory work, women have seldom the habit of methodical perseverance in pursuit ; they have, besides, to contend with one real difficulty—*i. e.*, being subject to interruptions from others which may often make it impossible to set apart an allotted time for their own occupations. But though they cannot command regularity of hours, they may gather up, if I may so express it, the same amount of time in fragments amid the other avocations of the day, and thus insure regularity of occupation. It is, doubtless, better to have two hours continuously for reading, but an hour twice a-day will do nearly as well ; and four half-hours, even, will accomplish a great deal, while the determination which keeps working through difficulties, adhering to the spirit of method where the outward form is impossible, is itself excellent discipline to the mind. On the other hand, as I said before, many things must be set resolutely aside. No interruptions must be allowed that do not come in the name of a higher duty ; no hindrances permitted, therefore, from visiting, or letter-writing ; nor from the children themselves bringing their noisy play to tempt the busy from their labour; nor even from the claims of the poor, to which some women devote more time than they really ought to spare from their families; nor from the apparent necessity of needlework, from which much that is ornamental might generally be retrenched. Even when of the most essential kind, it might, in most cases, be more cheaply paid for in money than by the total sacrifice of the time and faculties the mother owes to her children's higher interests. I know there are cases where the pressure of poverty and a large family force a woman to lead a life of continual drudgery; but there are few, very few, in which time is not given to some occupation which can make no claim equal to that which I am urging. And it must be remembered that those are the very cases in which a mother will be obliged to teach as well as to educate her daughters, so that, as a mere question of economy, it is better for her to pay a sempstress now, in order that she may be fit to undertake the far more expensive office of governess a few years later. But, in truth, it is not a question of choice or inclination; as well might a man, having once (by marrying) undertaken the charge of a family, consult his taste as to whether or not he can go through the labour of supporting them. A woman, in marrying, willingly incurs the duties and responsibilities of the mother's office, and she cannot choose which part of them she will attend to, and which neglect under the plea of unfitness. So long as she is unfit, her duty is clear—*i. e.*, to remedy the deficiency by every means in her power.

These remarks may perhaps seem to wander from my subject; but since, at every step, in considering female education I must assume that the mother is the teacher, or at any rate the directress of the whole, it appeared necessary to meet that plea of unfitness which is so frequently brought forward without any apparent consciousness that blame attaches to such unfitness, or that exertion would remove it.

We have seen that forgetfulness of the true human purpose of education, in over anxiety about practical worldly ends, leaves female education without any definite aim at all. Yet without a distinct purpose, and a well ordered method for attaining that purpose, nothing but confusion can result. Let the anxious young mother meditate well upon this, and before she sends for governess or masters, and embarks in all the toil and trouble of a school-room, let her try to settle definitely in her own mind what she is aiming at. Casting out all consideration of what particular acquirements are the fashion—of what Mrs. So-or-So does with her children—let her simply consider what she wishes her daughter to become in after years, and how present means can be made to conduce to that end. How many visions will then float before the anxious mind of the many chances and changes of that course of life which she must fit her child to meet. She will see her joyous and bright, first entering society ; the whole present full of delight, the whole future full of hope, gathering friends around her, whose character will depend on the tastes, principles, and opinions education is to form. She will see her placed in circumstances of difficulty in which her power of judgment and decision may influence her fate for years. She will see her, among others, exposed to evil influence, and yielding to or resisting it in proportion as education has trained strength of character and purpose. She will see her on the eve of that one fearful choice which fixes a woman's fate for weal or woe, and feel all that depends then upon the high or low tone of her mind, upon her power of controlling feeling, upon her habits of acting on principle; and all the consequences that must result from these to others, as well as to herself, as the new ties and duties of married life gather round her, will rise up to view. Or she may see her, free from those duties, walk onwards alone; she may follow her through the gay period of life till those years steal on when strength must be gathered up from within to meet the indifference of society, the loosening of early ties, the loneliness of home, the dreariness of the future ; and still then, as at all times, bearing her lot with cheerfulness or complaining, influencing others for good or evil, winning esteem or just escaping censure, according to the habits of her own mind, the tone of her own feelings and sympathies, and the worth of her own pursuits.

As the young mother looks through that long vista, tears of anxious fondness may perhaps more than once dim the vision, and drop on the sunny brow of the child whose future path her fancy has thus traced out. But will she not look at that child's daily training now in a new spirit from having sought to follow out its consequences ? Will she not feel that there must be a purpose in her education quite apart from questions of what she is to *know* by the time she is eight, or ten, or twelve, or in comparison with others? and that preparation for so wide a sphere of domestic and social duties admits of no such low standard as that of custom or fashion ?

The *universal* object of education, as we have seen, is to draw out all the capabilities of the human creature; to give as far as means and opportunities will allow the full measure of vigour, morally and intellectually, that each is susceptible of receiving, without regard to peculiarities of position or calling. But while this object ranks first, both in order of time and importance, it by no means interferes with the necessity of a peculiar training for the various active duties and pursuits that may fall to the share of each. It is a fruitful source of error, as we have seen, to look to this peculiar training for *principles of education*, because it must ever be fluctuating, and regulated by circumstances, but it is scarcely less essential than the other to the welfare of each individual. With the labouring classes this practical education generally takes the shape of learning some manual art, and is wholly removed from book-learning, except as the habits trained by means of the latter at school tell upon general character and capacity. With the great mass of men who are above manual labour, this second education comes in the form of professional studies or apprenticeship to business, when the latter is not of a kind to demand direct intellectual preparation. With the wealthy, who are exempt from professional toil, this period of their education should make them acquainted with all social and political questions on which, owing to their wealth and power, they are likely to exercise influence—should train them to be fit leaders of other men, and to feel the responsibility of their position. With women the training for the peculiar duties of their vocation depends rather on a peculiar direction given to the primary and fundamental education than on the acquisition of any special branch of knowledge.

A woman's active occupations as the mistress of a household are too slight to require long apprenticeship. Needlework, the only indispensable feminine art, is learnt from childhood. Her more serious duties as a wife, a mother, or a member of society, do not call for peculiar forms of knowledge; it is the generally well-disciplined and well-balanced mind that is needed to educate and influence others, not vast stores of information, valuable as they may be. We may say, then, that nothing similar to a man's professional training is required for women; but throughout their education it is needful that the teacher should bear in mind the position her pupils are to occupy, and modify, with reference to that, the general mental and moral training she bestows. She must consider, for instance, what are the peculiar difficulties and trials, to meet which in a right spirit, will call for the exercise of such or such a quality ; what intellectual or moral peculiarities the course of woman's life is most likely to foster or to check, and what, therefore, it is desirable to counteract or to strengthen by education. She must remember that she is not training one who is to take a part in active and arduous employments, but one who, by the silent power of example, by the general tone of character, opinion, and views of life will exercise domestic and social influence, who will wield a moral sway rather than the power of intellect or knowledge. The professional avocations of men, or the employments marked out by the possession of wealth and power, while they call for a peculiar range of study, give also a decisive direction to tastes and habits. With women, the direction of the latter rests more with themselves, and must therefore be a serious object throughout the course of education, since on the latter will depend whether the direction shall be a right one or not.

Another point to be considered by the teacher is the very short period allotted to female education, and the little chance that any errors that it may have fallen into will be corrected by intercourse with society. Not only is a man's education prolonged by college or professional studies, but the world into which he is thrown to struggle, and toil, and compete with his equals and superiors, must educate him in some measure, whatever be the deficiencies of his early training. The school is often a rude one—full of hard trial and bitter mortification to many—but still it is a school by whose searching discipline all but the most inert or the most worthless must derive at least some intellectual benefit; their powers of mind must in the course of years be strengthened, and their knowledge enlarged. The consequence is that, except among the utterly idle, the man is always intellectually superior to the boy; and the man of five-and-forty superior to what he was at five-and-twenty. But we do not find this so generally the case with women; nor is the difference surprising when we consider the different circumstances of their lives. At the age when boys exchange school for college, girls are taken out of the school-room altogether, and books and study as a compulsory occupation are set aside. When young men who do not go to college exchange the intellectual excitement of study for the far greater excitement of a busy life, young girls exchange a quiet and regular life of rational occupation for the frivolous idleness of society; for dress, gossip, and fancy-work; or, at best, for some art or light pursuit taken up as an amusement, and they may live years in the world without being aware of the pitiable barrenness of their own minds. Or, perhaps, they marry at the age when young men are just beginning the more serious part of their education, and sink at once to the homely cares of a household and nursery before they have acquired any tastes or habits that will keep up mental activity, having no settled pursuit, no love of knowledge, no motive for intellectual exertion till their children want education, and they feel themselves unfit to give it.

How is it possible that minds should not deteriorate through such a course ? If it be acknowledged that stagnation is death to the intellect, how can the faculties of women be expected to keep alive and vigorous under its oppressive influence? The result is what we might expect. Women gain in worldly experience and the sad knowledge of life, but *intellectually* their minds, far from enlarging and ripening, too often contract more and more as they advance through those long monotonous years from girlhood to old age. Home cares and trials, suffering, religious meditation and moral feeling—these have been their teachers during that time, and in so far as they have influenced mind and character doubtless improvement is seen; the spirit has been chastened and practical judgment has been ripened, but the intellect has been allowed to rust. In activity of thought and imagination, in desire for knowledge, in power of reasoning, there is in general no advance, while too many have fallen back, as their minds, after their early studies were over, ceased to be occupied with subjects that could keep alive the spirit of intellectual activity. How often, accordingly, is it seen that she who acknowledges that at eighteen she read history or poetry with pleasure, will at fifty read nothing but some book of light literature from a circulating library, just as a change of occupation from carpet-work or letter-writing.

It is hardly necessary to remark how many exceptions there are to the truth of this melancholy statement. In London especially, the mere tone of dinner-table conversation, in all but the most frivolous society, forces some degree of intellectual life, some curiosity about what is going on beyond their own circle in that great knowledge-gathering world, where life is so busy and so intense. Still, the above is but too true a picture of the ordinary state of things. The mere impress of life upon the countenance marks the difference in this respect between man and woman. The former loses the beauty of youth no less than the latter, but years have stamped his brow with thought, and given it not unfrequently a nobler expression in age than it had in early manhood; while a vapid look, or a settled expression of care, or the meek gentleness of long endurance, have replaced on the woman's face the sunny brightness of girlhood. He has ripened through the course of years—she has withered; his powers have enlarged and gained in firmness and weight what they may have lost in fire and brilliancy; hers have been smothered under small cares, small pleasures, and small interests. The most frequent exceptions are among women who marry but have no children, and thus rescued from nursery cares, to which so many mothers limit their views of the office imposed upon them by Heaven, have been driven to come out of their own narrow sphere, and to take an interest in social questions, or in their husbands' pursuits; or else among women who have either married late, or not at all, and who, left, therefore, as youth passed away, without the excitement of new ties and positive occupations, have drained to the dregs the wretched monotony of their idle life, and have then turned to mental pursuits in despair, to find in them at last a new spring of life—new interests, new energy, new ties to the human race.

This is exactly what any rational system of education would have supplied them with before. Leisure and inaction are the sure trials they will have to encounter. The teacher's object, therefore, must be to cultivate tastes, to excite desires which shall keep the mind awake in the utmost monotony of the outer life. She will feel how earnest must be in her pupil's mind the love of knowledge, the delight in the exercise of thought, the bent towards self-improvement to enable her to resist that *malaria* of idleness, and to supply her with motives of exertion which she cannot, like men, find on the busy arena of the world.

Assuming, then, these views of woman's life, and regarding education as that which is to fit her to meet its various trials and emergencies, and to preserve in her own mind a lofty purpose governing thought and action, let us see what is the course it will pursue.

The task of education is twofold. First, to cultivate moral and intellectual habits; secondly, to inspire love of knowledge. And this task is to be performed partly by means of regular studies unfolding the mental capacities, partly by example, by association and influence. Ordinary systems of education aim simply at a given standard of information. Certain things are taught which it appears desirable that the pupil should be acquainted with, and some vague expectation is entertained that good habits will follow. And this expectation is justified, doubtless, to some extent, since it is probable that a certain measure of patience, method, and power of attention must be acquired from any regular study. But real education makes the formation of habits the first object, to which acquirements of every kind must be subordinate. It reverses the above order, and selects the subjects of study with a view to their effect in disciplining the mind, rather than with reference to the actual value of the knowledge imparted. For instance, though it might be more practically useful to us to know several languages than to study Euclid, yet, if geometry were considered a better school for reasoning, it would have the undoubted preference over the former. And so on through all the variety of subjects that can be presented to our choice.

Here we see the marked division between *essentials* and *non-essentials*. The latter may include much that is valuable and most desirable, but the former have a character of their own; their object is not to enrich the memory with information, but to train those habits of mind, without which mental exertion is feeble and almost worthless. If one study tends more than another to exercise patience, or observation, or judgment, that study takes place at once among the essentials. Or should it be one which our means of home-education will not allow us to follow, we must, in seeking a substitute, be guided wholly by those considerations. If obliged to forego the requisite discipline in its best form, the purpose itself must not be set aside; for our pupils must still, by whatever means in our power, be taught to observe, to compare, to reason, to work with accuracy, and patience, and method. Mere information must always be held subordinate to this.

In female education, the class of essentials includes also what will cultivate those tastes and excite that desire for knowledge on which we must depend for exercising the same beneficial influence over woman's life that active and professional employment exercise over man's. In cases where the means of intellectual education are small, this great object must be accomplished by influence and association alone; and in any case the subjects to be included under this head cannot be rigorously defined. It behoves the teacher to study closely the tastes and capacities of her pupils, to ascertain through what avenue it will be most easy to introduce the love of knowledge; what branch of inquiry awakens the keenest interest; what form of truth will most readily kindle the desire to seek below the surface of things, and to feel a pleasure in mental exertion. Whatever promises this result takes rank among the essentials of education, even though not of great importance. When once the mind has been led to feel that noble excitment, we may hope that we have laid the foundation of future progress. The skilful teacher can perhaps generally awaken the tastes which she desires to see predominate; but, if not, she must do her best with those her pupil evinces, never desponding so long as the mind is not of that feeble cast which shows no decided tastes of any kind— which seems equally devoid of any natural bent or of energy to follow a path pointed out by others. These are the cases of greatest difficulty, and yet these are also the cases where it is most important to discover in what direction the mind can be made to work with most pleasure and alacrity.

Every pursuit, however worthy, which does not tend towards one or other of these two objects—to excite love of knowledge, or to form sound mental habits—falls into the class of non-essentials. It is a matter of choice, not of necessity; time may possibly be afforded for such pursuits during the period of tuition, or attention may be directed to them as

desirable to be followed up hereafter; but they form no part of the necessary work of education.

The difficulty of framing a plan of study is thus greatly simplified;
adherence to those two divisions, and to the principles which mark the
distinction, makes our task clear and definite. Still there is in each particular instance room enough for choice to bewilder the inexperienced;
and for this reason, I think it advisable to propose a general course of
study, and subsequently to take up its several portions with some detail;
not supposing that it will in any case, perhaps, be implicitly followed, but
to illustrate my meaning, and to aid those who may desire aid to apply
the principles I deem so important.

I must first premise, however, that it is not my intention to enter into
the subject of early education further than may be needed to prepare the
way for what is to come after. I limit my observations to the school-room
education of girls, beginning at twelve years old, and ending at eighteen.
Those six years constitute the proper period for that elementary instruction by means of which we hope to ground sound principles of moral and
mental development. Character is then unfolding and taking shape ; a
permanent form may be given to habits and tastes ; and, when health is
good, sufficient vigour of body and mind is developed to bear serious
application with benefit. The word *elementary* applied to the instruction
may disappoint some who, perhaps, expect that an education so anxiously
cared for shall produce some perfect fruit; but we may be satisfied if the
fruit, though unripe, is sound at the core; if our care has laid a secure
basis for future self-improvement; if, while cultivating worthy motives of
action, it has furnished the power and the desire to learn, and left nothing
to *unlearn*. Boys leave school at that age avowedly only just fit to begin
serious study. Why are we to expect more than such fitness from girls?

§ 2.—All the aims and endeavours of intellectual education resolve
themselves into the culture of the reason and the imagination. The various
important mental habits enumerated above are all subservient to the right
exercise of reason, while the latter, together with imagination, give the
tone to moral action and conviction. The proportions in which those two
great faculties are combined determine more than anything else the power
and cast of the mind and character. Wherever the one predominates so
much as to overshadow and depress the other, we find either on the one
hand want of accuracy, discrimination, and vigour, or, on the other, too
great rigidity and too little inventive power, with a deficiency of warmth
and enthusiasm. Educational studies, therefore, must tend to cultivate

and to maintain a due proportion between these two faculties, carefully forming the habits which minister to the right exercise of reason, and cherishing all that will help to refine and elevate the imagination.

One point is equally essential to both; namely, the cultivation of the power of language. How far language influences thought, how much of what the mind elaborates is owing to the faculty of shaping our conceptions in words, is one of those questions which it is hopeless to solve; but viewed in relation to education, we cannot doubt that it is no less indispensable to cultivate the gift of language than the gift of reason. Accordingly, Dr. Whewell remarks* that 'educational studies are mainly such as are fitted to educe two principal faculties of man considered as an intellectual being; namely, language and reason.' And, taking the same view, Dr. Donaldson limits the elementary education strictly to the studies which aim directly at the cultivation of these two faculties. 'Mental culture,' he says, 'or the discipline of the mind, depends entirely on that system of logical teaching which gradually imparts the habits of methodically arranging our thoughts, and exercises the reasoning faculty in the practical processes of deduction. . . . . Educational training will attempt what does not belong to its own province if it does not confine itself to the development of deductive habits—in fact, to teaching the method of language; for in man, the only reasoning and speaking creature, the thought is necessarily completed in the expression. Now, as far as the world has hitherto advanced, there are only two forms under which this instruction is possible —on the one hand it appears as grammar, which deals with the expression of our thoughts in language; and on the other it presents itself as geometry, which applies the rules of language to a methodical discussion of quantities, magnitudes, and proportions . . . . up to this time the known materials of deductive reasoning are exhausted in grammar and geometry.' †

The culture of the imagination is forgotten, or under-valued, by both these writers, when in the above-quoted passages they give such exclusive predominance to the cultivation of reason, and this omission has been common in theories of education; ‡ but so far as they go we may go with them, and accept grammar and geometry accordingly as the essential groundwork of educational studies.

---

* *Of a Liberal Education in General,* &c., p. 8.
† *Classical Scholarship and Classical Learning,* p. 19.
‡ The small work on *Home Education,* by J. TAYLOR, is a remarkable exception to this. His remarks on the 'training of the conceptive faculty,' as well on habits of observation, are well worth reading.

For those who are not accustomed to contemplate subjects of this nature, it may be well to explain a little further the nature of the benefit to be expected from the study of geometry. Dealing with a subject free from all ambiguity, in which certain strict definitions and axioms limit all that is admitted into, and supply all that is necessary for, the train of reasoning pursued at the moment, there is nothing to divert the mind from the one operation it has to perform, namely, to prove whether a given proposition does certainly follow from a proposition proved before. To borrow Dr. Whewell's words, ' Geometry really consists entirely of manifest examples of perfect reasoning : the reasoning being expressed in words which convince the mind in virtue of the special forms and relations to which they directly refer.' *

In another place the same writer has well expressed the influence of mathematical studies, and of geometry especially, on the mind. They 'familiarize the student,' he remarks, ' with the usual forms of inference till they find a ready passage through his mind, while anything that is fallacious or logically wrong at once shocks his intellectual habits, and is rejected. He is accustomed to a chain of deduction where each link hangs from the preceding, and thus he learns continuity of attention and coherency of thought. His notice is steadily fixed upon those circumstances only in the subject upon which demonstrativeness depends, and thus that mixture of various grounds of conviction which is so common in other men's minds is rigorously excluded from his.' †

Now, it must be obvious to any one who attends to this statement of the value of geometry, that it is not a scientific value only, great as that is, but one which tells upon our whole modes of thought and action in daily life. We all require to know whether a thing which is brought before us be proved or not, and *why* and *where* the proof fails. We all require to draw correct inferences from any facts or propositions that we are considering. When routine fails us, we shall no more act rightly unless we have reasoned correctly, than the blind man could walk with a safe step along a path he has not trodden before. We all require to act methodically, that is, steadily and regularly towards an established purpose, but we cannot do so unless we have clear ideas concerning that purpose, and the means of attaining it ; and close attention and correct inference are necessary towards having clear ideas. Therefore, although

---

* *Of a Liberal Education*, p. 29.
† *Thoughts on the Study of Mathematics*, reprinted in *Essay on University Education*, p. 138.

we might never throughout life have occasion to conduct a serious argument, or to use consecutive reasoning in matters of speculation, we should equally need the habits which spring from cultivating the power of close reasoning.

As a discipline for the reason, geometry is the only portion of mathematics necessarily included in elementary education. Arithmetic claims to be admitted on other grounds, and from its universal practical use is equally indispensable. To a certain extent its claims are indeed acknowledged by all; but women have hardly been supposed to require more than will suffice for keeping household accounts. The advantage resulting from the habit of ready and accurate reckoning, and from ability to understand the method of calculations which do not refer to domestic affairs, has been too generally overlooked, and consequently in very simple matters of business women are wholly, and often ruinously, in the hands of others. On such occasions, doubtless, there are often other things to be studied and understood besides the actual calculations, but if these offered no difficulty the rest would soon be mastered. The apparently hopeless confusion of business to an ignorant person is in the long columns of figures, and the new ways of dealing with them. All the processes of arithmetic should be made thoroughly familiar, and rapidity as well as accuracy should be aimed at in working them. Considerable progress may be made in this during childhood, so that at the period I am now speaking of, the more difficult portions only should require to be taught.

Geometry and arithmetic include all of elementary mathematics which can be called strictly necessary. But we have seen that in educating girls, essential studies must extend to subjects which shall afford an introduction to those pursuits in which we hope to kindle their interest. We must not leave them, when education is nominally ended, with well-sharpened tools and no employment for them, but rather initiate them into actual work, in hope of rousing the spirit of inquiry and of mental activity which will thenceforth find work for itself. In this view some extension of mathematical study becomes necessary in order to prepare the mind for understanding the great discoveries of physical science. Dr. Whewell justly regards that man as below the standard cultivation of his times ' who is not only ignorant of, but incapable of comprehending, the great achievements of human intellect.' * And without some slight knowledge

---

* See *Philosophy of the Inductive Sciences,* vol. ii., p. 511.

of mathematics it is scarcely possible to apprehend, even dimly, some of the mightiest of those achievements.

How dim that apprehension must still remain with such scanty knowledge as we can hope to impart, we need not be told; but it is certain that even some acquaintance with elementary geometry enables the student to approach any scientific subject in a different spirit from one who has never gone through that preliminary discipline. Not only is his mind open to the perception of some of the most important relations with which exact science deals, but he has some appreciation of the clearness and method which science requires, and a distinct apprehension of the difference between probability and demonstration, which is rare with those who are accustomed to deal only with the loose forms of ordinary language. A slight elementary course of algebra will follow up the same object. The mind will be opened to a new class of ideas, to the nature and power of symbols, without which it is impossible to have even the faintest conception of that weapon of giant strength, by the aid of which some of the most wonderful triumphs of science have been achieved. It is true that we cannot with such scanty knowledge attain to a clear conception, such as will satisfy the understanding, but we open to the imagination the magnificent arena of science; and we may rest assured that each time the imagination has soared to a lofty region and paused to contemplate order, and grandeur, and beauty, a refining and strengthening influence has been exercised over the whole nature.

To these first steps in mathematics I would add some knowledge of the principles of mechanics. Not only is this knowledge necessary, in order to understand the simplest problems of physical astronomy, but in itself the study offers many advantages. Few subjects present so fine an example of the deduction of far-reaching consequences from a few simple principles; and this, which can be appreciated without entering into the mathematical difficulties of the subject, makes it second only to geometry as an intellectual discipline. For when we can awaken the perception of the fruitfulness of great truths, when we have excited interest in them, and led the mind to turn frequently to the contemplation of them, we have given a habit of greater value than knowledge itself. In a lower but still important point of view, mechanics claim a place in educational studies, as enabling us to look intelligently at the ingenious and wonder-working machinery daily brought to perfection, exhibiting such beautiful applications to common use of those few great principles which form the basis of some of the grandest discoveries in science. Whatever prevents the young mind resting in indolent ignorance within sight and reach of objects of interest, whatever tends to form that intellectual condition in which the spirit of rational inquiry kindles whenever anything either not known before, or not understood, is presented to observation, is of value in education.   Some acquaintance with mechanics, leading to an interest in watching machinery, is also of use in calling out the power and habit of observation, and of that kind of observation that traces the adaptation of means to ends, which impresses on the mind the necessity of seizing leading points, and of distinguishing the essential from the accessory, in order to observe with profit.   Habits of observation are so essential to women, that no means of cultivating them should be neglected.   Those whose power lies in influence, and whose business is education, must depend greatly on their power of observing character, slight indications of feeling, minute circumstances as affecting health of mind and body; and there are few habits more difficult to give in after life to those who are naturally unobservant.   Certain moral defects are generally found in the latter, and contribute to the evil result.   These must be duly checked; but to aid that moral discipline the intellectual habit, and the knowledge of what constitutes nice and accurate observation, must be given by study.

Science has been in general omitted altogether from female education, or when attended to, it has been in so slight a manner, through such meagre catechisms of knowledge, that a superficial acquaintance with facts has been the only result, reaching to no comprehension of law or method.* I may be told that it is also omitted in the education of boys; but without considering what may be urged for or against this omission, I must repeat that deficiencies of this nature are of far greater consequence in the education of girls.   We cannot afford, in teaching them, to neglect any means by which the value of accurate and definite ideas and of strict reasoning can be impressed on the mind.   When the course of life is never likely to bring knowledge to a practical test, we cannot labour too strenuously to make the habits of the individual such as may supply the want of that test.

But apart from such considerations, how strangely poor and un-

* Since writing the above, I have heard of some schools where ' natural philosophy ' is taught by professors; but, as far as I am able to judge, the objects aimed at, and the results obtained, hardly give them a claim to be excepted from the above censure; and in home education the neglect is still so complete, that few governesses will be found competent to give instruction on those points, or even to direct the reading and questioning from books.

furnished is that mind which remains ignorant of the great laws of the physical universe, shut out from that magnificent field of thought and contemplation which seems exhaustless in its resources! Few things mark the frivolous intention of female education more than the complete neglect of any attempt to excite an interest in these vast subjects, or even to open the mind to their grandeur and importance. It is common enough to hear it said, that education is to give women *resources* in their monotonous home-life; but the resource of a real interest in subjects that are occupying some of the finest intellects in every generation is not of the kind sought for. It is not uncommon to find persons who have a smattering of several languages, just enough to read second-rate works with a master or a dictionary, or who have spent the price of a moderate library on music and dancing-masters, who have read many volumes recording military movements they do not understand, and court intrigues it is a gain to forget,—who remain contentedly ignorant of every great law which the intellect of man has been able to trace in the order of the universe, to whom it would be the same if the sun were still believed to · revolve round the earth, or if chemistry were still in the crucible of the alchemist; content, year after year, to measure ribbons by the yard, heedless of how that tool of vulgar use has been made to measure the starry heavens; to see motion in all natural things and in all machinery of human invention, and not care to inquire how men have detected and applied these secrets of nature;—to live daily in sight of steam-engines and electric telegraphs, but ignorant of all concerning them, except so far as they cheapen travelling, and convey intelligence quicker than a mail-coach!

A large course of physical science is manifestly out of the question in female education, and the exclusive pursuit of one science, even supposing that could be carried to any extent, is not only unfit for a school-room course, but, for reasons I may enter into hereafter, is not perhaps desirable for women at any time. I would propose such a course of reading as shall make some of the leading facts and great laws of the physical universe familiar to the pupil's mind. I desire that the course should be such as to awaken interest concerning these lofty inquiries, and to give power, in some small measure, of understanding the method in which they are conducted; it should lead the mind to contemplate some of the great results which, besides their intrinsic beauty, are, day by day, as mechanical invention waits upon the steps of discovery, advancing the civilization of the world and the power of man over external nature.

In the immense range of physical science, it is not easy to choose the subjects to which it may be most desirable to turn attention. Each, as we consider it, seems too full of interest and value to be neglected. Astronomy, which, in countless ages past, first kindled in man the spirit of inquiry into the order of nature, still stands unrivalled. The extreme interest of geological speculations, and the scope they afford to imagination as they range over immense periods of existence, are exceeded only by astronomy. The beauty of chemical laws and phenomena, carrying the mind in contemplation from the minutest and commonest things to powers that are almost sublime in their reach and magnitude, make one loth to turn from the study they offer, as well as from subjects in great measure connected with them, such as magnetism and electricity; all opening glimpses of a region of unseen forces, a world unknown to our senses, which, while it opens to the reason a field of the most abstruse investigation, strikes the imagination almost with awe.

Difficult as it thus becomes to choose where so rich a choice is before us, it is well, unless the pupil should evince a very decided preference for one subject beyond another, to be guided by the degree of mental discipline each study will afford, rather than by their comparative interest. For instance, with regard to natural history, looking at the study in that point of view, we may agree with Dr. Whewell that it has distinct claims as an educational study, arising from its opening the mind of the student to the nature of right classification, and thereby tending to promote that great aim of intellectual discipline, the substitution of clear and definite ideas for what before were loose and ill-defined. This study gives us, he says, ' in a precise and scientific form, examples of the classing and naming of objects, which operations the use of common language leads us constantly to perform in a loose and inexact way. In the usual habits of our minds and tongues, things are distinguished or brought together, and names are applied in a manner very indefinite, vacillating, and seemingly capricious; and we may naturally be led to doubt whether such defects can be avoided; whether exact distinctions of things, and rigorous use of words be possible. Now, upon this point we may receive the instruction of natural history, which proves to us, by the actual performance of the task, that a precise classification and nomenclature are attainable at least for a mass of objects of the same kind. Further, we also learn from this study, that there may exist not only an exact distinction of kinds of things, but a series of distinctions, one set subordinate to another, and the more general including the more special, so as to form a system of classification.

All these are valuable lessons. If by the study of natural history we evolve in a clear and well defined form the conceptions of *genus, species,* and of *higher* and *lower steps* of classification, we communicate precision, clearness, and method to the intellect through a great range of its operations.' *

For these reasons I would, when time and aptitude allow, include some study of natural history in an educational course, since it is by such considerations that we must be guided amid the difficulties of making a selection. Viewing other branches of science in that light, I conceive, then, that some knowledge of the great outlines of astronomy, of geology, and of physiology cannot, without strong reasons, be omitted from a rational education.

Astronomy scarcely needs to have its claims set forth. In an educational point of view we must value its completeness, its certainty. We see in it the example of the perfect success of the most rigorous scientific method, and the one form in which science has reached her highest development, the power of prophecy; while the extent of the results obtained, no less beautiful in themselves than important in their daily application, and the field opened to the loftiest flights of imagination, all point it out as a subject on which to be wholly ignorant marks us as alike indifferent to scientific truth and to the grandeur of man's intellect.

Geology opens, as I have said, a field only second in extent, and perhaps scarcely second in interest, to astronomy. A large portion of the facts with which it deals comes within range of ordinary observation, and thus interest is excited in a class of minds that are not easily stirred by what is remote and unseen. It has this advantage also of bearing upon and receiving light from a great variety of subjects. Natural history, comparative physiology, chemistry, physical geography, all contribute to the speculations of the geologist, and this vast range which we cannot hope to explore, while it seems, at first, to be an objection to including such a subject among educational studies, is, in some respects, my inducement for doing so. If girls were to study science with any hope of great proficiency, or for any definite practical purpose, it might be essential to limit the field, and to bend all their energies in one chosen direction. But this is not the purpose we have in view. Our object is to give to

---

* *Philosophy of the Inductive Sciences,* vol. ii., p. 515. Dr. Whewell does not admit chemistry to have any claims as an educational study; yet the beauty, precision, and *elastic power* of its nomenclature seem to fit it to give, in some measure, lessons of the same kind as those above pointed out.—(See *Ibid.* p. 514.)

minds that will be exposed to narrowing influences as wide an interest as we can in all that is worthily exciting human thought and enterprise; * and for these reasons geology, which points out the connexion between so many branches of research appears to me likely to aid the mental discipline of education. The more extensive the region into which we have just glanced, and no more, the less possible will it be to deceive ourselves with the notion that education and study are over at eighteen.

I have already explained the benefit to be expected from teaching some of the classifications of natural history. That study is also very favourable for forming habits of observation, the special importance of which to women I have spoken of above. Facts of natural history are among the first things that awaken a child's interest, and they may be made the means of teaching how to observe, compare, and to perceive relations and analogies long before any notion of scientific classification could be understood.

The claims of physiology to be included among the subjects of elementary instruction are twofold, and upon a very slight consideration become sufficiently obvious. The interest of the subject in itself needs no comment, and any study of natural history implies acquaintance with the outlines at least of physiology. It is a lamentable mark of ignorance, or of the absence of an inquiring spirit, when we are indifferent to knowing something of this frame of ours, this engine of life so wonderfully wrought and sustained ; and some knowledge of its structure and functions is most important with a view to a rational care of health. Persons who possess that knowledge, even in a very slight degree, will often avoid illness, while they will never suppose that their scanty information can be a substitute for a physician's knowledge when illness is actually present. Nothing so clearly reveals to us the depths of our ignorance as a few well-defined notions of the basis of real knowledge. Thus, the popular saying that ' a little knowledge is a dangerous thing' is true only when that knowledge is superficial as well as scanty ; not founded on accurate principles, but puffing up the mind with conceit for what has been obtained by a mere exertion of the memory.

It is most essential to women to have rational notions of the conditions required for health, since they are frequently, and in some cases almost constantly, in charge of the health of others. The degree to which even

---

* Reasons for encouraging a diversity of pursuits in women will be given later in this chapter.

the moral management of children is affected by considerations of health, how necessary it is that the latter should be always present to the parent's mind, is sufficient to recommend the subject to women. Physical well-being for life, all that makes existence a pleasure or a burden, may depend on the judgment shown in the care of health in childhood; yet most women are left to pick up their knowledge of what is absolutely indispensable from uneducated nurses at the moment they need to use it, while the moral and physical effects of their ignorance remain utterly unheeded. Nor is it as mothers alone that women would feel the benefit of having sound principles on this subject early instilled, and their minds turned to the study. In their households, and often through a large circle of their poorer neighbours, women of the upper classes are called upon for medical advice, and give it, unfortunately, with great recklessness, when ignorant of the simplest principles of medicine. The direct duties of sick nurse, which it falls to the lot of women in every rank to perform or to superintend, enforce the same lesson of the necessity of some knowledge of medicine founded on acquaintance with the principles of physiology, combined with those habits of accuracy, order and observation which are formed by looking at a subject scientifically. These are the .qualities which intellectual discipline contributes towards making a person fit to watch over a sick room or over the health of children ;—the moral qualities indispensable to complete the fitness, gentleness, patience, unselfishness, are cultivated by other means, but will not suffice alone.

Such are the reasons for selecting these few subjects from the vast field of science to make part of elementary instruction. Besides the direct knowledge imparted, such a course will suffice to awaken the spirit of inquiry, to show the scope and aim of physical science, and to bring to light the many links by which one subject is connected to another, and each to all, till we feel that interest on one point has opened so many sources of fresh interest on others, that the longest life and the most untiring efforts would be insufficient to exhaust them. The whole course of scientific reading will also carry on the discipline of the reasoning faculty begun in geometry. The method of scientific investigation, the mode of collecting and weighing evidence, the tracing of effects to their causes, the instances of abstract theoretical reasoning verified by experiment, the philosophic spirit shown amid doubts and difficulties ; all these afford lessons which the teacher will eagerly call to her aid in the formation of her pupils' mental habits, and which she will scarcely find in so admirable and accessible a form in any other class of inquiries.

We come now to the second branch of essential elementary education —namely, to the study of language, which in truth can be considered second to none, although for the convenience of arrangement I have placed mathematics and the scientific reading more or less connected with it in the first place. Much discussion, amounting to angry controversy, has been spent on the comparative merits, with regard to mental discipline, of the study of mathematics and language, as if there existed a necessity of choosing between them. But waiving all such useless attempts to exalt one noble branch of human knowledge at the expense of another, it seems to me a simpler, as well as a truer view, to consider them, in education at least, as complementary one of the other, each supplying some points which exclusive cultivation of the other would leave too much out of sight.

It seems almost a waste of time to point out how important is the cultivation of that faculty of speech which, together with reason, is the great prerogative of our human nature. The universality of the gift perhaps encourages a belief that its exercise is too natural and easy a thing to need much study. I would ask persons who think so to compare the language of children in different classes of society, and then to try the labour of teaching them. The ease in the one case, and the difficulty in the other of conveying a new idea, of explaining any simple matter, will afford the readiest illustration of the power of language over the mind. That power can never be measured in the constant action and reaction upon each other of modes of thought and speech ; but when we remember that whatever the inner life of thought, language alone gives it outward form and power over others, we need no more to make us desire to possess it in such perfection as our faculties will allow.

Nothing, perhaps, so clearly marks the really educated man as the *method* of his conversation, the logical order in which he habitually expresses his thoughts. Clearness of thought itself is undoubtedly the point of first necessity ; but without the study of words, and of the relations of language, even definite ideas are not brought forward with that clearness which affects the minds of others. The nice distinctions which the study of grammar brings to light are distinctions of thought; they are different modes of perception, different relations of ideas as affected by considerations of space and time, the *when* and the *where* which modify all our conceptions. The order in which the *matter* of discourse is set forth belongs to the whole mental condition, according as we are, or are not, able to see the just proportions of different parts of a subject, and to arrange them accordingly—in other words, to deal with it *methodically*; while the order of our *words* betrays whether we are accustomed to value accuracy and clearness, and to cast our thoughts into that form which is most favourable to strict reasoning; the two together are, as I said above, the sure indication of a really cultivated mind.

It has been generally considered that this study is best carried on through the medium of languages which have once been the organs of highly cultivated intellects, but whose forms are no longer subject to the fluctuations that affect those which are used for the daily purposes of life. Such are the languages of Greece and Rome; now dead to vulgar uses, but living for ever as the utterance of genius in some of its highest forms. Accordingly, Greek and Latin have been generally used for that part of mental discipline which depends on grammatical studies. But that knowledge is not attainable by all; and where it is out of the question, we must seek a compensation in the study and comparison of modern languages. Although their ruder grammatical structure may teach us less than the almost perfect forms of the Greek, still we shall learn to compare the modes of expression, and the different constructions, to sift the principles of grammar from the peculiarities of idiom, by which means the philosophical idea involved in such or such rules becomes more apparent. Dr. Donaldson justly remarks the almost dangerous force of the associations of words used ignorantly in our native tongue; how they seem almost to imprison thought, and render it difficult to appreciate what belongs to forms of expression only, and what to general principles; and he remarks accordingly that the effect of learning a foreign language ' consists in the contrast of the associations it calls up with those trains of thought which our mother tongue awakens.'[*] Mr. Mill also, in his *Logic*, speaks of the disadvantage with regard to clearness of conception which persons labour under who are acquainted with their own language only :—' One of the advantages,' he says, ' of having accurately studied a plurality of languages, especially of those languages which eminent thinkers have used as the vehicle of their thoughts, is the practical lesson we learn concerning the ambiguities of words, by finding that the same word in one language corresponds, on different occasions, to different words in another; when not thus exercised, even the strongest understandings find it difficult to believe that things which have a common name have not, in some respect or other, a common nature.'[†]

---

[*] *New Cratylus.* Introduction, pp. 10 and 11. Second edition.
[†] *Logic*, vol. i. p. 86. Fourth edition.

There can evidently, then, be no hesitation about teaching two or more languages, whether ancient or modern, whenever it is possible ; but this possibility may not always exist, and it remains to be seen what can be done for the study of language with the help of our mother tongue alone.   In some respects it presents peculiar advantages for study, such as freedom from difficulties of grammar and idiom, and the intimate sense we have of the value and meaning of words which secures us against being misled by seemingly equivalent expressions.   Etymologies are more easily traced than in a foreign language, and thus the history of the language, through its various phases of development, may be mastered with comparatively little difficulty.   Another important object of the study of language considered as mental discipline — namely, the acquisition of habits of accurate reasoning with an imperfect instrument—may likewise be attained by the aid of our native tongue alone. Geometry is the best school for the reason, and in some respects it is the easiest ; there is a lucid clearness over the path which leads so unerringly from step to step ; there is a light thrown upon the nature of demonstration which can nowhere else be obtained.   But amid the changes and uncertainties of actual life, when in business, in action, or in study, we have to guard against our own ignorance and the prejudices or party views of others, against the force of associations, and the influence of feeling obscuring the perceptions of the intellect, we find too little room for certainty, little or none for demonstration.   We must deal with words, and words too often involve theories, themselves involving doubts and consequences we are unable to calculate, while action and conviction alike vainly seek a surer guide than probability.   Here the habits formed on geometrical demonstration alone would be too liable to fail, or even to mislead us.   In this vast region of perplexity, which embraces almost the whole actual experience of life, we must be able to reason with and about words ; that is, we must feel sure that the terms we use stand for ideas as definite as study and an *honest purpose* can make them.   We must be sure that we are not deceiving ourselves with the jugglery of words, because no positive proof can be brought for or against what we maintain.   The method of strict reasoning is first acquired in the school where nothing can obstruct its progress ; but we must learn to carry that same method into more complicated subjects.   Each step is really made in the same manner from inference to inference ; the difference is in the grounds upon which the inference is founded.   It is obvious, therefore, that while the best means of acquiring the habit of performing that operation surely and rapidly is where the grounds are perfectly certain, it is equally necessary that judgment should be exercised in reasoning where the grounds are doubtful.

For this purpose it is needful that we should study the forms of language, the nature of metaphorical expressions, and of that wide class of terms which involve more or less of opinion, while they seem to state only facts. We must learn in what manner language can be reduced to the forms of strict reasoning, so that we may see where any ambiguity lurks— whether in the mere expression, which can be rectified, or in the nature of the subject, which can only be guarded against. These objects, for which some study of logic becomes necessary, will doubtless be facilitated by that command over several languages which aids us in detecting ambiguities, yet with somewhat closer labour we may manage to dispense with that advantage. It appears, therefore, that for several of the purposes which make the study of language indispensable in education, we are not seriously hindered by ignorance of other tongues, whether ancient or modern. Knowledge of the ancient languages, from which sprang so large a portion of those now living, whose literature influenced for generations the whole tone of thought and association in modern Europe, and influences it yet—is indeed most desirable; and whenever opportunity allows, it should be made the groundwork of linguistic study. The modern tongues also are valuable for their own sake, apart from the considerations we have dwelt upon here, and should undoubtedly be learned when it is possible. But the one indispensable study is that of our native language, whether with or without others. How, then, can we avoid returning to the oft-repeated accusation against female education, when we find that while it makes the teaching of modern languages one of its boasts, it has in great measure neglected the only essential one—that language which is our birthright, which is not only precious to us on the highest intellectual grounds, but which is dearer to us than we perhaps ever know till after the silence of years had made a long divorce of cherished associations, they all spring up around us again at the first sounds that greet us as we return to our native land. It is a great *privation* to be unacquainted with any foreign language; to forfeit the advantages which they give us as intellectual discipline, and to know only in the pale reflex of translation some of the finest masterpieces of human genius; but it is a *disgrace* not to have a competent knowledge of our own language, and of the literature which has made it glorious. How is it possible to believe that it is a love of literature or admiration of genius which prompts the desire to understand Tasso and Schiller,* while Milton and Shakspeare are known in mere scattered fragments, and Spenser, Dryden, Bacon, Burke, Addison, even the eloquent writings of our old divines, are almost closed books? It is indeed a strange perversion, but the method in the madness proves that the same evil principle runs throughout—the same sacrifice of the solid and rational to the showy and superficial.

That important part of education which relates to the cultivation of imagination belongs also, in great measure, to studies connected with that of language. I have spoken above of scientific truths and speculations as appealing strongly to the imagination ; but literature, and especially the higher forms of poetry, tend directly to cultivate and refine it. There is a strange distrust in many minds of this faculty, which in its higher manifestation is the loftiest power of the human mind ; and which, even when not gifted with the creative energy that makes it sublime, is at least the source of some of the most ennobling pleasures we are capable of feeling on earth. Its excesses, its perverting power, seem to be dwelt on more frequently than its elevating tendencies, and it is overlooked that those very excesses are the result of natural power misdirected and unchastened. It is probably this kind of dread which has caused the culture of the imagination to be, as I remarked before, overlooked in ordinary systems of education. But cultivation, while it calls forth and strengthens a naturally feeble faculty, refines, exalts, and directs the strong one, which if left to itself follows a wayward course, and produces the very evil we feared. The antagonistic power to imagination is the understanding; but it would be a strange delusion to expect that because the former was neglected, the latter would acquire strength. The feebleness we daily see in unimaginative persons is a sufficient proof of this. On the other hand, let the reasoning power be carefully trained—let a due sobriety of mind be habitually maintained by serious pursuits and duties, and the power of imagination need cause no alarm.

It is strange that the moral effects of want of imagination should be so constantly overlooked. The coldness, the want of tact, the want of sympathy of the unimaginative make them as unlovable as they are uninteresting, and peculiarly unfit them for holding a position of moral

---

* Even this result does not always follow from the ordinary teaching. Young ladies who have *spoken German* for years with a governess, have been unable to read Schiller. The limited vocabulary of gossiping talk does not include the language of a high class of literature. After years spent in learning the forms of French or Italian, it is common to find that their great writers are unknown. What, then, except obedience to fashion, prompts the learning ?

influence, such as that which belongs to women. Nor does it follow that they are free from the faults that are generally ascribed to a different tone of mind, from subjection to feeling, for instance, rather than to judgment, or from love of excitement. With regard to the latter, the desire for it may be all the stronger in proportion to the slowness of the mind in feeling it; and when the *intellect* is least susceptible of it there is the greater fear of its taking a more dangerous direction. Of this we may be certain, that imagination is a better safeguard against frivolity than either dulness or apathy, which leave the mind exposed to *ennui*. The unimaginative are not necessarily studious or reflective, but they are probably wanting in speculative faculty, and therefore not likely to think much or deeply unless upon some actual business they are engaged in, while for amusement they are likely to read novels which a taste for fine poetry would have rendered tiresome or offensive.

We may neglect this precious faculty, and in those who are naturally gifted with it, it will become wild and wayward, while the material interests of life will probably remain all in all to others. But it would be well for us to remember that all which gives a spiritual charm to the daily intercourse of life—all that gives generosity to benevolence, and a soul to love, and heroism to self-sacrifice—all that makes the earnestly religious mind live for the future and the unseen, and triumph over the power of the senses—all that makes the human heart glow with rapture, and thought soar through countless worlds to the throne of the Almighty, is due to imagination: the purifier, the consoler, the liberator amid the trammels, the sufferings, and the evil of our actual existence.

It is sufficiently obvious how much the study of language leads us to examine the operations of our own minds. Literature and poetry, by exciting interest in the delineation of character and feeling, and in the various manifestations of intellect and of moral sentiment, carry that habit still further; the young mind that has been properly guided through these studies is no longer an unobservant or unreflecting spectator of life. Historical reading will exercise the same habit on a wider scale; exciting the same train of thought when action and character are exhibited among large numbers and over long periods of time which before had rested upon individual contemplation.

As a mere narrative of events, history is important; no mind, raised ever so little by education above mere animal existence, can be so dead to all interest as not to care to inquire something of the fate of past generations—how the world we live in assumed its present aspects—when the familiar names daily upon our lips first bore their present significance? The feeling, almost amounting to emotion, with which we contemplate a ruin, an excavated tomb, a half-defaced inscription, proves how deep within our souls lies the source of historical interest. Those who most decry the value of the study, do so merely on the ground that we have not materials on which to found a correct judgment, or to arrive at certain truth. Correct knowledge of the outlines, at least, of history, of the course of events which have changed the aspect of the world and brought man in different countries to the condition in which he exists at present, is then properly a part of elementary instruction. And to give this correctly, geography is necessarily included in the study. But the real value of historical reading, as part of an educational course, is that it affords the first, and indeed for women generally, the only means of carrying beyond the scrutiny of individuals that study of human action and motives, and of the practical bearing and working of great moral and intellectual principles, which is so important a part of our knowledge. The scenes of home-life to which women are restricted, afford a very narrow sphere for this great study, and feelings and partialities come in to distract the judgment. But on the wide field of history we can hope to be impartial. There, through the course of ages and the extent of the civilized world, every motive of action, every delusion, every high impulse, every base passion, has played its part, and can be seen unveiled; and nothing within the narrow experience of individual life can afford to the teacher such valuable materials for forming her pupils' judgment, for enlarging their sympathies, and exciting in their minds the love of speculation on subjects of wide and stirring interest.

Such a study, it need hardly be said, is not for children. The mind must be gradually led up to the capability of engaging in it. When the rules of right reasoning have been learnt, together with the methods of sifting evidence and arriving at probable truth, then the intellect is ripe for that study which is to help in forming judgment on all those questions which most affect our social and individual welfare. In short, it is a study which must be begun in the school-room, for the sake of establishing right principles, but which rather cultivates a tendency towards pursuits to be followed hereafter than promises much result for the present.

Intelligent interest in social, moral, and political questions is very important to women, who not only hold a position in which their feelings and prepossessions, as well as their opinions, exercise great influence, but who also are all more or less concerned with education. We cannot

4

expect much skill in that difficult art of moulding character, of forming associations and feelings in the young, from those who have not themselves studied the principles whence motives and action spring, who are not habitually observant of these things, and interested in considering moral and mental development. Women who spend their early youth in trifling pursuits, enter suddenly upon one of the most responsible offices that can fall to a human being to perform, and begin their study of the human mind when they view it individualized in the child they love with an intensity which seldom perhaps leaves the most practised judgment wholly clear. They have to learn at the moment when they must begin to act, and what they love most consequently suffers most from their ignorance.

It is quite true that some persons have what seems an almost intuitive perception of character, and possess in consequence a moral influence which brings children especially under their entire sway. Again, we see mothers who seem to mould their children's feelings by the mere force of pure and high example, joined to the devotion of that love which truly 'passeth understanding;' but we have no right to expect such power, or such results. In educating girls, we must remember that they are to be fitted to have the charge of education, and we should give, therefore, that general impulse to their studies which shall direct their future reading to subjects bearing on that essential part of their natural vocation. Nor, fortunately, is it a difficult task to do so; at least I have had occasion frequently to note a difference in this respect between men and women. Supposing some taste for reading to be kindled for the first time in a man, he will, in general, turn, even without any distinct purpose in view, to what is practical and positive—to party politics, for instance, or applications of science; while women will be more readily interested in moral speculation, and all that bears on individual life and conduct. The fact, such as it is, admits of ready explanation. It is pointed out here merely as indicating the aid which natural inclination may be expected to give towards what should be an earnest aim in female education.

The studies now briefly passed in review, namely, elementary mathematics and outlines of certain portions of natural philosophy, grammar—studied through the means of one or more foreign languages as well as our own, if circumstances permit—English literature and history, both as narrative and as a moral study, form the course which, as far as I am able to discern, will best fulfil the twofold object education must strive to accomplish. The cultivation of sound mental habits and the necessity of kindling love of knowledge, have been kept in mind throughout. Each study has been recommended for a distinct educational purpose, since even what appears to have merely the extension of knowledge in view is chosen for the sake also of bringing the mind into a fit condition for meeting those sure trials of woman's life—leisure to be frivolous, and the absence of all ambitious motive for mental exertion.

I fear that some will think this course presents too wide a range for the studies of six years, beginning at twelve years old, while others may think it must necessarily be so superficial that its utmost compass will be little worth aiming at. I believe both classes of objectors would find themselves mistaken on the whole, though they would be right according to one view of the subject. To judge the question fairly, it is necessary to remember that the great purpose in laying down a scheme of educational study is to frame it on a *right method*. It is of real value only when every step made by the pupil is so ordered that it shall be the safe starting-point for a further step. If the course here proposed were offered as likely to produce a complete work, a finished pyramid of knowledge at eighteen, it might well be called too arduous, or be laughed at as too superficial; but my object is merely to lay a right foundation for future labour, by the means of certain studies, followed with method and a definite purpose. I propose that the scheme of school-room study should be the framework of a more extended scheme, where nothing will have to be displaced, no proportions changed, where every future acquisition will find its fitting link of association, so that the whole mental store may be laid up in harmonious order, instead of becoming a patchwork of incongruous fragments. The fact, therefore, that little progress can be made in those several studies is not, according to my view, an objection to the system, for I think there are sufficient reasons for wishing, in the education of girls, to break up the ground in various directions rather than to attempt leading them, perhaps somewhat further, towards one or two objects. When we have opened several paths before them, we shall leave them free and able to choose hereafter whither they will direct their steps. The studies here proposed will be more or less slight, according to the pupils' capacity. In their slightest form they will lay a methodical foundation, and train the mind to right habits, whether for study or practical life; in their most extensive form they can aim at little more. The edifice will be raised a few feet more or less, but the ground-plan remains the same, and if that be wisely laid, each addition made now or hereafter will be in harmony with the original design.

It is no reproach to women to say their knowledge is *small* upon any subject as long as it is *solid*, and that they are aware of its small extent. This is enough to distinguish them from the superficial, who are equally ignorant of the fundamental principles of what they pretend to know, and of the vast extent of the knowledge at which they have only glanced. Great knowledge is seldom within woman's reach, unless her natural powers be such as to defy obstacles. In education, were we to apply ourselves wholly to one subject, the work achieved must still necessarily be very imperfect at so early an age, and we forfeit the advantages of trying the tastes and capacities, and enlarging the interests and sympathies. Once more, it is not profound knowledge that women require, either for themselves or society, but the cast of mind that results from the love and pursuit of knowledge.

It has been objected that the mind itself is not benefited by great variety of pursuit; that the power of concentration, which is the source of vigour of thought, is injured by it, and this, no doubt, to a certain extent is true. But devotion to one subject, or to a very limited range, which favours concentration of thought in minds of any power and under favourable circumstances for study, is more likely, with ordinary minds and under the unfavourable influences of woman's life, to lead to contracted views and to indifference to all beyond the chosen pursuit. Where much depth is out of the question, it appears evident that we cannot be gainers by limiting the surface.

As a question of happiness, I believe devotion to one pursuit not to be desirable for women. They are not destined to 'achieve greatness,' and the means of doing so are seldom open to them, even had they the power. The exceptions are so few that we may lay it down as a general rule that no gentlewoman is independent enough to follow the bent of her own mind, till she has reached an age when neither tastes nor habits can be altered. In a lower rank of life there is less dependence on the forms of society; but this comparative freedom is only the result of another dependence—that of poverty, which drives a young woman to self-exertion. But among the few openings then before her, there is none which offers a hope of high distinction or a reward for severe mental labour. Unmarried women living under their parents' roof have neither time nor money at their disposal for any object peculiarly their own. Their movements, their hours, their society, are regulated by the views of others. When they marry, the increase of freedom is often little more than nominal, while in some respects they are more dependent than before. These are points which it is folly to lose sight of in laying down a scheme of female education, and we need but contrast this mode of life with the course a man pursues who is devoted to one study, and earnest in following it, to see how impossible a *successful* pursuit of that kind would generally be to a woman; and wherever we have given much time or labour, success is an indispensable condition of happiness.

The latter will be better consulted by giving to women a considerable range of mental occupations, which allows of one being pursued when another is hindered, and enables them to fall readily into the pursuits of those around them. In a life so exposed to narrowing influences it is desirable to create as wide an interest as we can in all that is worthily exciting human thought and enterprise. It is desirable to link an inactive existence with the stirring world without by all the ties which can be created by pleasure in the same inquiries, and sympathy in the hopes and endeavours of those who are labouring actively in the various fields of research. Mental sympathy, which men rarely give in full measure to each other—for the very reason that engrossed in labour or ambition, they can seldom come sufficiently out of themselves to enter earnestly into the hopes and object of another—this mental sympathy is the surest bond of friendship between man and woman. The latter has no feeling of rivalry, no mortification in meeting a superior, and frankly and freely, and with something of that glow of feeling which always perhaps animates the intellect of women, she can feel for his difficulties, rejoice in his success, enter into his views and hopes, or try to lighten his toil. Such friendship, which vulgar minds may deride, and to which vulgar gossip may often give another name, is a truly precious treasure, and in a different manner beneficial to both. Even this reflex glow from the ardour of active life or of a noble ambition, gives something more of animation to the lonely and secluded existence of many women; and would it not be well if in married life this element of happiness were more often found? The additional charm thus given to the most affectionate intercourse needs no description; but would not the charm work in some degree even under less happy circumstances? Would there not at least be more peace, more cheerfulness, greater mutual respect, if *minds* could meet, even when *hearts* are partially estranged?

§ 3.—In laying down a plan in a work like this, the *method* is truly everything, since it can but seldom happen that its details can be followed step by step as they are given. Means, situation, ability, health, all bring in a variety of considerations that tend to modify in each family the adoption of any system of education. The utmost a writer can do is to set forth and illustrate general principles, the parent must still judge ultimately of their mode of application. But it must be remembered that minds accustomed to act upon system are alone capable of doing this with profit. They alone, when a plan requires to be either enlarged or curtailed to suit particular circumstances, are fit to discern how the alteration should be made without sacrificing the main purpose. Unmethodical minds are not aware that the importance of a thing is often less owing to its own intrinsic value than to the place it occupies, to the relation in which it stands to something else, and they change or displace at random, according to convenience or inclination.

It will be evident from the foregoing remarks that the one indispensable condition is that the master-principles of education, together with a spirit of method, should govern the teacher's mind. No course of study, however varied or expensive, can otherwise be expected to yield much fruit; while under such a teacher far narrower means may be made to attain the essential points. It is not the book but the method in which a book is studied which disciplines the mind. We may learn grammar, and know nothing beyond the dry parsing of a sentence. We may read poetry and not acquire one notion of taste, or feel our imagination either elevated or refined. We may read history and not derive from its perusal one lesson of morals or politics. We may go through the most valuable scientific treatises and bring away nothing but facts. We may pore over Euclid and never learn to reason upon anything beyond the propositions there demonstrated. No cunningly devised system will educate without an educator. As well might we expect machinery to do its work without being directed by one that understands its parts and their movements. A ruling mind is needed at every step in education, and more especially in the home education of girls, where so much is left to choice, and where, as I said before, the errors committed will rarely find correction in after-life.

The success of self-educated men, which appears, at first sight, to be in contradiction to the extreme importance I have ascribed to the teacher's influence, is rather, if rightly viewed, a corroboration of it; for all the qualities I have mentioned as indispensable in one who would direct education already exist in the minds of those who are impelled to direct their own education and to seek knowledge for themselves. Love of knowledge, patience, resolution, the art of making small means minister to great purposes, these must belong to him who has been capable of feeling the need of education and of supplying the want by his own unassisted efforts. The labour of studying without help must also necessarily quicken intelligence and exercise judgment, and train some habit of reasoning, and some care in seeking the right method to work. When this spirit is in the learner, the teacher sinks in importance. The strong motive is the schoolmaster never absent from his post. Yet I believe that most self-educated men would confess how much waste of time and faculty would have been spared them by good teaching. At any rate, these exceptional cases do not alter the general truth, that the quality of the teacher's mind is of more importance than the means and circumstances of the education.

I have said before that in speaking of the education of girls, *teacher* is really synonymous with *mother;* at least that the latter must inevitably exercise a degree of influence which makes any other almost nugatory. It is not, indeed, necessary that she should be able to give instruction in the different branches of study, but that she should have maturely considered the purpose of that instruction, and be able to keep the ultimate purpose steadily in view. In a word, the tuition may be left to others, but the spirit and method of the education must be given by her. Till women, therefore, are better prepared for this portion of their maternal office— till they are more often sufficiently educated to feel at least an equal interest in the duties of the school-room as in those of the nursery, we can hope only for partial improvement.

Even with the most scanty means, the mother who is thoroughly impressed with the value of education and with the essential purpose of mental discipline, will not lose sight of, or feel herself constrained to neglect, its most important parts. I am anxious to press this remark, lest some should object to my plan of *essential* studies that it is beyond the compass of many who can afford but little in the way of teaching for their children. In the first place, we may remark the inexpensive character of the studies I propose compared with accomplishments and foreign languages. But, supposing the most rigid economy necessary, I should wish to prove that a well-educated mother will still manage to secure for her daughters some of the best results of mental discipline, in defiance of homely cares and want of assistance.

Good books are so cheap in the present day, that it must be very seldom that education is really hindered for want of the means to procure them. If regular tuition cannot be provided, while the mother's own time is very much taken up with other duties, she may so manage still that the qualities drawn forth in her children by the necessity of studying, in great measure, alone, and the greater effort of patience and intelligence required, shall compensate, *as regards mental discipline*, for the slighter progress made. Even where, as must happen when means are very narrow, books and leisure for regular teaching are altogether scanty, the circumstances and practical duties of life may, by a judicious mother, be made to serve, in great measure, as substitutes for study in exercising judgment and observation, in forming habits of decision, of method, and accuracy. The very privation of books and leisure may become a means of stimulating a desire for knowledge which will seem as the privilege of a more favoured condition, and every glimpse of which may be treasured as the working man treasures his rare holiday.

Young persons so trained will, of course, be very ill-informed; and for boys, to whom a certain amount of positive knowledge at a given age is indispensable to insure their favourable entrance into a profession, such disadvantages would be a real misfortune; but girls have no intellectual task awaiting them—their well-being will depend not on what they *know*, but upon their general cast of mind and character. Let mothers comfort themselves, therefore, with the assurance that even such hindrances as I have described cannot rob their daughters of some of the best fruits of mental training, and that their minds will be ripe for intellectual cultivation, should the opportunity ever present itself. Unfortunately, few parents seem to appreciate the advantanges that may be derived from the peculiar circumstances of their position. It is common to hear mothers regret that they cannot afford to give their daughters the same education that other girls receive, and with this sterile expression of regret their care ceases. The natural consequence is, that their daughters, being allowed to grow up amid desultory household occupations, remain no less incapable of the systematic industry, management, and economy, of the sound judgment, foresight, and decision in practical matters, which those homely duties might have taught them, than of the logical reasoning and clear apprehension which result from intellectual cultivation.

If this should seem to be in contradiction to what I have said of the value of intellectual culture, or if any unreflecting persons, willing to get rid of the toil of study, and to see women confined once more within the limits of household occupations, should infer that intellectual labour is useless in female education, I can only reply that the inference is unfair as the conclusion would be unsound. I have here supposed the case of a mother fully aware of the benefits of mental discipline, having studied and reflected upon the subject herself, and striving, in the midst of the homely duties to which she is forced to give her time, to form those habits, and infuse into her children's minds those tastes which will make them naturally turn to the pursuit of knowledge, should leisure to do so ever be theirs. It is hardly necessary to point out the contrast between such a mother and one who neglects the better means of education she might have commanded. Neither must we forget that the social position which allows time and money to be spent on education is also that which affords abundant leisure and an opening to all its perils and temptations. The mother placed in that position is not herself occupied with household business, except in the way of general superintendence; and therefore, in neglecting studies for practical matters she would not be setting an example of obedience to duty, but merely of capricious preference of the homely to the intellectual. Necessary needlework, or other still more menial occupations, may, as I have pointed out, be made to afford valuable lessons; but not so a frivolous occupation. In the one case the highest use is made of the poorest means; the highest aim is kept steadily in view through the most unpropitious circumstances. In the other case the amplest means and fullest opportunities of working out the best purposes of education are scorned and neglected. The moral effect of following such a course would be worse than the intellectual; for where there is time for noble and elevating occupation, and children see the preference given to the servile or the trivial, a lesson is taught whose baneful influence will not easily be effaced.

The fashion of the day, however, points so strongly towards a variety of elegant accomplishments that there is, perhaps, little need of this warning against the deliberate choice of homely occupations. In some respects it is more often necessary to remind mothers of the importance of household skill, and that they are educating not *artistes*, but women to whom the care and comfort of families will one day be trusted. But the warning may stand as a protest against more than one form of error or ignorance. The preference of the frivolous to the solid is equally, if not more mischievous than that of the homely to the intellectual, and far more common. Both proceed from the same blindness to the real purposes for which it is desirable that the human faculties should be trained.

CHAPTER III.

§ 1.—In considering the course of study to be pursued during the six years to which my remarks on school-room education refer, the subject will be divided, for the sake of clearness and convenience, into different periods. But there are certain points of moral training which cannot conveniently be so treated, and which it will be well therefore to consider in the first place. It is true that the whole course of intellectual and of moral culture must proceed hand in hand; and the results of the former,— knowledge, ripened judgment and power of reasoning, will bear upon the whole tone of character; but it would be an interruption to refer at every stage of our remarks upon study to the moral improvement which should be going on at the same time, and to the difficulties from moral causes which the teacher may have to encounter. We will glance, then, here at certain indispensable points which can never be left out of sight through the whole course of education, such as truth, and the control of temper, while others will be referred to in speaking of the studies selected for the purpose of fostering or checking some characteristic quality.

I wish also to say a few words on the effect of health upon character, which appears to me to be too little considered in education.

The first business of the governess, before she can decide on any plan of lessons, must be the careful study of her pupils' dispositions and capacities; the former especially, as the most difficult, and as affecting her future labours far more than the state of their knowledge or their power of learning. Supposing, as I do, that children are not placed under her care till twelve years old, character has already acquired many fixed lines, and is more developed for good or for evil than the intellect. If the governess is left to enter upon this task unaided, it will prove both a long and a troublesome one; for children rarely betray at once to a stranger either their best or their worst qualities; nor without knowing something of their previous life and training does she possess the key to their peculiar habits or turns of feeling. We may venture, however, to hope that the cases are comparatively rare in which the mother's knowledge of her children does not come in to aid the observations of the governess. She, whose care it should have been to watch every change, to note each new shade of character as it developed from the first hours of conscious existence, ought to be able to furnish the governess with information which the most careful observation would hardly enable her to obtain for herself till perhaps much time had been wasted, and many attempts made in a wrong direction. Even if the mother in detailing the early education of her children should betray her own ignorance of the subject, her very errors will enlighten the governess. The latter will see *where* she is too look for deficiencies, and what is the root of any faulty conduct she may observe.

I have little doubt that a journal of a child's life in which should be carefully noted peculiar traits of character, indications of intelligence, or of deficient understanding, of strong tastes or dislikes, as also the first occurrence and occasion of certain faults, the system adopted to subdue them, and the result obtained, would be of great service to the governess who undertakes the subsequent management of the same child. Doubtless, also, such a record would be very useful to the mother herself in dealing with younger children. It might save many of those painfully mischievous attempts to subject different characters to the same treatment, by pointing at once to the differences which exist in circumstances or conduct which the inaccuracy of memory would class as similar.

A journal of the same description kept subsequently by the governess would in like manner have considerable advantages in helping her to pursue her plans more systematically; referring back from time to time to the experience of the past month or year, and enabling her to measure accurately the progress made both morally and intellectually. A careful mother would naturally desire to see this journal, and the knowledge that it would be subjected to her inspection would insure regularity in keeping it. A record so kept and read, and talked over together by the mother and governess, would assuredly give to both a more accurate estimate of what they had accomplished and of what remained to be done, and secure a more steady co-operation on the same system, than could be attained by mere unwritten observation and the desultory communications made in conversation.

Moral training is the proper business of those early years when the whole nature is in its most pliant state ; awake to impressions and feeling, but unfit for mental exertion. When the mother has given her earnest care to this most important duty, a girl of twelve years old should come into the hands of a governess requiring little more in this respect than watching upon those points of character which change or develop as childhood passes into youth. Violence, sullenness, obstinacy, fretfulness, impertinence, disobedience, deceit, and the timidity which leads to falsehood for fear of punishment, all these are manifested early, and should be so restrained by early discipline, that at the age we are considering here, the ripening of reason and self-control should alone be needed to confirm the work effected by parental authority and management. The germs of all that is valuable in character should be already trained, ready to expand and strengthen under the influence of intellectual cultivation; but if the task of childhood and that of youth must both begin together, progress will unavoidably be slow and the end uncertain.

Unfortunately this is too often the case. Children with prematurely forced intellects are babies in conduct, and then the labour of education is heavy indeed. Tempers requiring the utmost care may by that time have been soured by injudicious management; the mother is reduced to that most humiliating confession, that her children 'are quite beyond her control,' and gladly gives up to a stranger the task appointed to her by Heaven.

One great mistake that educators fall into—and it is partly founded on peculiar religious views—is that a child's nature can be changed; that the heart being evil and corrupt, all its natural tendencies must be thwarted and repressed. Now, those who have considered the subject more philosophically agree that most natural qualities have a good as well as an evil side, and that the evil is to be subdued only by cultivating some quality of an opposite character, and by bringing all those influences to bear which shall draw out the good. The natural tendency will remain the same, but a strong opposing principle rises habitually against it, and all the force of association tells on the side of good instead of evil.

For instance, the punishment which follows each outbreak of violent temper in a child, though in some measure necessary to enforce self-control, does little or nothing towards counteracting the inward disposition which leads to violence, while it may, if frequent, break down the fine spirit which often accompanies such tempers. But if every endeavour were turned to cultivating kindness and love towards all living creatures, and a humble view of the child's own merits and claims upon others, the very sources of angry emotions would be gradually dried up, while the warmth and eagerness which generally form part of the same disposition remain unimpaired. In like manner with the timid, the endeavour should be to encourage boldness and to rouse decision; to accustom them to responsibility, the latter being made a mark of honour; to excite sympathy for the great deeds of fearless and heroic natures. Fear, therefore, should never be appealed to, though at the moment, fear is the readiest instrument to accomplish a particular purpose. With the sullen we should, upon the same principles, avoid, as far as possible, any punishment which can be borne with dogged obstinacy, while striving to cultivate a habit of frankness and cheerfulness, making them feel the pleasure of finding sympathy in all the small troubles and difficulties they openly avow; the desire for sympathy so created will gradually drive out the sullenness.

In this system of management we call to our aid the power of association, which, in education, may be called almost creative. By watching, training, and discipline, the mother forms habits of action; but the *active practical principle*, on which Dr. Butler * so well shows that the permanence of habit and its influence on the mind depend, is owing to the motives that are brought into operation. Now education creates motives by the power of association in moulding tastes and desires. By persevering discipline, for instance, we can give habits of industry, of regularity, of obedience; but we can ensure the duration of these habits after the discipline is removed only by forming in the mind those associations which will excite the *desire* to work and to be useful, and to strive after worthy objects. Habit influences action, association influences thoughts and wishes; both are indispensable instruments, but the power the parent possesses of moulding the mind through association is the highest power one human being can exercise over another. It may be compared to the mighty efforts of physical science in compelling the great laws of the universe to be the ministers of man in accomplishing what must otherwise remain for ever beyond all human achievement.

No set rules can be given for a task like this; it belongs mostly to the mother, and must be wrought by example, by influence, by patient instilling, little by little, by everything she does, and every word she utters of praise or of blame, that tends to associate the notions of pleasure or of pain with this or that action, habit, or state of mind. Natural peculiarities may indeed sometimes baffle her efforts altogether, or appear to do so for a time, but judicious management, patiently persevered in, will generally triumph. She must be careful, however, not to work upon one mould for all children, or to cherish the vain notion of producing one and the same result with different materials; the same ultimate object must, of course, be kept in view, but the general direction given will take its peculiar shape from the peculiarities of the individual. Vulgar methods

---

* See Theory of Habit: *Analogy of Religion, Natural and Revealed.* Part iii., chap. 5.

of education force certain modes of conduct and certain habits of study during the period of youthful subjection, and seldom indeed does the pupil receive any notion of the real purpose of any part of this tedious discipline: but the aim of the mother who knows the value of association is to mould the inner life in accordance with the habits she imposes for a time; to kindle the love of goodness, the desire for knowledge, the pleasure in active benevolence, which shall be lasting guides when her authority is withdrawn.

Let those who doubt the power that education derives from association consider for a moment what it is which, apart from constitutional peculiarities, makes the great difference between one man and another; or, to take a wider, and at the same time a simpler view, between one class of men and another, when even original peculiarities become unimportant, since taking a thousand men in one class and a thousand in another, there will probably be found among them an average number of the various types of original character. What, then, makes the difference? What marks the distinction between the savage and the civilized man—between the gentleman and the boor? What but the different circumstances and influences which have been around them from childhood, and which have combined to associate the ideas of pleasure, of greatness, of virtue in the mind of the one with what perhaps in the other is associated with vice, or pain, or degradation? The thousand shades between these extremes make the various shades of tastes and desires, likes and dislikes, by which motives and character are formed. Miss Martineau, in her *Household Education*, makes some true remarks on the difference that the tone of a man's tastes and pleasures makes on character. ' Of all the solemn considerations,' she says, ' involved in the great work of education, none is so awful as this—the right exercise and training of the sense of pleasure and pain. The man who feels most pleasure in putting brandy into his stomach, or in any other way gratifying his nerves of sensation, is a mere beast. One whose chief pleasure is the exercise of his limbs, and who lives without any exercise of the mind, is a more harmless sort of animal, like the lamb in the field, or the swallow skimming over meadow or pool. He whose delight is to represent nature by painting, or to build edifices by some beautiful idea, or to echo feelings in music, is of an immeasurably higher order. Higher still is he who is charmed by thought, whose understanding gives him more satisfaction than any power he has. Higher still is he who is never so happy as when he is making others happy— when he is relieving pain, or giving pleasure to two or three or more people about him. Higher yet is he whose chief joy it is to labour at great and eternal thought, in which lies bound up the happiness of a whole nation, and perhaps a whole world at a future time, when he will be mouldering in his grave.' *

When we consider how rarely ordinary systems of education even attempt to sway these notions—how recklessly they create associations of pleasure with idleness, luxury, and selfish indulgence—how they neglect to form any such associations with mental occupation, with benevolence or the power of usefulness, we may see how far we are yet from having used the instruments which nature put into our hands.

In childhood it is idle to address the understanding, when everything invites to mould the feelings. Even later, when reason is acquiring strength, and the mind is capable of conviction, we find convictions are barren of action unless we can influence the motives which lead instinctively to action. This, as I said above, the mother is able to do with her children by the power of association. With these two mighty instruments —association and habit—education, if commenced early enough and perseveringly continued, has a power we can scarcely limit. But if a mere system of isolated checks and reproofs is acted on in childhood, it becomes very difficult to adopt a better one at a later period. It is while the child is still the passive subject of unquestioned authority that he can be brought fully and unconsciously under the influence of such habits and associations as we wish to form. When the will has acquired strength, when character has become in some degree marked, when other influences have had time to tell, and when growing reason is announcing the period for self-government to have superseded that of blind obedience, then it requires the co-operation of the young creature herself in the work of moulding her future tastes, desires, and action, and that co-operation is, in such cases, most likely to fail.

Mighty, then, as these instruments of education are, it requires knowledge of human nature, close observation, great patience, and steady foresight to make a right use of them. Nothing is so easy as to reprove or punish faults at the time they are committed; but much thought and method are necessary to train the principles of better action. Just as it is easy to teach a lesson, but laborious to make every effort of to-day tend towards a purpose requiring perhaps years to bring it to perfection. Mere instruction, in short, mental or moral, looks to the present, works by

---

* *Household Education*, p. 24.

means of day by day expedients; *education* looks to the future, and works
with a view to the whole course of life.

§ 2.—Perfect sincerity and love of truth stand first among the points to
be aimed at in moral training. With little children this subject presents
some difficulties; yet if we are not anxious to do too much we shall find
that to a certain extent they can easily be made to understand the difference between truth and falsehood in any simple matter of fact, and that
what cannot be explained is in part placed by intuitive feeling beyond the
necessity of explanation. For the child blushes in telling a falsehood, and
resents any attempt made to deceive him; thus nature helps us in one
of the most momentous tasks of education. With this we ought to be
satisfied till the understanding is better developed; too great rigidity
sometimes intimidates a nervous child, and sometimes in one who loves
opposition fosters the very evil it purposes to repress.

Imaginative children will lie for the pleasure of creating the fiction,
but when seriously questioned they soon feel the moment when it would
be wrong to persist in what they at first said for fun. It is unwise to take
any further notice of such a fault, or to attempt to alarm the conscience
before the ground for the displeasure can be understood. If gently discouraged, these freaks of fancy will soon be confined within legitimate
bounds. Timid children lie from fear of punishment, and require very
careful treatment: and again, conceited or over-sensitive children will
occasionally tell a falsehood to avoid being known to have done a wrong
or even a foolish thing, when they would not have shrunk from punishment could they have escaped the censure of those whose approbation
they value. In such natures there is evidently much to work upon, and
when we have succeeded in attaching a stronger sense of shame to untruth
than to any other fault a child can commit, the evil will soon disappear.

It is well with children whose truth cannot be trusted to avoid as far as
possible asking any questions that can give occasion for falsehood. It is
of importance to avoid the recurrence of the fault; and thus the habit is
broken, and conscience, which would have grown hardened by repeated
failings, becomes more sensitive during the pause from conflict between
the natural tendency and the new sense of duty. When the child is old
enough to feel the tacit reproof, it is sometimes a useful lesson to ask any
necessary questions pointedly of another person, and to take the occasion
to explain to her that we dread asking her what we wanted to know while
she is still so childishly ignorant of right and wrong as to fall into the

grievous fault of untruth—a fault which, besides its moral guilt, is thus seen to make her useless. The advantage of treating it as a childish fault is two-fold : first, the pride of the young creature being roused may prove a powerful auxiliary against her inclination to falsehood; and secondly, the conscience will not be dangerously lulled by the indulgence shown, which is known to be in consideration of the age of the offender.

If a child has been allowed to grow up to twelve years old in careless-ness about truth, the task of correction becomes a very heavy one. It is true that at that age the understanding may be appealed to, and all the reasons that make falseness in any form both odious and disgraceful, may be explained, appealing to any spark of honour or high feeling that may exist in the child's mind ; but, on the other hand, the bad habit has acquired strength, the easiest mode of escaping from a difficulty has been resorted to, till it is hard to rouse courage to prefer a bolder course, while conscience has become feeble from neglect. Still we must persevere; nothing must be left untried which may help to lay that foundation of moral integrity, wanting which, the whole character is tainted with unsoundness.

Nothing perhaps will affect the young creature so deeply as finding that loss of confidence and esteem is the natural penalty of untruth which you could not spare her if you would. Words of repentance and promises of amendment cannot restore things where they were. Deceit creates dis-trust, and the latter *will* not pass away till some steadiness in self-conquest shall have given an earnest of the sincerity of the promises. It would be mere weakness in such a case to use any mitigated terms in expressing the contempt you would feel for any grown-up person who could be guilty of such a fault, and that so painful a feeling is only softened towards the young offender in compassion for her weakness and ignorance. It is only because you see that she is still a mere child in sense and feeling that you can show any indulgence for a vice which would otherwise forfeit your esteem for ever. The more gentle your habitual language and manner, the more will the child feel the sternness of this moral indigna-tion, and the more will she be pained by the grief you may show in having been so disappointed in one you loved and trusted. The lesson will be painfully severe, and the effect upon the mind of the young creature must be anxiously watched ; some could not endure it long. I believe it would be lost upon none but the utterly cold and feeble. It must not be for-gotten that the more severe the reprobation the parent or teacher is forced to express, the more careful should she be to let it be felt that in the youth

5

of the delinquent she sees earnest hope of amendment. The young must never for a moment feel that they are despaired of, for if they despair of themselves, farewell at once to energy and hope of improvement.

But checking downright falsehood is a very small part of the training required to form a truly upright character. There are many subtle shades of untruth and of insincere dealing which require to be watched and subdued. Every shadow that mars that lucid candour which is so well named *single-minded* should be felt to be so much leaning towards evil.

There are many faults which are too commonly tolerated which have more or less of this character, or induce habits which would easily lead to indifference about strict veracity. The trick of exaggerated language is one of these, that of making excuses when questioned or reproved is another, and another again is the habit of inaccuracy in repeating what has been said or heard, intending probably to give, if not the very words, at least a complete equivalent, but neglecting to consider whether that supposed equivalent does not imply some admission of fact or feeling—some inference or opinion which the actual words said, or the actual thing done, did not imply—by which means a false impression is given under colour of a true statement. This falsehood by inference is so common as to deserve very serious attention at the age when opinions are forming, and when it becomes most essential in order to form our own that we should judge those of others in a fair and candid spirit ; but this subject is beyond the comprehension of children, all we can do with them is to form the habit of implicit accuracy. If a statement be made professedly as a repetition of another person's statement, require the precise words, or a confession of where the recollection of them is not clear, and treat the matter as of little value when the memory is confused. So with narrative, strict adherence to facts should be required, no colouring epithets allowed to pass without showing the child how they tend to alter the view of the case, to give her impression, instead of simply furnishing the person she is addressing with the means of forming an opinion.

Few things will help to establish in the young mind a more rooted conviction of our supreme value for truth than seeing that on all occasions great and small, these apparently trifling things are borne in mind by ourselves, and that any, even the slightest symptom of indifference to exact truth in others, tends to lessen our esteem and to destroy our confidence, both in the judgment and feeling of those who are thus careless in forming opinions, and inaccurate in making statements. Want of attention to these points allows the young to run on to the very verge of grave error, while the line between the carelessness and exaggeration which are tolerated, and the falsehood which is looked upon as criminal, is easily confounded.

Perhaps in no other habit of the mind does the influence and example of those around them affect the young so powerfully as in this complete integrity of word and action. Many cases have been seen in which parents who could not have consciously trained a single good habit in their children, have unconsciously trained this first of all virtues by the force of their own example of unswerving uprightness and singleness of motive. They have loved truth, and they have spread so pure a moral atmosphere round their children that it would seem as if no falseness could live there, and the young creatures grow up true and honest, while scarcely hearing a precept in favour of truth, or a denunciation of falsehood.

Some persons who assiduously cultivate sincerity seem to consider that bad manners are the outward badge of this virtue. The mistake is no less foolish than mischievous. The only occasions on which sincerity and good breeding can come into collision are when the necessary expression of opinion by one person wounds the feelings of another. It is evident that such occasions should be avoided if possible, since it is a plain rule of Christian morals never to wound the feelings of others unless forced to do so at the call of a higher duty. If an opinion *must* be given, or if we stand in a position in which our silence will seem to give sanction to what we morally disapprove, let the opinion, though gently given, be open and uncompromising. If we are bound to speak what others will receive as the truth, or at any rate as our honest conviction or view of the truth, the duty is clear, and at any cost must be accomplished. But that duty is comparatively a rare one, especially for the young. We do not so often stand as judges upon or witnesses against each other as the apostles of this virtuous ill-breeding would have us suppose. Let us be kind and gentle, and thinking no evil, severe in our scrutiny of our own motives, and not curious to seek into the motives of others, unless they may serve to extenuate their faults, and we shall find that we are but seldom placed in the position of either sacrificing truth, or of offending against good feeling and good manners.

Adherence to these same rules of not judging others will help us in those difficult occasions when children question us about objectionable conduct in older persons, conduct which they see is in opposition with the principles they have themselves been taught, while yet their parent or others, from whom they hold that teaching, seem to remain on a footing of

kindness or intimacy with the offenders. In accordance with the above
rules, the young may easily be made to understand that there is no want
of sincerity in this ; because we do not venture to judge the motives and
feelings of others. If we see what is wrong in action, it pains us, but we
regulate our dealings with the individuals according to the claims they
may have on other grounds upon our affection, kindness, gratitude, or
compassion, or mere outward respect ; and we do not feel it to be at all a
part of sincerity to express an opinion of their faults, or to show our sense
of them by abstaining from any office of kindness or good breeding. But
if the child is in danger of being really puzzled or misled by the apparent
esteem of its parents for an unprincipled person, some further explanation
may be necessary. It is better in such a case to be quite open upon the
subject ; admit the faults which the erring person does not care to conceal,
or which have come to the knowledge of the child, but take that occasion
to impress on the young mind that weak and faulty as human nature is, each
one of us is bound to be indulgent to others while severe to himself; that
we must expect to find evil mixed with almost all that is good, and therefore must welcome all the good without ever making the conduct of others
the standard of our own. The knowledge of our own motives, of the
degree of weakness or of strength with which we have resisted temptation
or withstood better influences, warrants the utmost severity towards ourselves, while the absence of this very knowledge makes judgment of others
rash and unjustifiable. When, therefore, we blame their conduct, we
must allow for the many things which perhaps make them objects rather
for our pity and sympathy than for our censure. This mode of reasoning
is perfectly intelligible to children, and it will save them at once from
confusion on moral points, from mistaken sincerity, and from uncharitable
temper.

The case when this difficulty is truly distressing is where the faulty
person is one of the parents; when a father or mother is unable to conceal
that the principles he or she has most carefully inculcated upon the
children are disregarded by the other parent, whose authority remains not
the less sacred, and whose claims to respect it is so important not to forget.
It is hard to say to which of the parents this position is most trying. A
father must feel that the mother's influence is too powerful to allow almost
of any hope that the effects of her example may be counteracted ; while
the mother, who dreads for her children their father's laxity of principle,
is obliged to submit to his authority, and often to see her most anxiously
arranged system of education interfered with or set aside at the bidding of

one who has never given an hour's thought to the subject which engrosses her whole mind.

Nothing can entirely avert the evil of such a state of things, or prevent its being the source of great perplexity and suffering; but the course I have indicated above will, I believe, be the safest—silence, so long as silence is possible, and then perfect openness on points which can no longer be veiled from the children's observation, with the expression of earnest grief rather than of blame, and of every feeling that can mitigate censure against the individual. It will be needful to dwell particularly upon the facts that respect for the parental office, and gratitude for care and affection, cannot be altered by perceiving errors in the parents' principles or conduct; for the shock to the young mind of discovering such error is so great, that there is fear of a sudden revulsion of feeling. Ignorance of the world makes the young very rigid moralists, and when their belief that all they love is pure and excellent is first shaken, the revelation is torture to a sensitive mind, and the evil effects may last for years— perhaps taint the feelings through life, unless carefully watched and judiciously treated.

There are many points of a comparatively trifling nature in which it becomes impossible to disguise from children that what the one parent thinks right is disregarded by the other, and that they disagree about their children's management and education. It requires great judgment to deal with such cases without sacrificing truth, or betraying the feelings which disagreement of this nature, on a subject we have much at heart, can hardly fail to produce. One most important point for both parents to remember is, that discussions of this kind between them should *never* go on before the children; if they retain any remnant of self-command, they will refrain from exhibiting to them the unseemly spectacle of discord. The one who holds the highest principles will certainly be anxious to avoid this evil, if only for fear lest children should hear from lips habitually revered some unguarded expressions of ridicule for rules or precepts they have been taught to respect.

The mother, being forced to submit to the authority of her husband, will take care to avoid the occasions on which he might be provoked to express his will authoritatively. She would rather be silent when the children are present, or seem not to hear, or leave the room that she may not be forced to hear, than allow a discussion to arise before them, and to let them find themselves in the new position of judges between conflicting opinions, in which the very questions most interesting to them, their pleasures, their studies, the treatment due to them for good or bad conduct, are at stake. A mother will, as I said, make many sacrifices to prevent the disagreement being discovered. But when concealment is impossible, then perfect frankness about the opinions, and avoidance, as far as possible, of blame of the individual, will again be her only safe course. She may fairly say to her children, ' Your father thinks differently from me on such or such points; I believe I am right, for I have carefully considered the subject, while he has not had the same means or leisure that I have had to study it. When you are older, you may reflect upon it yourselves, and decide, according to the best of your judgment, which of us is right; in the meantime, I have the charge of your education, and must act upon my own views, unless your father were positively to forbid it, when it would be my duty to submit to him in whatever does not involve the sacrifice of real principle.'

Sentiments of this kind, simply and frankly expressed, will often save the mother the grief of seeing all her labour made barren by miserable dissensions and divided authority. There is this consolation also, that the highest-toned character will in the long run exert and retain the strongest influence. The highest standard of right that has been held up to the young mind is that to which, when not under the immediate impulse of passion, it will turn instinctively, as if with some oft-suppressed yearning after the heaven of truth and purity.

To be true at all times requires no small degree of courage, and to the enervating education of women, which tends so much to destroy the very spring of that quality in the mind, must mainly be attributed any peculiar insincerity that our sex has been accused of. Women are not left merely to feel the timidity almost inseparable from weakness and a dependent position, but they are trained up to believe it wrong to think for themselves: to fear appearances, to fear opinion—even that of the foolish and vain, whom they cannot respect—to fear showing their feelings or characters, in short to *seem* to be fashioned on the ideal of female excellence which happens to be in vogue at the time, however little their real being conforms to it. There are points on which this deference to opinions, valueless in themselves, is indispensable for women ; but how difficult it is to reconcile such a theory of life with that fearless uprightness which God and man require of every human creature ! Yet a woman is expected to reconcile them, and when she fails men easily forget all the influences which have been ceaselessly at work to transform her timidity into cowardice, and her natural position of dependence into one of moral slavery.

Other considerations also make it indispensable to educate girls to a more fearless love of truth. The position of women is one in which so much is generally to be gained by a little artifice or petty management, while it is often so vain to insist openly on her clearest right, that the temptation is fearful to any one whose own sense of honour and integrity is not such as to revolt from the least approach to underhand dealing. The danger is the greater, because the evil may begin in such slight shades that they blend and melt away into the engaging prettinesses of feminine manner—those coaxing, winning ways, which add a real charm even to lofty character. The line between manœuvring and tact, without which the best fail in home influence, is a delicate one to draw, and it must be left to the innate feeling of the upright mind to keep distinct what precepts fail to distinguish.

Men's faults and their virtues alike combine to throw them helplessly into the hands of any woman who is not scrupulous in using her power; and the less a woman really loves, the more complete is her empire, if she choose to exert it; while the alternative is too often subjection to a capricious and arbitrary will. If mothers, therefore, shrink themselves from power purchased at the cost of singleness of mind, they should surely spare no efforts to train in their daughters, not sincerity alone, but moral courage, till they feel that manœuvring in all its shades is become a moral impossibility to them, and that they would sacrifice anything sooner than their own self-respect in stooping to artifice. Only by training more vigorous minds and characters can we hope to get rid of the faults which an opposite system has encouraged.

The habit of acting upon a sense of duty is closely connected with integrity, and the idea of duty itself is one of the earliest that a child can be made to understand. A little creature, scarcely able to speak, knows that it is doing wrong in disobeying an order, and that sense of wrong-doing, the earliest indication of conscience, is the foundation of the notion of duty. Next, the child can be made to understand that its parents, in their conduct towards it, are acting under a sense of duty to God, to whom they are answerable for the right guidance of their children. There is a simple grandeur in this conception which will sometimes powerfully affect the child's mind, and give a new character to its obedience. It is with a view to cultivating the sense of duty more than with regard to any special point of conduct, that obedience is the one great virtue of childhood. By insisting on it, by claiming blind, uncompromising obedience, we are teaching the child to submit its own will to the only duty it really understands; and far therefore from encouraging, as some persons suppose, a weak habit, unfit for a creature who is hereafter to be governed by reason, we are laying the foundation of that habit of obedience to the call of duty which is the very source of moral strength and lofty action through life.

When the understanding begins to ripen, and the reason is able to act, the season for blind obedience is over. Orders given then should be explained; the motives of them unfolded. The young creature should be led to examine principles, and lay down rules of conduct, and to feel that whatever reason and conscience approve, duty commands. Then the old habit of obedience will come in to aid in this difficult task of self-regulation. The duty of the man to obey his conscience stands on precisely the same grounds as the duty of the child to obey its parents; it is the highest rule of right which the reason of each is able to perceive.

A child has no steady will, though the impulse of the moment creates wilfulness; and those who are afraid of breaking down strength of character by exacting implicit obedience, forget that there is no strength shown in obeying impulse. The mind is not active, but passive under such a course. A man's strength is in his power of self-control; his very power over others is often in proportion to his command over himself. When, therefore, we oblige a child to control itself in foregoing its own wishes, in resisting impulse, in repressing anger or insolence, we are doing our best to endow it with that power which essentially makes man a moral being, which enables him to walk with a determined purpose through the difficulties and temptations of life, neither passion's slave nor the puppet of circumstance, but his own master; resolute and self-possessed. When this power is wanting, even the clearest convictions of what is right, and the most religious feeling about duty, will fail to insure a steady course of action. Then it is that 'the flesh' remains so weak, while 'the spirit is willing.'

We all know these things; there is nothing new in these beaten paths of morals; but why is it then that education so seldom steadily aims at training the power of self-control. The rule of obedience is left too lax with young children; it is maintained too strictly at a later period; the habit of self-command is equally neglected in both cases. In childhood. that habit, as we have said, is best cultivated by acting at the bidding of another; but in youth, by acting upon convictions and a self-determined course. The blind obedience of the young child was an instrument, not an object in itself; the aim of moral discipline is to give the power of self-guidance, and it has lamentably failed if it has only made a creature fit to be guided.   Authority, therefore, over the child should always be exercised with the view of fitting the youth to be independent of authority.

All the strong and resolute points of character are for this reason full of promise, though a weaker nature may give less trouble in early life to parents or teachers.   Obstinacy, which joined as it sometimes is to feebleness, is one of the most hopeless faults to deal with, is also occasionally the indication of a resolute temper, and deserves to be carefully and cautiously treated.   The teacher should sedulously avoid entering into a contest with an obstinate child, or insisting upon anything which by dint of resolution the child can succeed in refusing to do.   There should be nothing conditional either in a task imposed or in a punishment inflicted. It will not do with such tempers to threaten for instance confinement till a certain thing is done, for the obstinate child is reckless of many things which the teacher cannot disregard, as health, the necessity of exercise, &c. If the fit of obstinacy has arisen at lesson time it is better to close the books, saying that in such an unreasonable mood a child is not worthy to take up the time for which we have so much demand.   If punishment is necessary, let it be definite, and such as cannot be resisted, demanding no concessions and thereby giving no occasion for contest.

Obstinacy may also sometimes be attacked through the pride which usually accompanies it.   We may take an opportunity of expressing our respect for true resolution when it is guided by reason, and shown in a consistent course of action, and even own that we hope the obstinacy of the child may indicate some degree of strength, while the pettiness and folly of its childish manifestations excite our pity; if we can persuade the determined spirit that we are seeking to lead it in a right direction, not to break it down, we shall have gained something.   It will more readily respect what we show respect for, and be ashamed of that which excites our contemptuous pity.   Thus we may overcome the obstinacy while we husband the strength of character which will assuredly be all needed to walk steadily in the path of duty.

The sacredness of duty like that of truth, is not taught in a few set harangues or on a few great occasions.   Here again example is the most powerful auxiliary, and its influence is strengthened by all the force of the associations of love and reverence that cling round a parent's life. Long before children can understand the principles on which we act they can discern whether our conduct is consistent or not, and feel the difference between the uncertain guidance of those who have no fixed principle of action, and the calm unswerving rule of those who act under a sense of duty. The former provokes rebellion, and frequently keeps the children in a state of unhealthy excitement and irritation; the latter influences them as men are influenced by perceiving some great law of nature, they neither cavil nor question, but submit to its regular operation.

Unfortunately in education many conscientious parents are guilty of a painful degree of inconsistency. They act indeed upon a sense of duty, but want of knowledge makes their conscience a blind guide. They will not err with regard to morals, but they are ignorant of the means of enforcing the principles, and cultivating the habits they most value. Thus while their motives are fixed, their conduct is unsteady, and children cannot be expected to understand the reason of this unfortunate contradiction. This is one striking example of the inefficiency of moral goodness without intellectual cultivation, and also of the evils resulting from education being trusted to the ignorant. Yet there is no alternative till women receive mental training of a higher order.

Love of justice is another characteristic of a truly upright mind; indeed it is the very essence of uprightness, love of truth manifested practically in our judgments and our dealings with others. Women have been accused of being deficient in this quality, and I have said elsewhere * what may account for this deficiency as far as it really exists, and excuse it, as far as excuse is possible for such a fault. There is no need to recur here to that part of the subject, except to say that it will be almost impossible to cultivate love of justice in children, unless they feel that it regulates all our dealings with them. There is often great laxity on this point. Sometimes severity, more often indulgence preponderates, and under this uncertain rule a child does not know what to expect and gets no example to guide his own practice. Of course it is not meant that a child is always to receive the just measure of punishment for every fault, but he should always be made to feel what in strict justice he has deserved, and that any mitigation is owing either to compassion on account of such or such circumstances, or because good conduct in other respects has deserved a reward, &c.; in short, some reason should be assigned and explained, which will leave on the child's mind neither a doubt about the future, nor a belief that you yourself disregard the justice according to which you profess to have drawn up the rules he has transgressed.

---

* *Thoughts on Self-Culture,* p. 146. Second Edition.

But though it must be optional with the parent to remit a deserved *punishment*, no consideration should be allowed to deprive a child of deserved *reward*, whether the latter come in the shape of something promised before, or in that of approbation, which is the dearest of all rewards to affectionate children.

It is when the child feels he deserves such encouragement and does not receive it, or worse still, when his efforts to do right are met with impatient, angry words, because while doing his best he still falls short, that the feeling of being treated with injustice swells in his heart. I am not speaking of real unkindness, but of the petty acts of a wayward sway, when the heart may be full of affection, but a hasty temper, or ignorance or want of method makes parents neglect the labour of close inquiry or observation, which is indispensable for acting justly.

The sense of justice exists in the minds of children long before they can understand what it means, and working upon this natural foundation, it may be made as abhorrent to them to commit an act of injustice as to tell a falsehood. Gradually as the understanding expands the grounds can be explained to them on which certain claims are admitted as just, while others are rejected. The want of integrity that lurks in not allowing in the case of others, what we should insist upon in our own, can then be unfolded and illustrated. If mothers had been more careful to do this with their sons, we should not have waited till now, to see some of the rights of women recognized by our legislature. Had they so taught their daughters, there would have been less submission to oppression, but fewer of those hasty judgments in which excited feeling speaks where reason should have spoken, and which expose women to the accusation of being unjust.

Selfishness is generally at the root of the injustice of men, ignorance and impulsive feeling of that of women; thus the former are mostly unjust in action, the latter in judgment. They are not trained to reason upon what touches their feelings, and we must remember that in the narrow experience of women it is mostly on points more or less personally interesting, that their judgments are called for, and this forms the habit of mind which influences them throughout. This habit of not submitting feeling to reason, joined to want of experience in sifting evidence, blinds them to the fact that they either do not know enough to come to a decision, or that they are uttering a feeling, not a conviction of the understanding; and stating perhaps with regard to the conduct of another, their own prepossessions and inferences instead of the simple facts of the case.

This view of the character of injustice in women points out the course of training required to preserve the young mind from the error. The *intellectual capacity for being just,* must be cultivated no less than the moral love of justice; and that can be done only by strengthening the reasoning power, to counterbalance the natural predominance of feeling; and by forming habits of accuracy and discrimination in all matters of opinion. The necessity of the invigorating influence of severer mental training is thus felt at every step of female education.

In all that has been said here of the love of truth and of the practical qualities that belong to it, it has been considered in a moral point of view only. The love of intellectual truth is distinct from this. They blend only as we lift our minds to God, as the source of all truth and all knowledge, as well as of all perfection and goodness; that is, of all the soul pants to know, as well as of all the heart desires to love. Love of knowledge and love of truth in the intellectual sense are one, and I have already said how important I conceive it to be that the love of knowledge for its own sake should be cultivated till it becomes the very spring of intellectual life for women; giving energy to pursuit when their outer life offers no mental stimulus. I shall have occasion also to return to this part of the subject, and will only remark here that the habitual contemplation of great truths, the serene yet earnest delight that the pursuit of knowledge affords, exercises a calming influence over the mind which is most favourable to the healthy moral condition. The strength of feeling and of prejudice is subdued or kept under control by the habitual exercise of reason, while the mind is quickened in its perceptions of truth. Supposing other things therefore to be equal, we may consider that the love of intellectual truth tends greatly to favour an upright and consistent course of life.

§ 3.—We come now to the consideration of another class of qualities.

There are few serious vices that affect daily happiness so much as faults of temper. What women suffer from such faults in men, is so well known that the only wonder is how they can still so often treat them as light offences. In their own case they are saved at least from the danger of forming so false an estimate, for no one excuses ill-temper in women. It is too inconvenient a fault where submission is required, so that just as we expect perfect self-control from our uneducated servants, overlooking the difficulty and the struggle, so men, while holding women as their inferiors, expect from them a degree of moral strength shown in self-conquest which they rarely dream of exerting themselves. However, in this particular instance the spirit of exaction has done us too good service to be quarrelled with; truly may we welcome anything which has helped to exorcise the familiar demon that turns home into a place of torment, and places those who love each other best in the position of persecutors and victims.

With young children, violence is the most common form of ill-temper, and the finest natures, those that have most strength and spirit morally and physically, are often most prone to it. Fretfulness on the other hand is more commonly a symptom of weakness either moral or physical. We may generally presume that an habitually discontented child is not in a condition of complete health. When a child gets into a violent passion it is not the raving, the insolence, or even the blow given under the influence of that temporary madness that causes us any anxiety. The child is often as sorry, and as much ashamed of itself, as we can desire when the fit is over, especially if left to the workings of its own feelings, without repentance being dictated to it, before the irritation has subsided. Some children may be met sternly and punished at once unless they make the desired effort to control their violence, and this strong effort of self-conquest frequently repeated, though under the influence of immediate fear, may sometimes help to train a habit of self-control. But such a course would be full of danger with a child of delicate nervous organization, or with the high proud spirit which contest drives to exasperation. With the nervous child, punishment or even an angry remonstrance, while the evil mood lasts, is only increasing the agitation which is already, in its mere physical effects, beyond control; while with the high-spirited the expression of anger, or the threat of punishment, only gives the occasion for the contest which the furious spirit loves. It often wants a vent, and the more daring, the more frantic the act it is driven to, the greater the relief obtained. Then if not injudiciously meddled with, the reaction begins; but the first words of the wise speeches and moral exhortations that most teachers have ready for such occasions, kindle again all the excitement and irritation that was beginning to subside. Perfect coolness is necessary in such cases, as few words as possible, and no punishment till the child is in a fit state to understand why it is inflicted and to feel its justice.

The time for exhortation comes afterwards. Then the child should be made to understand that our real deep concern is not for the outbreak which is like some violent but transient fit of illness, but for the state of mind which makes such an outbreak possible; for the proud spirit which

cannot brook opposition, the ungentle, unchristian feelings that make *self*
so prominent, so careless of inflicting pain; the quick sense of injury and
tendency to fancy it, with blindness to faults which are constantly calling
on the indulgence of others, and ought therefore to keep the mind humble
and patient even should the injustice complained of be real. The child
must be taught how to watch for the first symptoms of her besetting sin
and to exert self-control to repress it then, before it has grown to its full
strength: try to make her feel how lowering it is to become the blind
slave of feelings which we are ashamed in our sane moments of ever having
entertained. Pride, which before was our enemy, may thus be enlisted on
our side. According to the age and character of the child the teacher
may either slightly touch upon this subject, or enforce and illustrate it by
examples showing what miserable weakness there is in the human creature
who, striving by violence to domineer over others, has no power to
conquer self, is too feeble to make real feelings and settled convictions
triumph over the temporary excitement of passion.

It is not very common to find violent temper in women; though probably there is as much violence among children of the one sex as of the
other. The whole tendency of female education is to repress all manifestations of it; and as one of the first things a girl can be made to understand
is that violence of manner or of language is utterly unwomanly, she learns
to be ashamed of what is held to be unworthy of her sex, just as a boy of
no very high feeling is ashamed of betraying fear. But women have to be
on their guard against other forms of ill-temper, really worse than
violence, such as sullenness, peevishness, &c. These may even be fostered
by the very means taken to repress the violent manifestations, when
imperfect treatment has attacked symptoms only, leaving the root of the
disease untouched.

Violence may remain unchecked from mismanagement, but it cannot
escape notice, while other forms of ill-temper may by the unobservant
pass wholly unregarded. These are the forms which interfere most with
habitual cheerfulness, and require to be corrected on that account no less
than for the unamiable qualities they foster. In general all forms of
sullen temper, in which I include the peevish and discontented, are worse
than the violent; more ungenerous, more exacting and meaner in motive
and feeling. Violence is much more likely to be controlled by reason,
since a sudden impulse may by a strong effort of self-command be
restrained. Accordingly while almost all high-spirited children are
occasionally violent in temper, we generally find this fault corrected, in

women, at least, at a later period; but sullenness seems to infect the whole mind, and from its nature is so much longer in operation that the difficulty of overcoming it is proportionably greater.   The manifestations of it likewise being less openly offensive than those of violence, it is not struggled against so seriously, and even if partially corrected, often settles into a discontented, peevish tone of mind, full of sensitiveness and irritability.   It is sad to think how many homes these faults have poisoned!

Trials and wrongs of a serious nature are borne with courage or resignation by those who cannot command themselves to meet trifling accidents or disappointments with cheerfulness.   Many a woman has endured from her husband far more than any human being can be required to endure from another—she has forgiven him neglect, violence of temper, disregard of her interests and feelings, contempt for her understanding and for her just claims to have a voice in family matters that are of equal concern to them both—she has shown the enduring spirit of a martyr where resistance to oppression would have been just, and often beneficial, and yet with all this abnegation of self, she meets him daily in little things with a fretful, irritable tone which robs the most self-denying act of its charm, and brings back over every happier moment the cloud of past suffering and wrong.

We must remember with girls that their position and mode of life while they check violence tend to foster the more concentrated forms of ungentle feeling; there is no complete remedy but striving from early childhood to cultivate a frank, cheerful temper as well as kindliness of disposition.   Children should never be suffered to go over a quarrel twice. Once settled, let neither word nor tone of voice be allowed to betray that it is still fresh in the memory.   It would be well if in after-life women could remember this rule of never 'harping upon the past.'   If wrongs have been too deep to be easily passed over, let us pray in silence till we have strength to forgive, but once forgiven nothing should betray that they are still remembered, the poison of their sting should never be left to taint the heart.   A frank and cordial manner, a tone in which no smothered bitterness still echoes, must be the condition of real peace; and if a woman cannot so far command herself when she has conceded the essential points, the weakness is sure to bring fresh suffering on her own head.

I have spoken here of cases in which there are real trials to be borne, the natural effects of which on an undisciplined mind will show themselves in peevishness or irritability, but there are too many cases in which habitual fretfulness has no such excuse.   In the first instance perhaps it may have arisen from suffering health, or from injudicious treatment in childhood; but long indulgence has made it the ordinary expression of every trivial annoyance till it wears out the kindest patience and threatens to blunt the truest affection. It is by thus looking forward to their future effects that we learn the importance of faults that in childhood attract less attention than others which are in truth more easy to correct. The duty as regards physical and spiritual health, of preserving an equable cheerful frame of mind is the point that is lost sight of. We check a child's temper or impertinence, but we do not sufficiently watch the signs of inward emotion, which the timid or the reserved, or the cold and proud will not express, but which influence character all the more sometimes from this silent indulgence. In short, in this as in so many other things we deal with symptoms instead of causes, we do not search out the evil and strive to set up a counteracting influence. If a child is fretful the great object is to remove the causes of discontent, and cultivate the taste for cheerful things. If she be sullen or reserved, try to make her feel the pleasure of sympathy, show that you trust to hers, and that it gives you comfort; be frank and warm in the expression of your own feelings, tender in manner, so as if possible to rouse the force of association in favour of qualities the very opposite to those which belong to her natural disposition.

One great enemy to a cheerful disposition is the habit of murmuring, of continuing to complain after the complaint has been proved to be unreasonable or useless. Where difficulties are to be surmounted, wailing over them is only wasting the time and energy which should be spent in the struggle. Where they are unavoidable and insuperable, complaining destroys the alacrity or the calmness which a reasonable person should show in bearing what no efforts can avert. Just as a quarrel should never be recurred to a second time, so children should never be allowed a *second grumble.* Good-humour, whether in obeying an order, in obliging a companion, or in enduring a privation, is most essential, and the habit will be greatly promoted by never tolerating a second remonstrance, or any repetition of expressions of annoyance or reluctance. A point once yielded must be yielded without reserve; a thing once decided upon must be done promptly, and, if a service to another person, graciously as well as readily.

The wretched habit of scolding and lecturing which is so common among those who have the care of children is of the worst possible example. Let a reproof be more or less sharp as occasion may require, but always short; many a monitor has destroyed his own work by over-talking. The child felt the justice of the first reprimand, and would have submitted in silence, but it is repeated, and repetition is irritating, even when it does not—as almost always happens—lead to some exaggeration. The least evil resulting then is that the spirit of rebellion is roused again, while if the expressions of reproof have been exaggerated, respect lessens as the sense of injustice is kindled in the child's mind.

The least that a teacher can do is to set an example of the conduct she enforces on her pupils; never therefore let her return over the past, never cast up again faults confessed or atoned for and forgiven. There are occasions indeed when the past must be referred to, when the repetition of a fault is what gives it a serious character; or when what would be quite unimportant *once* threatens by frequent occurrence to form an evil habit. But these things should be gone over calmly and gravely when the child is in a state to be convinced of the error or the danger her past conduct points to. This is very different from the outpouring about past offences on the occasion of some fresh irritation which betrays an accumulation of wrath, so that the child suddenly finds that she is reproved not for one fault alone, which she knows to be deserving of reproof, but for a score of delinquencies she had thought passed over or forgotten. Nothing tends more than this with sensitive or timid children to destroy that confiding frankness which it is so essential to maintain. They feel that they are perhaps watched with secret displeasure even when all seems right. When the teacher forgives it should be a frank and entire forgiveness; except in grave cases, and for the single fault of untruthfulness a child should never feel an instant under suspicion. In the same manner with regard to granting indulgences, do it cheerfully and freely or not at all, and never seem to repent of it. A child should be able to read clear as light in the countenance and manner of those who have charge of her, all it concerns her to know of their sentiments towards herself.

Good-humour should be maintained no less in struggling with mental difficulties. When temper is lost over a troublesome lesson it is better to treat the fault as one so childish and silly as to make the person who can be guilty of it hardly fit to be allowed to study. This will more readily create a feeling of shame than if the fault had been met with sharp reproof; and when by conquering the ill-temper on the next occasion, the child has discovered how much that very emotion had tended to cloud her understanding, she will be more earnest in future endeavours. When real difficulties have to be overcome, the teacher should be more anxious

6

about the mood in which they are met than about the result. The knowledge proposed to be gained, if not mastered to-day may be mastered to-morrow or next year, but every day, every hour does its work in forming good or bad habits. The pupil must be early accustomed to encounter difficulties with patience and courage, without hesitation and especially without those miserable lamentations many children are allowed to indulge in, which impair energy and enfeeble the understanding. The word 'impossible' should be unknown in a school-room. It is the teacher's duty to know her pupils' disposition and capacity, and to regulate their tasks accordingly. If they have had experience of her knowledge they will soon trust her. It is the child's nature to trust its elders, and when we hear so much about the necessity of winning children's confidence and respect, the truth is, it is only by dint of inconsistency and ignorance that we ever forfeit them.

A quiet, unhesitating authority—a rule unswerving in its exaction of what has once been established, great gentleness making the sternness of moral disapprobation, if called forth, to be more sensibly felt—these qualities in a teacher will insure around children that calm atmosphere which is so essential to allow the faculties full play without moral disturbance. The feeling of necessity gives great unity and intensity to exertion, and thus it is desirable that in study as in conduct, the absolute necessity of obedience should be felt till good habits are formed and the sense of duty has acquired strength to maintain its post as the great taskmaster of life.

§ 4.—The great antagonist of all forms of defective temper is, as I before remarked, the cultivation of the benevolent affections, of which the daily home manifestations are gentleness, unselfishness, and a sense of the duty and pleasure of being useful.

Gentleness is a compound of good-temper, tenderness and refinement, and carries with it a spell for turning away wrath and winning its way even to rugged hearts. It is compatible with every vigorous quality of mind and character; indeed the latter without it, will avail women little in some of the most difficult circumstances of their lives. If she whose position, as far as it rises above that of a mere subordinate to man's will, depends wholly upon influence, will not be at the trouble to make that influence lovable, she must expect to find herself powerless, while the right of the strongest prevails.

A better standard of home manners among children would do much to cultivate gentleness. The words, the tone, the action, which good breeding would banish in company, good feeling should banish from the home circle. Not that the drawing-room manners should be the standard, though they may serve to point a contrast; the feeling which is at the bottom of the conventional form, or which the latter strives to simulate, is what we must arrive it. Let children learn how all those rules of good breeding are framed to produce the same outward semblance, which a gentle, loving spirit devoid of pretension and presumption, would naturally assume. They can be early taught to see that the privilege of familiarity is to be more unreserved, more confiding, to give and receive more open and earnest sympathy, whether in suffering or in pleasure, and not to be more selfish, more inattentive to the wants and feelings of those we love than we should be to those of strangers. In this, as in most other points in education, example is indispensable. Where children see a want of deference and gentleness to each other among their elders, where there is none of the courtesy of kind feeling to inferiors in station, where the tone to servants is imperious, and where they themselves are treated with a disregard to good manners, it will be vain to expect more than a varnish of good breeding. The roughest and rudest school would not turn out the unmannerly cubs society is too much afflicted with, if the tone of home manners were one of refinement and unselfishness; and since women are the first victims of domestic bad manners, it is strange that as mothers, they are not more careful to form them on a better model.

Close and delicate observation on which *tact* depends is very essential to give due effect to good manners. Girls should on no account be allowed to grow up unobservant of the *minutiæ* of life and feeling around them. The most amiable will wound or irritate, will say the wrong thing, or withhold sympathy when it is most needed, because they do not see, what to the observing is clearly revealed. Never let slight attentions be neglected, teach the pleasure of gratifying an unspoken wish. The presence of old persons, or invalids, or little children, affords an excellent school for training this quality, and carelessness in observing should be reproved as much as any other heedless habit.*

In serving others, whether at their request, or under a sense of duty, great stress should be laid upon the charm of prompt and cheerful kindness. A very young child can be made to understand that a service slowly

---

* A French writer uses a happy expression when she says—'La prévenance c'est la menue-monnaie des affections, c'est l'art si doux et si feminin de compâtir aux petites peines, de partager les petites satisfactions, de *caresser la pensée.*'—*Le Mariage au Point de Vue Chrétien.* Par Mde. de Gasparin. Vol. i. p. 113.

or grudgingly yielded, the cost of a sacrifice painted on the countenance and exhibited before the person who has consented to accept it, destroys its value. In the same manner she will easily feel the difference between the generous and the ungenerous spirit of liberality—that which merely *gives*, whether time, or trouble, or money, and that which makes the gift a messenger from heart to heart.

In ordinary conditions of health, the subordinate position of women, which enforces much self-denial, combined with the natural strength of their affections, preserves them in great measure from the hateful vice of selfishness ; though many are led into selfish acts through an irritable temper, the habit of acting without reflection, through frivolity, indolence, or mere ignorance. For it is well to remember that the thoughtless are inevitably selfish, however guiltless in intention. But the warm feelings of women, and the mere habit of submitting at home to the will and fancies of others, make it rare for them to follow a deliberately selfish course, and prevent that complete immersion in self of which we see examples in men who are full of high and kind feeling when it is distinctly appealed to—a selfishness which blunts the very perception of claims or rights that militate against their own.

When women are really selfish, it is when a thoroughly frivolous education, the absence of moral discipline, and a life of trifling and amusement have exercised their combined influence over a cold or a shallow nature. In their utter ignorance of life, such women are unconscious of the existence of any deeper feelings, any higher duties, than they acknowledge themselves. They have no perception of anything nobler in human life than their own petty pursuits. We see them accordingly sacrificing their husbands' public or private interests, sometimes perilling his character, for the gratification of some whim, incapable of sympathizing in any serious pursuit he has at heart, even forgetting the claims of their children in a course of careless indolence, or in the race after the wretched pleasures of their butterfly existence. But, thank God, such women are rare, and in those whom defects of nature or education may lead into temporary disregard of others, one touch of real feeling generally dispels the mischief, and brings the self-denying, self-devoted character of the true woman to light once more.

Whether the danger of growing selfish arises from ill-health or thoughtlessness, the surest corrective is the cultivation of the benevolent affections, and of the sense of the duty of usefulness. The feeling that no human being has a right to be a mere idle drone in this great working world may be early awakened in children, and is a powerful antagonist of selfishness. Every kindly impulse should be cherished, but no reliance placed on impulse alone. It is not simply where we love, or where strong feelings point, that charity is enjoined by Christianity, or that the duty of usefulness, a part of charity, is seen to end. We have little time for sickly selfish fancies, when the wants, the cares, the happiness, the sufferings of our fellow-creatures are become our care; that which, according to the nature of their claims upon us and the degree of power we possess, we feel it a duty to attend to. The approaches of selfishness will still further be combated when the young mind is able to understand the power of influence and the moral responsibility entailed by it; to see that not one of us, however humble, can stand alone; that we influence and are influenced— support and are supported—injure and are injured, by each other's opinions and actions, and that each one of us therefore by the whole tenor of our conduct and thoughts is making an impression for good or evil in that small circle of our own generation that surrounds us, and through them on how many more whose very being is unknown to us?

Then again the social instincts of human nature may be pointed out; those laws of our moral being which, as Dr. Butler says, make it ' plainly appear that there are real and the same kind of indications in human nature, that we were made for society, and to do good to our fellow-creatures, as that we were intended to take care of our own life, and health, and private good.'* These things all tend to prove that it is not by following nature, but only by sacrificing one part of our nature to the other, that man ever attempts to make *self* the one pivot of action and desire. As well might he, because the necessity of sleep is part of his constitution, neglect food or motion, which he is equally constituted to require.

Views such as these presented to the young mind when it first begins to reflect upon life, and its own relations to what surrounds it, will have more influence in making a selfish course appear utterly wrong and unnatural than hours of lecturing about selfishness.

Long, however, before reflections of this nature could be appreciated, the *habit* of attending to others may be trained—that active habit of kindness and usefulness which is so opposed to all morbid feelings, whether of selfishness or of compassion. Little children can easily be led to think it a pleasure and a privilege to be allowed to do something for others—a

---

* BUTLER'S *First Sermon upon Human Nature*, p. 5. Fourth edition, 1749.

privilege which the weakness and ignorance of their age seldom allows them to enjoy, but which successive years by adding to their power will enable them to use more and more freely. They will also early feel pride and pleasure in finding that their power of rendering service entitles them to consideration from others — that in proportion as they are useful they rise above the mere childish condition. Services to be rendered at home to a sick or aged person, attendance upon father or mother when they are engaged in anything that requires assistance, all these should be held up as pleasures. They may be made the reward of good conduct, and the privation of them the punishment for impatience or ill-temper, which evidently prove the mind to be for the time in an unfit state to have charge of another person's comfort. Every little service rendered by a child should of course be received with pleasure, never with praise, as if some act of virtue had been performed, but with the simple words or manner expressive of gratification in being oneself the object of active kindness. Undoubtedly it is the mere duty of children to attend upon their parents; but if the latter take the care and attention as their due only, without a loving word to reward the labour of love, the young heart loses half the joy such performance of duty ought to bring, and parents must not wonder if the time comes when they receive only the attention that duty prompts, while the alacrity of affectionate service is shown where it is greeted in the same spirit that offers it.

But parents who sternly accept the services of their children, or are even exacting in requiring it, do them a less injury than those who with mistaken indulgence require nothing of them; who look upon it as a toil or a hardship that a child's play, or a young person's pursuits or amusements, should be set aside to attend to the wants or comforts of their elders. In the first case the heart is defrauded of a joy only ; in the latter it is robbed of a high feeling ; it is hardened against a call of duty. And the mind, allowed to remain blunted to the perception of the duty of being useful at home, is not likely to be awake to the necessity of being useful abroad.

One great danger of delicate health is that of falling into selfish habits. Considerable attention to our own wants, comforts, and sensations is forced upon us ; the wants and comforts of others are often unavoidably sacrificed to us, till we run the risk of considering this the natural state of things, and the poor self becomes the centre of all thought and endeavour. When young persons are subject to ill-health, it should be an object of great solicitude to prevent this moral disease growing upon the physical one.

The young invalid should have this danger of her position clearly pointed out to her : all that is done for her so willingly and carefully should be dwelt upon, and her thoughts turned frequently to consider what means of kindness and usefulness are left to her in her comparatively powerless state.   If others run about for her, perhaps she can write or work for them.   There may be a younger child to teach, or a little thing to watch while it plays about, and would disturb those who have more business on their hands.   Or an aged relative may just require the presence of some person in the room, or such slight services as any may perform who are not actually deprived of motion.   Even if in the latter state, the notion of usefulness must not be abandoned—the mind must not be left to the dreary worship of self.   Many little offices of kindness may even then be performed in the way of needlework, or accounts, or hearing a child read; and if by no such small things, then by what is greater and nobler than any manual service, by the example of patience and courage, by the daily conflict carried on between the soaring spirit and the suffering body, the sight of which may influence for ever the minds of those who frequently behold it.

'They also serve who only stand and wait,'

said our great poet; and we must be ready to accept any form of service towards our fellow-creatures that God is pleased to call upon us to undertake.

High-spirited imaginative girls easily fall into the error of forgetting the value of small things, and because they cannot reform prisons, undertake great works of benevolence, or spend their energy in missionary labours or plans of national utility, they sit down and mourn over woman's destiny, and let each day float down the stream of time with its freight of small duties and cares unobserved and unattended to.   They require to have the peculiarities of woman's vocation of usefulness explained to them.   All the rough work of the world is done for them ; in all classes that are above manual labour they generally, at any rate after marriage, know nothing of care or toil beyond their own homes.   A few eager spirits may wish it were not so, but the great majority find this the most happy and suitable condition for the feeblest half of the human race; it follows then that all the small daily cares that make home an abode of comfort—the kindly service, the prompt feeling and sympathy, all the labour of love that softens trial, or soothes sorrow, or comforts in sickness, is their debt to society.   It is not merely a matter of feeling requiring that the service should be requited with feeling, but a question of duty, into which the idea of requital does not enter at all. This view of woman's vocation guards her at once against the danger of despising small means of usefulness, or of being absorbed in trifling things. When trifles are duly considered in their relations as parts of a wider system, we need not fear that they should tend to foster frivolity.

§ 5.—One very essential point, both as regards health and temper, is the cultivation of habitual cheerfulness. To women it is doubly necessary. When we consider woman's life, we see that it is less subject than man's to sudden vicissitudes of fortune, to bitter mortifications and failures of ambition ; but, on the other hand, it is far less brightened by hope, less supported by the feeling of power to conquer fate by energy and exertion. Even among those who do labour to better their fortunes, the means are so small, the paths so few, that success itself affords to the mind no better stimulus than the hope of earning a subsistence, and perhaps of avoiding a miserable dependence in old age.

Among the large classes of women who are exempt from all necessity of labour, depression is not unfrequently the tone of their whole lives—a grey sunless day sinking into a cloudy twilight. Marriage, the one event that can bring change, is too often sought from motives which leave little right to complain that it has not brought happiness; and if shrinking from this uncertain lot a woman remains unmarried, then her years glide by in joyless monotony. Like some cheerless heath spreading out under the fading twilight, where no sound of human activity or gladness meets the ear, so the long future stretches out before her, and the spirit in which she will tread it must depend on the state of her own mind alone. Even in the ordinary trials or depressing circumstances of life which come alike to us all, a man has his business or his profession to distract his thoughts ; it may be irksome at first to attend to it, but it is a real blessing in the end. If he have no business he is free to seek the relief of change ; he can subdue gloom or irritability by the help of bodily motion on foot or on horseback, or seek society if he is in a mood to wish for it. But a woman must bear her depression in the midst of the same daily occupations which the very depression has made distasteful to her. Her business or relaxation is equally among the home scenes which recal and keep alive every painful association; and if she have no power in herself to resist the influence of circumstances, they will inevitably affect the nerves, and perhaps permanently depress the spirits.

Another reason makes it essential to women that the tone of their spirits should not depend on external stimulus; it is this : that not only are the occasions when they can enjoy such stimulus comparatively rare, but the excitement itself is generally frivolous in its nature ; it rouses no energy, it makes no call on the intellect, it comes in the form of pleasure only,—and to rely on pleasure for so inestimable a blessing as cheerfulness, is like depending for light on the flickering glare of a gas-burner, while the broad sunshine is unheeded without.   The source of cheerfulness, then, like every other spring of action in woman's life, must be from *within*, from habitual self-regulation.

But the strength required to be cheerful under a naturally depressed condition is greater than is generally allowed by those who have not themselves been obliged to struggle against the opposite tendency; a habit of cheerfulness deserves therefore to be sedulously cultivated from early childhood.   It is true that in childhood depression is rare except under circumstances of real suffering, bodily or mental ; but the latter is more common than ordinary observers suppose.   When surrounded with substantial kindness, when real wants are supplied and reasonable indulgence shown, we are apt to take it for granted that a child has all it requires and must be happy; but some children require more, and are far from happiness in this apparently enviable condition.   The *more* they want arises from a craving of the mind which is sometimes overlooked altogether, and sometimes when perceived is, perhaps with the best intentions, purposely set at nought.   It is an over-sensitive nature in the child, or an easily excited imagination or nervous system, that makes it require sympathy, and long to pour out feelings or fancies that come with a sort of nameless oppression, half pleasure, half pain; and kind-hearted persons think they are doing right to check this, which they believe tends to weaken the mind, and thus they will not afford the relief and support the child wants, but leave it to struggle alone.   Now if it were true that by such a process we did strengthen the over-sensitive nature, this course, however painful, might often be right; but it is not so—the mind recoils from the touch of coldness or sarcasm—thought and feeling are repressed outwardly, to be cherished all the more in secret.   Boys, who in addition to this injudicious treatment at home go through the rough worldly apprenticeship of school, grow hard, and often, as a natural consequence, selfish; while girls become depressed, morbid in fancy and sentiment, and with that painful feeling of isolation which springs from the consciousness of living spiritually alone while surrounded by those who are nearest and dearest.   It scarcely needs remark how directly such a state of feeling at a later period leads a girl into the danger of taking the first man who speaks words of love to her, for the one being fated by Heaven to give her the sympathy she has craved for so long in vain.

However wayward or foolish, then, a child's fancy or emotions may appear, it is most important that the young creature should never feel itself misunderstood, or looked upon with derision. Give sympathy first, and then the child will easily be led to believe that greater knowledge and experience of life will correct the views or sober the sentiments which she has now expressed. Whenever it can be done with truth, it is advisable to point out that those views or sentiments are quite natural at her age, or with her turn of mind; that others have felt the same, and have gradually come round to other feelings. By this means the young mind is saved alike from the temptation of continuing to maintain from vanity what she believes to be peculiar or interesting, and from the feeling of half sadness and half fear which possesses acutely sensitive minds, when, in their inexperience, they believe that they stand alone in sentiment or opinion. The difficulties of dealing with cases of this nature are among the many things that make unimaginative persons so unfit to have the charge of children at any age. However kindly or high-minded their influence may be, it throws a chill shadow around, beneath which many a root of bitter or unhealthy feeling has sprung up to a sickly growth.

Everything round children,—the voice, manner, tone of thought of those who are most with them,—should be cheerful. The nature of a healthy child is to be happy; it requires no outward stimulus; active or passive enjoyment is the normal condition of its existence; but it is easily disturbed, not only by illness but by bad management or uncongenial influence. At a later period, when nature has no longer undisturbed sway, the severer the mental labour required, and the higher the sense of duty inculcated, the more careful should we be that no sternness accompanies them. Cheerful alacrity in conduct, as in study, is the quality to aim at. The love of knowledge and the delight it is calculated to afford should be kept before the mind, not the dry necessity of working up to any fixed point. And so with conduct: we may instil into the young heart the conviction that the peace of a satisfied conscience is a treasure, for the loss of which no joy to be gained by a sacrifice of duty can compensate—we may inspire the love of truth and goodness, that love that ' casteth out fear,' and makes gloom seem almost alien to religion. Every encouragement should be given to all forms of healthy innocent enjoyment, to merry games, to light-hearted fun; more especially should this be our endeavour at the age when the happiness of early childhood—that happiness in mere existence—passes away; when the restless spirit begins to stir within, and to inquire and sound its own sensations and sift its enjoyments; then double care should be taken to surround it as far as may be with all things bright and fair, and to keep the mind not only active but joyous in its activity.

We are perhaps too apt to look upon religion as the proper source of cheerfulness; unfortunately with some minds, it rather leads to calm endurance, than to a cheerful struggle with the ills of life. The mind naturally subject to depression learns from ordinary religious views to despise this weary existence while looking forward to happiness beyond; but not to seize and cultivate all the means of cheerfulness and innocent enjoyment which can make this life happier to ourselves and others while it pleases God to leave us upon earth. Religion is indeed the only true source of resignation and fortitude under real calamity, under those dire strokes of Fate which unpeople the world to us with the closing of a grave, or make life so bitter that if earth were our only heritage, it would be mere weak folly to stay and bear its tortures. Here it is that religion comes in with its sublime motives and hopes, and strengthens the fainting, and calms the maddening soul. But in the petty trials of every-day life, the mind, however pious, will be swayed by its constitutional tendency to cheerfulness or despondency. A very uncharitable judgment is sometimes passed on those who are habitually depressed, when it is supposed that if they really believed in what they profess to hold sacred, they could not be cast down by earthly trials. Persons who judge in this manner not only overlook the considerations I have urged, but also forget this fact, that the very trial the naturally depressed have always to contend with, *is inability to hope;* there lies the very root of their suffering. If they had power to draw consolation from a distant prospect of happiness or assurance of good, and thus to derive cheerfulness from religious trust, they would not be so powerless to see the cheering tints which, to more happily constituted minds, brighten also the gloom of daily life. There is another danger in trusting to religion principally as the means of cultivating a cheerful spirit—namely, that naturally depressed minds are at least equally likely to seize upon the terrors as the consolations of religion, and then another victim is added to the many whom religious melancholy has led to the very threshold of a mad-house,—if not through its gates, to the less dreary refuge of the grave.

Highly-wrought sensibility, great susceptibility of feeling, the quick and exquisite sensation of pleasure or of pain,—all these, which are common to the delicate nervous organizations of women, are foes to habitual cheerfulness; not only because what are slight wounds to harder natures are deeply painful to them, but also because after every excitement follows a reaction : the nerves are unstrung, and whether pain or pleasure has been the exciting cause, depression follows, just as a period of complete exhaustion follows some over-exertion of physical strength. This is one of the points that requires very delicate handling in female education, and in which the remedy must come entirely from cultivating an opposing principle of strength. Repression, even could it be successful, would be dangerous in other respects ; with natures such as I am speaking of, the feelings, denied all outward manifestation, would only prey upon the mind, and either affect health or give a morbid tone to the whole character. Girls must undoubtedly be taught to control emotion, and to be reserved in expressing strong feeling ; but the feeling itself should never be checked—it is the very life of woman. Better were it for her to remain over-sensitive or weak, the creature of warm impulse and erring judgment—anything but hard and insensible. In the former case she may be unhappy and win little respect, but in the latter she becomes a thing out of nature, and closes our hearts against her. The world has suffered enough from women's feebleness and ignorance ; but life would be a dreary wilderness, a cold arena of discussion and strife, without woman's tenderness and sympathy.

Nature provided against this, the worst evil, by giving to women generally great strength and warmth of feeling in proportion to their mental power ; it is the duty of education to correct what might become dangerous in this natural tendency by using every means to strengthen the reason. Unfortunately the common method has been the reverse of this. The exuberant sensibility has either been coldly checked and silenced, or where this has not been aimed at, the weakness has been encouraged by the frequent appeal to sentiment and the neglect of all vigorous cultivation of the understanding ; while moral training itself has been exclusively based upon religion, the highest of all appeals to the feelings.

Parents should be on their guard with a foreign governess, lest instead of repressing she should rather cultivate sensibility as something interesting, and encourage the exhibition of emotion. One of the striking characteristics of the English is their calm self-possession. This may be carried too far ; the calmness may be cold as foreigners generally esteem it to be, and the repression of emotion may tend to repress feeling too much, and to produce that unlovable disposition that neither gives nor values sympathy. But, except when thus exaggerated, calmness and self-possession are among the most valuable features of character, and deserve more especially to be cultivated in women, whose naturally quick susceptibility and irritable nervous temperaments require all the force of habit to keep them in that equable condition in which judgment is fit to act, and reason able to maintain the empire over feeling. Exaggerated sentiment, whether expressed in language or in violent emotion, is also likely in England to expose persons who fall into it to ridicule and misconstruction. It is repugnant to English tastes and habits, and is not only harshly judged, but it is also perhaps more dangerous when combined with other features of our national character. The feeling or emotion which with the easily excited and easily changed mood of the majority of foreigners evaporates in mere words or in tears of joy or grief, becomes far more intense when joined to the deeper and more earnest disposition of the English : the first outburst is not more violent, but it cannot pass away so rapidly; it shakes the over-sensitive mind to its very depths, leaving a morbid tone—a fitful state of excitement and depression, that is unhealthy to body and mind.

Madame de Saussure, in her work on Education, speaks more than once of the craving for strong emotions as a fault women are likely to fall into. That this is not true of Englishwomen we may well rejoice to say, for it would be difficult to describe a state of feeling more likely to be injurious to purity and refinement of mind as well as to happiness. One glance at the calm sphere of domestic joys and duties which constitute woman's world, suffices to show that suffering, if not degradation, must be the result of that restless craving. Not only, however, do we find that it is a common fault among foreigners, but Madame de Saussure speaks of a *' prétension à l'impressionabilité '* as one of the characteristics of the times, and I can hardly fancy a worse form of affectation, or one more calculated to excite disgust in all who value delicacy of feeling. Madame de Saussure compares it with the affectation of learning,* which had exposed women to so much ridicule, and justly considers it far more reprehensible; but in truth the latter is a harmless folly, which scarcely deserves to be brought into such comparison.

---

* ' Vanité pour vanité, celle-là (la pédanterie) ne serait pas si profondement corruptrice que l'envie aujourd'hui si fréquente d'éprouver soi-même et d'exciter des émotions. '—*Education Progressive*, vol. iii., p. 134.

Whether the Germans may be accused of this odious affectation of a fault I know not, but there is an excited tone about their correspondence and in their works of fiction which proves the existence of the fault itself. Friendship borrows the vehemence of passion, joy is ecstatic, grief is despair, religion is a rapturous sentiment, and thought itself is expressed in high-flown imagery; distinctness and accuracy being too often sacrificed to a vague grandeur of conception. These are forms of language too prevalent in Germany not to indicate prevailing mental defects, which we should be sorry to see gaining any ground in this country. These are, therefore, points deserving serious attention in engaging either a French or a German governess; it is probable that the influence of the latter might be more injurious, because stronger, than that of the former. The vague sentiment and enthusiasm of the Germans has a deeper root than the vapouring exaggeration of the French; they are more earnest, and therefore more likely to influence; they are more sad, and have therefore more affinity with the English mind and would be more readily imbibed by the pupil.

Whenever we apprehend danger from the over-excitement of the emotional part of our nature, the surest means to avert it is by the sedulous exercise of the faculties on subjects which for a time preclude the sway of feeling. Let the high sensibility be directed to channels of active bene-volence, where the force of habit will tend to lessen passive impressions, and therefore to calm emotion and sober fancy, while strengthening the desire for exertion in the cause of others. Cherish all quiet, cheerful forms of pursuit or amusement. Give full and warm sympathy whenever you can feel justified in doing so, and thus win the right to attack all morbid sentiment without incurring a suspicion of coldness; and carefully but unobtrusively draw the thoughts away from regions where feeling and emotion can be kindled, to find mental excitement in new forms of knowledge or speculation, or in wider observation of life and action. By such means we may hope to preserve the exquisite sensibility which is so great a charm, while ensuring a considerable measure of that serene cheerfulness which is so important to happiness and that strength of judg-ment and habitual command of reason without which the most lovable natures fall miserably below the influence and the power of usefulness that ought to be theirs.

Another difficulty with regard to repressing quick susceptibility in girls is that this very susceptibility is what makes them keenly alive to praise and censure, and there are few points in female education harder to deal with than this. We have seen that the constant care for appearances tends to deaden moral courage, yet we cannot say to a girl, 'Be indifferent to opinion so long as you are right, pursue your course with self-confidence, only avoiding presumption.' The advice would be full of peril and moreover almost impossible to follow, for it involves a false assumption, the self-confidence could never have any real basis. The quiet routine of domestic life affords no sufficient criterion by which our own powers can be accurately tested. A boy tries his strength among his equals from the moment he goes to school. He learns his own value, be it high or low; later the same lesson is given on a wider stage, therefore it is that diffidence is less pleasing, and conceit far more inexcusable in men than in women. No young woman can have so tried her own capability or worth as compared with others, as to arrive at a reasonable appreciation of herself, or to have reached that assurance of power on which a rational self-confidence is grounded. This is one cause, both of timidity and of that eager snatching at some wider exercise of their faculties, which is occasionally seen, and which is reproved or ridiculed as love of excitement by those men especially who though they have the widest sphere of activity opened to themselves restrict their exertions to the stable or the kennel.

In this inability to feel confident of herself, how could a woman be indifferent to opinion, even were such indifference safe ? Truly, the most excellent of women may not dare with impunity to disregard even the trifles of public opinion. The small pleasures of such independence are far from being worth the penalty which will assuredly be exacted. The higher a woman's tone of character, the more earnest her desire to tread a wider path of usefulness than most of her sex are content with, and the greater her capacity for doing so, the more will she consult her own happiness and the interest of her own pursuits and influence, by scrupulously attending to the trifles which the world expects a woman to understand. There is no better reason for teaching women to detest frivolity than this, that they never can throw off the yoke of trifling things.

While girls are thus forced to measure many actions of daily life by an uncertain standard, it is evident that the quick susceptibility, by means of which they read only too easily the feelings of others concerning them, may often become an instrument of torture, yet we dare not encourage indifference. The best safeguard a young girl can have is in perfect respect, reverence, and love for the guides of her youth, which makes trust in their approbation take the place of self-confidence. It is in this respect that parents who over-value their daughters, and express their joy and pride in them in a manner offensive sometimes to good taste, fall into a less dangerous error than those who are ever ready to find fault, or who even withhold the expression of their praise or esteem. The girl who is depressed at home from not feeling sure of approbation or sympathy, will have no ground of self-confidence abroad. Want of experience may lead her to vacillation in conduct, and hesitation in manner, seeking to please, and afraid to offend; or else to defiant determination to take her own way, not aware that what she calls honest and straightforward, the world will call presumptuous and singular. But, on the other hand, she who knows that she is valued and approved by those who know and love her best, and whose opinion is to her all that is wise in public opinion, will be in a state of calm yet safe indifference about the judgment of others; she has self-reliance, but it is not the confidence of presumption. There is a source of rest and strength in this feeling, even if it be not altogether well-grounded, and we may be sure the experience of a few years will correct any error fostered by a too partial estimate; while, on the contrary, the uncertainty and restlessness caused by the opposite system are poison to a life which, in all essential things, must be bounded by home.

The quiet self-possession which springs from the feeling of being loved and valued at home for what we are really worth, by those whose opinion we respect, is also a great safeguard against vanity. The vain are for ever oscillating between the weakest dependence and the most assuming self-confidence, if indeed that word can be applied in any sense to the capricious mood born of the approbation or flattery of others. The estimate formed at home must be upon solid and permanent qualities of heart and mind; the estimate formed of young girls in society can only be founded on the impressions made by manner, voice, liveliness of conversation, accomplishments, or more commonly by dress and appearance; these, therefore, assume an undue importance in proportion as the opinion of society, and not home approbation is the test of her own merit which a girl is led to depend upon. I believe the almost unavoidable importance that opinion assumes in a life which affords no means of testing our worth or powers as compared with others, gives the appearance of vanity to many a woman whose heart is really free from it, accordingly it is often a less enduring fault in women than in men, the weakness of early years only, corrected by experience and the earnest duties of life. Men have not in their youth the natural inducements to vanity that women are surrounded with, nor do they throw it off with the follies of youth.

But where there is a natural tendency to vanity, there is scarcely a fault that a mother should watch more assiduously or check more severely; whereas unfortunately it is encouraged not only indirectly by the whole system of education, which looks to appearances instead of realities, but even directly as a thing to be desired in itself. Parents have been heard to say that they wished their daughters to be vain; that a woman was unendurable without vanity. In other words, that a woman was nothing worth without the applause of society, and that the surest way of winning that applause is early to make it the ruling principle of life. And according to their aim they are right. It is another instance of the ' children of the world being wiser in their generation than the children of light,' for there is that perfect harmony between the means and the end, which ensures success.

The dangers of vanity to women are manifold. Its gratification must be sought out of home, and that alone is sufficient condemnation in the eyes of all who look to woman's real happiness; it leads, of course, to prefer display to knowledge, brilliant appearances to unassuming realities, flattery to affection and sincerity. A vain person also is generally one of slow and rare sympathies. The mind engrossed with the thought of the impression it wishes to produce, or has produced, has little leisure to read the feelings of others, still less to forget itself in their happiness or misery. Vanity is a perennial source of selfishness and weakness. It makes even great and good actions, when the nature is capable of such, subservient to a little purpose. Self is still the centre, applause the breath of life; and talent, affections, home joys, and the real esteem of mankind are sacrificed to the petty triumphs, on which the soul, starved from better food, has been taught to live.

Vanity in women most commonly attaches itself to personal appearance, and if it stopped there would be simply ridiculous. But this frivolous form of the vice too commonly leads to another which is too hateful for ridicule, to vanity in the power of playing with human feelings, self-gratulation in making a manly heart bleed under strokes given in sport; triumph in seeing a woman's life wither under the loss of ties a despicable self-worship has withered. She who began with being vain of a mere outward form, ends with being vain of a crime !

It is true that personal vanity does not always lead to coquetry, and that coquetry itself may be of a less dangerous character than here

7

described; but the former must be contemptible, and the latter cannot be altogether innocent; it cannot be free from guile, it cannot be guiltless of sporting with feelings which every simple and honest heart will hold sacred; it must be indifferent, to say the least, to exciting the storm it has no power to quell.

The miserable system of match-making, so prevalent in England, by which girls are dressed up and taken out into society to find husbands, is of course a hot-bed of vanity and coquetry. It is not what they *are*, but what they can *seem* during a few gay hours which ensures the triumph; it is not the esteem to be slowly won, but the feelings to be quickly excited, the passion to be kindled and kept in play, that secure the desired object. No wonder, while such is the parents' aim for their daughters, that frivolity and vanity should preside over their education.

Those who have other aims will watch the first buddings of vanity, and take every precaution to prevent their expansion. Some people wishing to check a vain child, decry her appearance or abilities, and fancy that by thus slighting her, they will lead her to think less of herself. But such a system would, even in the case of mere conceit, act as a temporary check only. The wrong feeling would be mortified, not changed. On the contrary, praise warmly given at times, adds force to the censure expressed on other occasions.

It is better to be quite candid with young girls, both as to their appearance and abilities, they should have no flattering discoveries to make in society, and though they will find advantage of looks or manner valued more in proportion there than at home, that will not do much mischief when they have learned the value of the higher praise which a woman can win at home only. The consciousness of possessing well founded regard and approbation in her own family must, as I said before, replace to her the self-reliance which public success gives to a man, and from early childhood we may be building up the associations which shall make such regard and approbation a heart-felt joy, and mere drawing-room praise a thing of small account, like any of the other pleasant sounds or scenes that excite a momentary enjoyment, and are forgotten as soon as they have passed.

§ 6.—The state of the health and of the physical constitution generally affect more or less all the points we have dwelt upon in this chapter; and this view, so important in education, is one which appears to me not to be attended to as it deserves. Irritability or good-temper, cheerfulness or discontent, alacrity or sullenness, selfishness, susceptibility, diffidence, and timidity, all are influenced by the physical elements of the constitution, the favourable or unfavourable organization, or nerves, or by mere differences of strength, and it must be the educator's ceaseless task so to watch, that while health is cherished to the utmost, yet that as childhood passes away the spiritual nature may more and more rise above the dominion of the physical, and attain to as much freedom as is compatible with the mysterious conditions of our double existence. In childhood our great care must be to remove all physical hindrances to mental and moral development, and in youth to awaken the courage which looks steadily at the physical condition, whatever it may be, and determines to conquer or to endure in patience.

I must not be supposed to refer all moral or mental symptoms to the bodily condition, for no doubt excellent health has often accompanied a most distressing state of moral feeling, I simply mean that the connexion between the two is too intimate to be ever safely overlooked, and that although many children, for instance, may be ill-tempered and discontented without suffering in health, there is always a suspicion that the latter is not right, and that if the irritability or the depression are simply mental they will, at any rate, be greatly aggravated by neglect of physical precautions.

Temper in most children suffers almost immediately from any bodily discomfort, and habitual fretfulness under circumstances when a child ought to be happy and contented, is perhaps always the sign of something internally wrong, it may be of some constitutional peculiarity which medical investigation alone would detect. On the other hand a fit of passion will disturb the circulation or digestion, and frequently repeated may interfere materially with health. Observations such as these are almost inevitably made in every nursery, but they are not consistently acted upon in the management of the children. Illness or naughtiness is apparent at the moment, and no sufficient trouble is taken to ascertain whether the cause was moral or physical. One child, for instance, who has made itself ill with a fit of passion is petted and coaxed as an invalid, while it really deserves punishment, and might receive it in a beneficial form either by taking a dose of medicine or being sent to bed. Another child, on the contrary, who is not obviously ill is scolded as naughty, while in truth it is suffering from that general nervous irritation which proceeds from bodily derangement.

Another point not sufficiently considered in the management of pas-

7—2

sionate children, especially if of a nervous organization, is the violence of the physical agitation which accompanies the mental paroxysms. It should be remembered that all emotion, even though springing from some moral source, is partly physical in its effects. The habit of years enables us to control these signs by which every passion, whether joy or grief, love, hate, or fear, betrays its presence, and in some constitutions they may be entirely suppressed; in general, however, even after the mental emotion has sub-sided the nerves are still shaken, the lips quiver, the heart is still disturbed in its action, the breath comes quick or laboured, and if this be so in the full vigour of life, how can we expect it to be otherwise with the tender frame of the young creatures who have not yet learnt to control or to con-ceal any physical sensation? yet how common it is when a child has had a violent fit of passion to hear it commanded suddenly to stop crying, to banish the signs of ill-temper, to speak certain words under threat of punishment, while there is actual physical impossibility of obeying? If the disobedience be then treated as a fault, the child feels the injustice; and supposing the original sin to have been one of temper, the evil is only increased; a new burst of violence may even follow from the irritation caused by fruitless attempts to obey a command which should never have been given. When a child has been shaken by emotion, the latter should have ample time to subside. Where there is reason to believe that the child is willing to make an effort, it is well to express that belief, speaking gently but without any relaxation of firmness. Lying down a few minutes will help to still the beating of the heart, and the throbbing of the temples which show how the delicate frame has suffered; and a glass of cold water will sometimes restore the power of self-command by helping to overcome that involuntary sobbing, which ill-judged persons *scold at* as naughtiness and thus increase, while it is completely hysterical in its character and requires the same quieting treatment as any other nervous affection.

It is common to hear it said that a child is in ' a naughty mood ;' and it is true that irritability, peevishness, in short every form of perverse temper the little creature is liable to often does recur in fits, not apparently owing to outward circumstances that have provoked it, but to the mood within. This surely points to some cause that deserves to be sought out. Injudicious teachers choose that time to be more than usually exacting, and thereby provoke the rebellious spirit they intended to break.

The naughty mood should on the contrary be a time for forbearance. There is probably some physical cause at work, if we could detect it ; digestion or circulation is wrong, and at any rate the mind being in a sick state, it is manifestly not a moment to test its strength. It might be dangerous to let a child see that such considerations, which he cannot understand, affect our view of his conduct; but unless they do so, we shall certainly fail very often in our treatment of him. Let all irritating things be avoided as far as possible at such times; it is better to be blind or deaf to slight things, which if noticed must call forth rebuke, since the disturbed mood is perhaps only waiting for an occasion of contest, the excitement of which gives a morbid pleasure. If it could be done without incurring suspicion of the motive, it would be well on such occasions rather to abridge the lessons, and increase the sleep or the exercise according to circumstances. Sometimes this may be openly avowed, when the alternative for the lessons is not agreeable enough to induce a child to remember the naughty day with any satisfaction. The book may be closed on the plea that the child is evidently unfit to attend or derive any profit from it, and an hour in bed, or spent in walking up and down, as circumstances may suggest, may be substituted for the lesson. Tiring out the limbs, while breathing fresh air invigorates the nerves, is one of the best modes of subduing irritation.

I knew a child who, from seven years old till she was thirteen, was subject to the most fearful violence of temper unless she walked many miles every day. Everything was vigorous in her except her power of self-restraint. Had she been confined to a school-room, and forced to do, or punished for not doing like other children, those years would probably have been spent in constant disgrace and wretchedness, and moral victory would perhaps only have been purchased at last by the sacrifice of the physical strength. But a more rational system was adopted. She was allowed to take the full amount of exercise her peculiar constitution required, going out sometimes for hours with her father; she went to bed earlier than the other children, great attention was paid to all the detail of health, she did few lessons, and those more often alone than with her sisters. The result of this mode of treatment was, that her health was excellent; gradually more equilibrium was established between the moral and physical power, and as she grew beyond childhood, nothing remained of the intemperate nature, while she retained great strength and quickness of feeling, and a vigorous decided character.

The necessity of submitting children of different temperaments to the same treatment, is one of the evils of schools which we ought to avoid in home-education. It causes undoubtedly some increase of trouble if several children do not sleep, walk, or study the same number of hours, but the very difference of age within the same family must render this necessary to a great degree. The mistake is in not perceiving that considerations of health are the most imperious necessity of all, and that to sacrifice them to apparent method in following a set of rules, is to be truly ignorant of the very nature and objects of method. In a work like the present, rules must be laid down which give the appearance of rigidity to a system, but nothing more is meant than to state what seems the best course when no superior reasons interfere. The whole moral, physical, and intellectual constitution of the individual child must be taken into account before any system can be decided upon; and then none given in books will probably be adopted without modifications.

One child is eager to learn, or of an anxious, earnest mind, and works its brain more during two hours than one of an idle, volatile disposition in three; if therefore they are kept an equal time at lessons, the last hour will over-task the more eager child, and very likely tell upon health, producing nervous irritability or depression. If by a further mode of injudicious treatment these symptoms of mental exhaustion are treated as ebullitions of temper, there is a very good chance of ending with a fit of sullenness, or tears, in short, with the very evil it was intended to subdue.

Again, one child requires a course of stimulants both moral and intellectual, while another is in need of sedatives, but careless teachers, or those who are too ignorant to watch minute symptoms, treat them alike, and the depressed will too probably become sullen, and the excitable captious, if not violent.

The physician is not sufficiently brought into the counsels of those who are engaged in education. There is too generally a half superstitious repugnance to giving due weight to physical causes, as influencing moral and intellectual development. In some minds there is an unreasoning religious dislike to acknowledging anything but the condition of the heart and faith as having power over conduct. Another too prevalent feeling, amounting to a superstitious dread, is that with which the slightest approach to the subject of mental deficiency or derangement is avoided; yet who can tell how much of real and fearful insanity might have been averted if the early symptoms of mental malady, or of that want of balance in the faculties which indicates lurking evil, had been watched and guarded against from the beginning.

The word insanity suggests at once every image that is painful and abhorrent to our minds, but we must remember that there are almost numberless shades of mental as of physical derangement, and that slight symptoms of many fearful disorders show no revolting aspect, and will lead to little or no mischief if checked in time. Dr. Mayo* classes under one form of derangement those in whom, while the ordinary faculties of the understanding are developed, the moral sense cannot be cultivated so as to have its just authority over conduct. There would be in such persons a capacity for transacting business, but an incapacity for truth or justice. Now without considering extreme cases, what strange differences do we find in children with regard to the obtuseness of the moral faculty! Would it not be safer to regard it from the first, in the light of an indication of possible disease, of partial disturbance, than to content ourselves with moral exhortations which the very character of the evil deprives of all force? Would it not be better to seek any remedial measures that science can suggest than to let the child grow up to be at the mercy of circumstance whether he shall remain a mere selfish brute, impassive to the highest motives that govern other men, or whether he shall commit some fearful crime which will make the very mother who bore him wish that she had dug his grave by the side of his cradle?

What again is that extreme waywardness which we see in some children and which does not always pass away with childhood; that apparent delight in being naughty which later takes the form of craving for strong emotions even of a painful kind? We take it for granted that such conduct is voluntary, but is it really so? is not the young creature suffering under a debility of will which it may depend on our care and treatment to restore? And our treatment will necessarily depend upon the view which we take of the evil. At first we naturally look upon such things as the mere naughtiness of a child, but when ordinary remedies fail, or when the evil outlasts the usual period for such childish ebullitions, then it is surely time to look more closely into the nature of the symptoms and their tendencies and to shrink from no view however painful which may help us to decide on the best means to be adopted.

The case of the girl I mentioned above is one in which physical treatment had a marked beneficial effect upon the mind; the following is an equally remarkable instance of the failure of ordinary modes of mental and moral education in dealing with characters of an unusual stamp. The child I allude to here had a temper so violent that it baffled alike all measures of severity and of gentleness. She made home a place of torment to herself and others. Several persons in an older generation of her family had been

---

* *Elements of the Pathology of the Human Mind.* Chap. x.

noted for ferocious tempers and *eccentricity*, not to use a stronger term ; but still the notion of infirmity of the brain does not in her case seem to have presented itself, or if it did, it was thrust aside without any one daring to seek advice that might have thrown light upon the fearful surmise. The parents still trusted to moral training alone and the gradual influence of religious feeling to eradicate the evil.

She was approaching her sixteenth year when she was taken seriously ill, and from that time all symptoms of ill-temper and even of irritability disappeared.   She died at the end of a few months, having been a pattern of gentleness and patience throughout her long and trying illness.   The connexion, whatever it might have been, between the bodily and mental condition was thus proved,—too late.   Who can say what might have been the result had a physician skilled in the treatment of mental disorders or in tracing the delicate connexion between mental and physical symptoms been called in as soon as it became evident that the ordinary motives and power of self-regulation of well-constituted minds could not be awakened in her ?

But how fearful to confess that we dread insanity, or even slighter shades of mental derangement ! True—but do we avert an evil by refusing to look it in the face ? and is it not far more dreadful to allow such an evil to steal on unperceived ?

Nor is it with regard to the physical treatment alone of children betraying unusual mental symptoms that the advice of a medical man accustomed to close observation of mental and physical phenomena is likely to be of use. Slight things, which to the inexperienced seem of no importance, often suffice to indicate to him that want of proportion and balance on which perfect mental health depends, and would suggest to him precautions in the moral or intellectual discipline which might counteract a threatened evil, or help to call forth a too feeble faculty.

The necessity of watching moral symptoms as the earliest indications of a disturbance of the mental faculties, or as marking a predisposition to insanity which may become fearfully developed should favourable circumstances occur, is very forcibly laid down by Dr. Mayo in the work alluded to above.* What he says there of tendencies of a dangerous nature lurking in moral and intellectual peculiarities, but especially in the former, which are usually looked upon as of little consequence, puts in a strong light the importance of the view I am endeavouring to advocate.

---

* *Elements of the Pathology of the Human Mind.* By Dr. T. Mayo. Chap. ii.

For instance : how seldom do parents consider in any serious light whether their children are more or less cheerful, whether they are hopeful or desponding, confident and resolute, or undecided and prone to regret ? When such points are thought of at all it is with a view to their influence on active life, as leading to success or failure in pursuits, and therefore with girls they are perhaps uncared for altogether.   But Dr. Mayo sees in these states of the mind the first conditions of mental health or disease. After carefully going over each separate point, and marking where the enfeebling influence begins, and in what manner it operates, he sums up as follows :—' If unavailing regrets, if hopefulness and either of its consequents, disappointment or despondency, if fear in any of its varieties beset us—if the moral faculty be not strong enough to supply us with fixed principles of action,—if a large development of self-love afford us its appropriate source of regret, and if our moral constitution has rendered us unsusceptible of influence from sympathy, we are dangerously situated *quoad* insanity whatever may be the vigour or feebleness of those elements of our characters which lead to active pursuits.' *

Yet these are the things which ordinary education passes over as scarcely worthy of observation ; trusting to the experience of life to correct any defects which may follow from them, and may be regretted as unamiable, or as detrimental to worldly advancement.   Should the experience of life, however, include circumstances tending to develop the lurking seeds of evil, what will be the misery of those who in their ignorance left them to germinate unheeded ?

Dr. Mayo's views of the importance of intellectual pursuits as bearing upon mental health are also full of value ; his remark on the recklessness with which professional objects are held paramount to all others, and a boy's career determined according to his intellectual capacity, and the incitements of ambition, without reference to his moral peculiarities, and the whole tone of his mind and character, are no less interesting in their bearing upon the education of girls,—in which as these worldly objects can hold no place, intellectual cultivation and the methodical preparation for future duties and trials are neglected altogether.   The mistake in both cases is fundamentally the same, and proceeding from the same ignorance and the same error in principle.   I have already had occasion to point out this fruitful source of bad education ; † and here we find it denounced as tend-

* *Elements of the Pathology of the Human Mind.*   Chap. ii. page 35.
† Chap. i. p. 7.

106   INTELLECTUAL EDUCATION.

ing to deprive the mind of valuable safeguards against the disturbing forces which in the course of life might threaten to unsettle or overthrow the balance of the mental faculties.* I might quote many passages which would put this subject in a clearer light than I can hope to do, and enforce it with an authority to which I cannot pretend, but I prefer recommending the perusal of this short work to all who are engaged in education.

There are some cases of a very singular nature, in which the blunting of the moral feelings appears to be part of the disease, or at least accompanies its progress; cases in which young creatures formerly full of affectionate feelings, and whose truth there had been no reason to doubt, become practised impostors in simulating illness, and utterly indifferent to the misery they are inflicting. In two instances which came under my own observation, and which were subsequently referred to hysteria, inability to move or make the slightest exertion was the assertion made by the patients and persisted in, till real weakness induced by total want of exercise of the muscles had verified it in great measure. Attendants and friends in both cases suspected deceit; in more than one instance, it was evident to all except the parents, who could not believe in a fraud, the effect of which was to wring their hearts and destroy the whole enjoyment of life to the young creature whose natural impulse they maintained must have been for activity and freedom.

Undoubtedly this is the *healthy* natural impulse, but we are speaking of a condition in which the feelings become morbid. It is most unnatural to make choice of being prisoner to a couch during the gayest years of life ; and we cannot therefore understand such a preference unless we look upon that as well as upon the tendency to deceit and the indifference to the grief and anxiety of others as part of the malady itself. This was the view that forcibly struck me in both the instances I have alluded to, and it has since been strongly corroborated by an expression of Dr. Mayo's in the book above quoted, where he says that 'mendacity is a symptom of the hysterical constitution.'†

And what still further confirms it is, that in one of the cases I am alluding to, the moral nature remained pure and even beautiful in all but the two points connected with the illness; while in the other case, when the illness passed away almost as suddenly as it came on, and the patient

* See Dr. Mayo, pp. 41, 90, and 91 ; also p. 42 (quoted before).
† Page 159.

returned to active life, all the worst moral features and points of character which had been a source of the deepest anxiety were at once softened, and gave promise of complete reformation. In neither case was the intellect impaired.

Now I am not supposing that in cases of this nature the whole illness was an imposture; the limits of the latter it would probably be very difficult to define. We cannot tell in which part of that curiously united physical and spiritual being the evil began, I am simply deprecating the one-sided method of looking to that part only in which the symptoms are most apparent. In the case of strange ill-temper I mentioned before, the moral infirmity was alone made the object of care, neglecting the consideration of physical causes. In these cases of hysteria the physical infirmity was most apparent, and the moral symptoms were neglected. Had the mother been able to admit the supposition from the beginning, that falsehood and a morbid craving for pity might be parts of the disease, doubtless very different reports would have been made to the medical men in attendance. Their observation would perhaps have received a different direction, or physicians who have made these subjects their more especial study might have been called in, and their treatment might have been combined with measures tending to influence the patient's mind during any intervals when it was in a more sane condition, in that particular respect in which we must consider such a mind to be diseased. I believe also that had the patient known from the beginning that he was not considered to be in a fit condition to make accurate statements about his own illness, that a degree of delusion was known to attend it, and must be guarded against, I believe that had this been the case recovery would have been facilitated, by smoothing the way for the patient to make exertion without a sacrifice of pride.

How far such treatment would be advisable in other respects, is of course a question for a physician to decide ; all I would suggest is, that parents may add fearfully to the mischief of illness by refusing to look at its mental as well as its physical manifestations. With regard to girls, their peculiarly sensitive nervous organizations make such precautions additionally necessary. Hysteria especially is, in one form or another, so common among women, that its symptoms and effects deserve serious consideration in the course of their education. When we remember the many *clairvoyantes* of the present day—the visions, the conversations with spirits, carried on mostly through the medium of women, and other strange delusions which only come to the knowledge of the physician or the clergyman after they have shaken health or racked the heart and conscience, we may surely admit that it would be well if sound medical knowledge were brought in to aid a stricter mental training, in giving to the reason and the will greater power over the irritable nerves and excitable imaginations of young girls.

We must remember that the tendency of human nature to action is so strong that a retired sedentary life, such as most women lead, is almost sure to aggravate any disturbance of the completely healthy condition. Many forms of mental suffering now frequent among them would probably be much lessened were they exposed to the toils and hardships of a man's life. It is true that the same kind of suffering is still found in the labouring classes, which is some proof that it belongs to the female mind independent of circumstances; but it must be remembered that needlework is the great occupation of women in those classes, and the fact of stitching for bread instead of for amusement, will not do away with the bad mental effect of having the fingers only employed while the mind is vacant, and while the limbs are fatigued, not from healthy exercise, but from remaining in one position.

A retired, and in great measure, a sedentary life is however unavoidable for women ; let us then, at least during their education, bear this fact in mind, and provide physically and mentally as well as we can against its possible evil effects.

It is truly singular, considering the anxious tenderness of mothers, to what a painful degree the question of health generally is neglected in the education of girls. When evil becomes apparent, then indeed there is no lack of solicitude ; but if it come in an unusual form, if it creep on by very slow degrees, or attack mind or disposition before the body suffers, it is too apt to be passed blindly over. At any rate the question of health is not taken into account as one of paramount importance in settling all the details of life. It is not sufficiently remembered that with delicate organizations, everything that interferes with bodily health, or with the free development of the physical powers, reacts upon the mind, affecting the brain or the temper, according to circumstances ; while everything that either jades or irritates the mind tells injuriously upon health. Now, as education is necessarily in some measure a system of artificial stimulus to, and of artificial restraint upon the natural inclinations, we cannot be too careful to watch and guard against evil effects, and to give free course to nature, wherever it is possible in compensation for the restraint we are forced to put upon her in other respects.

Confinement to the school-room is generally much too long, and girls being continually on their good behaviour under the eye of the governess, and made to sit upright all the time of their lessons, do not get the relief which boys may find, who, though nominally in school as many hours, are left more to themselves, are idle part of the time, and loll about in any position that gives them rest. When lessons are over, they are at liberty to take as much or as little exercise as they please. The natural impulse is for action ; when therefore the young creature prefers quiet while fun and games are going on around, we may be sure that there is a degree of languor and lassitude which requires repose. But girls, weary or not, take their formal walk, and even if the limbs get sufficient exercise and no more, the brain and spirits do not get the combined rest and exhilaration which boys find in their games of strength and skill. The walk is often, indeed, made another lesson, by enforcing the necessity of keeping up conversation in some foreign and scarcely familiar tongue with the governess, to whom the process must be fully as dull and as unfit a preparation for after-work as it is to her pupil. Boys have another healthy antidote against possible over-work at school, in the freedom and idleness of the holidays, a boon generally denied to girls who are brought up at home. In a word, there is seldom any period of complete relaxation during the usual course of girls' education, they are incessantly being taught, or lectured, or advised, or watched. When we add to this the wretched custom of wearing stays, which still outlives back-boards and narrow upright chairs, and by which the figure is confined and distorted, while the muscles lose strength by the habit of artificial support; if we put all these things together we must allow that they go far to justify the sarcastic remark of a medical writer, who in speaking of the naturally healthy constitutions of girls, says, ' their one disease is education.'*

Even the stricter moral discipline of female education involves a degree of restraint which may tell injuriously upon some delicate nerves. Take the case of violence, for instance, when boys have had a pitched battle, or in any other open way have vented the ill-temper of the moment, Nature has had relief after her own fashion,—a fashion not to be encouraged certainly ; but let us at least remember while obliged frequently to thwart the natural impulse, that in doing so we exact severe effort which in return demands forbearance at our hands, lest the still feeble powers should be overtasked. In time the habit of control, together with the cultivation

---

* *Philosophy of Living.* HERBERT MAYO. Page 114.

of the benevolent affections, will prevent the angry emotions from rising, and then the physical struggle is at an end. The peevish, fretful tempers which are more common among girls than among boys, are, I believe, caused, in great measure, by want of attention to these points, by not giving Nature all the help and soothing we can, when taxing her powers, and repressing her natural inclinations. In the case mentioned above, when boys have finished their battle they are generally goods friends again ; but the girl who has been forced to smother all resentment, and preserve outward good behaviour, is far more likely to cherish inward rancour or discontent; then again, the sullen or peevish fit must also be concealed, and a depressed state of spirits is too often the consequence. From this it follows that the moral discipline being indispensable, it is most incumbent on the teacher to watch lest the efforts which are breaking down evil in one direction should be fostering it in another. They should remember that peevishness, fretfulness, smothered irritability, besides being in a moral point of view scarcely less obnoxious than violence, tend to depress the spirits, and that every form of depression is more or less inimical to health. On the other hand, it is cheering to reflect that when moral discipline has accomplished its work, and created habitual self-regulation, health derives no small benefit from the serenity of mind that accompanies it. The absence not only of irritation and angry emotion but of uncertain impulse and wavering motives is no less favourable to a healthy condition of the nerves, and of the great organs of the body than to the free development and action of the mental faculties.

I have already spoken at length of cheerfulness as one of the most important features of character to be cultivated as the antagonist to many forms of ill-temper, I will only add here that it is no less essential to bodily than to mental health. Even illness, even severe and protracted pain, seem to lose some of their power over the frame when the mind is able to preserve an equable tone of spirits; and many forms of lesser suffering are actually kept down by cheerfulness. The nerves remain free from irritation; there is none of the agitation that is kept up when sad recollections and gloomy forebodings alternately sway the mind. The spirit is at rest and the calm spreads to the bodily organization.

All these considerations of health and of the action and reaction upon each other of the mental and physical constitution deserve the mother's earnest thought from her children's earliest years, but still more during that period immediately succeeding childhood which I propose studying in the following pages. Many childish defects as well as childish illnesses are then over, and moral training should already have made considerable progress, but then a new class of difficulties present themselves, and ignorance and want of observation in the teacher may allow that which should be mere temporary disturbance to produce permanent evil.

At that time growth is often rapid and out of proportion to the strength, health in some cases remains uncertain for a considerable period, and new faults we were not prepared for seem to spring up to baffle us just as we were rejoicing over the success of our earlier task. A new phase of existence in short is opening, and the intellectual and moral nature share in the disturbance of the physical constitution. The eager and volatile will then sometimes grow languid in body and mind, even to depression. The quiet and cheerful become subject to irritability which if not watched might settle into peevishness of temper. The dull and unimaginative awaken to greater quickness and susceptibility, which may but too easily degenerate into that morbid sensibility which has poisoned the happiness of so many women; and in the highest toned natures there is a fearful increase of sensibility to every touch of feeling or fancy as youth unfolds. There is a paradise of beauty then to imaginative minds over which the second dawn of life steals with its magic light, bringing to view a thousand fairy forms and rainbow tints which the veiled eyes of the child could not perceive. Deep in the soul that ideal beauty had lain folded up, at times only a glimpse may have been revealed, while the unconscious fancy hovered over some image it could but dimly discern, then slept again till all the slumbering powers of nature awake at once and a glory is shed over earth and heaven.

It needs a delicate hand to deal with young creatures under the influence of this new excitement, and health of mind is as easily to be wrecked at such a time for want of care as that of the body. The quiet secluded life of girls favours the morbid action of feeling or imagination, accordingly we find that a dreamy languor alternating with fits of excitement and ecstatic delight is a common feature at that age, and may easily turn to evil if injudiciously treated. Some persons think they arrest a tendency to morbid sentiment or imagination by checking all expression of what they call romance, forgetting that the highly coloured visions of fancy or of an over-wrought sensibility are far more likely to be softened and sobered in tone if expressed in words, than if dwelt upon in solitary musings. There should be nothing to chill, not a shade of ridicule, or all hope of confidence, and therefore of influence, is lost. So long as the latter is preserved it is both easier and safer to guide than to repress; the mind may be gently turned from day-dreams to the region of fine poetry or of art, or to the contemplation of nature in her beauty or the grandeur of her laws; while at the same time studies may receive a new direction towards subjects fitted to draw out the power of reasoning, and thus to counteract the over activity of the imagination.

I have said above that when considerations of health dictate unusual forbearance with a naughty child, pains should be taken to conceal it. This precaution is necessary because the little thing could not be made to understand the reasons by which we are actuated, and might try to conquer indulgence by simulating the mood that had obtained it before. But when childhood is past, quite another method must be adopted. The reasons that influence the teacher in dealing with a young girl must be explained to herself, for she would quickly detect mystery or concealment, or lose some portion of confidence and respect if she suspected inconsistency.

If the moral tone, or the power of mental exertion appear to be affected by health, let it be frankly avowed, and let the treatment be as gentle as it is decided, while striving to rouse in the young mind the spirit of resistance to the dominion of physical sensation, and a sense of shame in relinquishing the great distinctive gift of humanity, the power of self-regulation, at the prompting of bodily infirmity. We too well know that this can never be fully carried into effect, but few can tell who have never tried it what a principle of mental vigour this feeling will maintain through years of depressing health. The young girl should be allowed to know that we consider her irritability or foolish sensitiveness as occasioned in great measure by delicacy of health, while we hold it to be altogether in her own power to prevent an accidental fault from becoming fixed in the character. Let her learn how sadly often amiable dispositions have suffered in this manner, and how women with whom delicate health is one of the most frequent trials of life, labour under a peculiar necessity of learning to bear up against the deteriorating effects which it is ever tending to produce on the mind. This is a very fitting time to begin to lead the young girl to consider some of woman's special duties and trials, and to understand some of the means adopted in the course of her own education to strengthen her for the peculiar mode of life which lies before her. This openness will, with any well-constituted nature, win confidence, at the very age when it is most essential to possess it; while the feeling of being trusted gives to the young both strength and self-reliance.

I trust that these few remarks on a subject so vast as that of the mutual influence upon each other of health, character, and mental development may have some effect in turning attention more earnestly to these points as essential considerations in education; that they may convince some mothers that it is their children's *whole nature* which they are bound to study, one part in combination with the others, in order to see where efforts are needed to maintain or restore that harmony of all the powers which is the true type of mental and physical health. Truly may they rest assured that evil allowed to grow unchecked in one direction will not stop in its progress there. Neglected health will enfeeble mental vigour; neglected symptoms of mental deficiency will gain strength, and perhaps overturn the whole balance of mind and power of self-regulation as certainly as neglected moral evil would blight the fairest hopes that intellect and bodily health could give of a happy and honoured career.

CHAPTER IV.

EARLY TEACHING.

I HAVE already stated that it is not my intention to enter upon the subject of early education. The management of little children requires a quite peculiar study and much experience, and I leave those to treat of it who are so qualified. Yet it seems necessary, in order that my readers may understand what point I start from, to explain briefly the very little I expect a child to have learnt before twelve years old, the age at which my remarks on education begin to apply.

Many persons will perhaps think it strange that I should include the whole period till twelve years of age under the denomination of early childhood, not yet to be subjected to a regular system of school-room education. It is more common to find mothers anxious about what their children know or can perform, at eight or nine, or too often earlier still, and seriously considering twelve years old as an age when real progress in many branches of study should have been accomplished. In my opinion such progress is not only impossible in most cases, but undesirable in all.

It is a crying sin against childhood to cut short its careless, healthy idleness, to substitute books for play, the forcing of the tender brain for the free development of bodily strength in exercise, the weariness of lessons for the spontaneous development of the mental faculties among visible objects, and the many relations of persons and things that are daily unfolding to the child. Nothing is to me so absurd as to see a baby of four or five years old gravely set down to a lesson ; and the sight of such a creature immured in a school-room adds sadness to the absurdity. It is not sufficiently considered how much a child inevitably learns in the first few years of its feeble life. The slender powers are probably taxed quite as much as is good for them by the daily efforts of apprehension and memory which must be made before the power of expressing even a child's thoughts, feelings, and wants in intelligible language and coherent sentences can be attained. Experience is exercised, the senses undergo constant training, the names of a vast number of objects are learned, with many facts concerning them, relations begin to be perceived, sensations to be distinguished, recollections to be stored, and anticipations for the morrow to be formed. If we conceive how much all the nascent powers are thus unavoidably exercised we shall surely feel that it is wise to let the gradual development of nature take place according to nature's laws, without risking by premature forcing in one direction to stunt the growth in another.

Rousseau's greatest claim to be forgiven the mischief of many of his writings lies in his strenuous opposition to early teaching. Had his entire system of education been practicable, it would have ended in a miserable caricature of human nature; but he deserves the praise of being the first to raise a powerful protest against the folly of working the infant brain. Every writer who deserves to be an authority on these subjects, whether in physiological works or treatises on education, has since him held the same opinion, and it is so far established that no one ventures to *profess* the contrary view, though it is daily acted upon by the impatience or vanity of parents. They agree in the mischief done by early cramming, but they will not allow that the lessons *their* children learn can come under that denomination. Early prodigies are still boasted of, the precocity which already threatens health is stimulated, and because the forward child is not unhappy under this system, they believe he is not injured ; while it is urged, with regard to duller children, that they do very little all the time.

To this plea there are two answers. *First*, that spending a long time doing very little, is one of the worst lessons that can be given; it is laying the foundation of a bad mental habit, which it will be most difficult to correct when real study begins. Ten minutes' teaching that requires earnest attention from the child is better in every way than an hour spent in dawdling over a lesson. One of the most valuable habits to which a child can be trained, and one of most constant use, is to do quickly and with determination whatever must be done; it is evident that hanging with half attention over a lesson during twice the time it really requires is in exact contradiction to this valuable rule.

Secondly, we may answer, that although during the hours spent in the school-room the brain be not overworked, the physical frame is at least deprived of the advantage of all the exercise of limbs and lungs which children would take if left to themselves during those hours which they are forced to spend in unnatural quiet.

But while baby-lessons are a sad spectacle, it is possible to give a child certain elementary instruction without its ever feeling the irksomeness of being taught. Thus a child may learn to read without knowing how, and that is undoubtedly an important step gained, not so much with a view to lessons as to giving the child a power of quiet amusement, by which means the time and nerves of those around him are greatly spared. But even this should be subject to the condition that the child has no repugnance to what is presented to it, half in fun, half in earnest. If there is no taste for the game of searching out first letters, and then words, and no wish to read the explanation of the pictures in his book, it is better left alone. There should be no compulsory lesson before seven years old at soonest, and then I would carry the compulsion no further than to exact an equal time of complete stillness and silence as the alternative for not doing the lesson. The latter will generally be preferred; and once the habit given of attending regularly to the same thing at the same hour, a step nearly of equal importance with learning to read has been gained. Even should the lesson be decidedly rejected, the penalty enforced will not be without its use in helping to form notions of submission to rules of order and self-control. When a child shows this decided aversion to lessons, it is easy to make him bear the penalty of his idleness in another way also, by refusing to read to him the amusing stories he will not read for himself. It may be explained to him that it was very well when he was too young to learn to read that he should trouble other people, but that now he is able to learn if he chooses their time cannot be given up to gratify his idle whims.

When the child can read, the fear is lest advantage should be taken of it to impose fresh lessons upon him, to task memory and attention with dry matter-of-fact that can have no interest for him. It were better to teach orally any little things it is desirable that he should know, and to

8—2

leave the newly acquired art of reading for pleasure only, till the habit of finding delight in books is well established in the young mind.   There are some who do not seem capable of acquiring that invaluable habit, but the point is seldom fairly tried; when the brain is forced over lesson books, and attention tried, the natural relief is in noise and idleness, and thus the association of pleasure it should be the educator's endeavour to entwine with the habit of reading is connected with the escape from it.   Let the little creature sit on the carpet with its stories of dogs or birds, or book of fairy tales, devouring new wonders, going back to the old with fresh delight at every call upon his imagination.   Leave him to grow absorbed in the interest which makes his cheeks flush and his eyes sparkle.   Let him have in all its fulness the first taste of the most elevating pleasures human nature is capable of enjoying—those pleasures which are wholly apart from the world of sense.   After having owed such keen delight to imagination aided by books, he will be more likely to rise hereafter to the region of poetry or of lofty speculation on nature's truths, that most sublime field in which imagination works, than if his young faculties had been wearied plodding over catechisms of the *ologies*, bringing just within range of his memory what remains a dead letter to his understanding and fancy.

Fairy tales have fallen so sadly under the ban of educational censure that they would require a longer apology than I have space for to reinstate them in favour.   In my opinion it is at once a false view of fiction, and a narrow view of truth which would force children away from those pleasant old paths ' to dwell in *dull realities* for ever.'   I believe fairy tales afford a far more healthy form of amusement to children than most of the stories of so-called real life that our modern libraries teem with.   Those wonderfully good or clever little boys and girls who instruct and reform their parents; or those young reprobates held up as patterns of corruption for doing the mischief which most children have a sympathy with, and yet cannot feel themselves to be so very wicked for loving; these are what really teach untruths, for they give false notions of actual life, and lead to false expectation and estimation of character.   Like novels which I had occasion formerly * to contrast with the reading of elevated fiction in poetry, they have all the evil of fiction unredeemed by that exercise of the fancy which more imaginative works afford.

That there are exceptions to this general censure need hardly be said.

* *Thoughts on Self-Culture,* p. 335.   Second edition.

Miss Edgeworth's stories and the charming series by Miss Martineau, which has but one fault—that of being too short—must always remain models for children's books. There may be others with which I am not acquainted, and there are books of a different class in the present day which are open to none of the above objections,—works which bring before children's minds facts of natural history, explanations of common things, in so attractive a form that they learn to take delight in that world of marvels which observation discloses in every road-side hedge, in every sandy beach, and even in town shops collecting the productions of every clime in one spot.

But admitting these exceptions, I am still convinced in general that wild poetical tales of romance or fairy-land, afford the most free and healthy scope for a child's fancy to unfold in, and open the surest way of leading him to turn to books for pleasure. There is no fear of his being misled by the poetic fiction of the talking of birds or trees, nor by the beautiful visions of magic transformations, nor by the account of good or wicked fairies dealing poetical justice among the guilty and the sufferers in a world which he very clearly sees is not our own. The child could not express in words his sense of pleasure in being thus transported into a different region ; but we who have chafed longer within the bounds of what we can see and know, and beat our wings so often against the bars of the prison-house, we know how the human soul pants after the ideal and soars away to it as to a more genial clime. Why then should we deny to children the first feeble efforts of a faculty which will more than any other refresh the flagging spirit through the weariness of later years ? There is no sense of justice in depriving children of such imaginative reading as comes within their comprehension, unless we would afterwards on the same principles take out of their hands not only every beautiful heirloom of genius which has made the poetical mythology of Greece familiar to us, but Spencer and Milton, Dante and Shakspeare, to replace them in their hours of amusement by fashionable novels or gossiping biographies. We may dread to see a child too prosaic, but need fear nothing from his imagination. Let it be watched, and carefully tended and directed, but let us not forget that the creative power of the human mind is there.

From fairy tales the child will naturally proceed to tales of adventure, to poetry, old ballads and legends awakening the first dawn of historical interest; then to travels and lives of great men. Once within the bounds of real life, of what appeals in some measure to his own knowledge and experience, he will generally be the better pleased the more of actual

truth there is in what he reads. 'Is it really true?' will be the frequent
question, as the spirit stirs within him at the account of heroic deeds, of
the self-devotion of martyrs, of the courage of affection.   His imagination
and feeling lift him to the height of actions whose motives he can scarcely
understand.   Such excitement, together with interest in the accounts of
far distant lands, of wonderful natural productions, the strange history
of the animals living around him, or roaming afar in those forests and
spreading wilds whose description he has delighted in, will take the place
of the marvels of fairy-land.   It is thus that the love of reading
allowed to develop itself naturally will lead on a child of any intelligence
step by step till the time comes to employ that intelligence in serious study.
It is said that some children dislike pure fiction, that their interest is never
roused except by something true and real.   If so, the peculiarity requires
some watching before we pronounce it to be a virtue.   I should be inclined
to suspect it was caused by incapacity to rise to a fanciful conception, by
coldness or inertness of imagination, which would require therefore to be
counteracted rather than to be encouraged still more by being kept within
bounds of the commonplace it sympathizes with.   I should fear that such
a child would show less interest in the heroic than in the homely, and
might respond as slowly to a lofty sentiment as to an imaginative thought.
I do not say that it would always be so; in the great variety of mental
constitutions there may be some so happily framed as to have by nature
all the qualities of a warm imagination, with the calmness and sobriety
which usually belong to a colder and more prosaic turn of mind.   But
these must be rare; and the absence of interest in fiction would not alone
indicate to me a more favourable mental condition in the child.

I have said that seven years old is the earliest period at which regular
teaching should begin.   After that half-an-hour every day may fairly be
exacted, and an increase of half-an-hour each year till twelve years old
will be borne without fatigue by any children in good health.   Other
matters requiring care and order, but not trying to the brain, may be
attended to in addition.   To make my meaning clear, I will briefly enu-
merate what acquirements I should expect to find in a girl of twelve years
old.   She should read and spell English perfectly, write a neat hand, and
be able to write a clear and simple letter.   I should expect her to know
an outline of Bible History, and of the spread of Christianity, and to be
well acquainted with the four Gospels; she might know also something
of the leading events of ancient and modern history, gathered from a mere
skeleton narrative, aided by reading the lives of great men, and perhaps

committing some principal dates well grouped to memory.* In the same manner she should have some slight notion of geography, partly learnt as a lesson, but in greater measure by following upon maps the travels I suppose her to read for her own amusement. I should wish her memory to be well stored with such poetry as she is able to take pleasure in, never having learned a piece unless it has first excited her own interest. If this rule be followed, there is no need to trouble ourselves about what can or cannot be appreciated at a given age. Some children have delighted in the Psalms, some in heroic ballads, some in Shakspeare, and some even in the versified eloquence of Racine or Corneille; while others of the same age could hardly feel the beauty of a fable, or of the simplest hymn. There is no gauge for the fancy or intellect, the only safe rule is to leave them free, and try their powers.

I should expect to find my little pupil familiar with the four first rules of arithmetic, and doing sums neatly and quickly. I believe the method of mental arithmetic now taught in schools is also an excellent exercise of the mind and memory, and one which many children take pleasure in. I should also expect, if circumstances have allowed it, that she should read and speak French or German, or both. This is the one form of knowledge that is more easily acquired by little children than by older persons; they learn different languages by ear without pain or effort, and thereby save much valuable time hereafter, which would otherwise be spent over dictionaries, in learning *words* when the time has come for learning *things*. If parents, therefore, are not restricted by considerations of expense, I shall say that the best plan would be as follows:—A Swiss *bonne* at three or four years old to be in constant attendance on the children; and at nine a German governess, sufficiently familiar with French to keep that up, while teaching her own language. Thus by the time a girl is twelve years old, she would speak and write two of the most difficult languages of Europe with as much ease as her own.

There is one other acquirement I should wish to find in my pupil, and that is some knowledge of music. I am aware that after all I have said against the undue importance attached to accomplishments, this will sound inconsistent; but I hope to prove that it is not really so. My objection to accomplishments is to their being allowed to usurp a place among the

---

* The only object of even such acquaintance with history at that age is to render intelligible the biographies and the poetry the child may read. Also in reading travels it is well that she should have some notion of the past history of the different countries, at least to the extent of knowing if they were early civilized or not, whether powerful or subject, &c.

essentials of education, and among the serious pursuits of life. But I have too true a value for the fine arts themselves as a source of pure pleasure, as a solace in hours of sadness or solitude, as a means of cultivating some of the fine qualities of the imagination,—and I rate their social influence too highly, not to desire that a reasonable time should be given to cultivate any real talent for them, or to gratify any real desire to learn them; only remembering to keep them in due subordination to the proper labour of education.

My reason for beginning music at an early age is this. The taste for it is often not shown till very late, frequently not till the voice develops, and singing offers a charm which was wanting in instrumental music. But to begin the rudiments at that age is painful labour, and still more painful waste of time, for there is rarely then an hour to spare; yet without much time and hard labour none will overcome the difficulties of music thus encountered all at once, and vocal and instrumental together. And after all success would be very doubtful, for the mere necessary manual suppleness and dexterity are very difficult to acquire when the muscles have lost the pliancy of childhood. I would obviate these difficulties by making them familiar in early years. Then if at fourteen or fifteen, a decided taste for music shows itself, real study begins from a favourable point. If, on the contrary, there be no wish to cultivate the art, the time hitherto devoted to it—and which should never exceed half-an-hour in the day—can be given to something else, and yet leave no regret for labour wasted; since I believe it hardly possible to find a study which is more adapted than music to train a child's memory, attention, patience, and quickness of apprehension. So many things have to be learned at once, or at least combined as soon as learned, that it affords an exercise different in some measure from any other subject in which a child could be instructed. Nor is the manual dexterity thus acquired without its value. Persons who are accustomed to use their fingers in any delicate operation, especially if requiring strength as well as delicacy, become skilful also in other things and light of hand: a woman should be both.

Among manual arts there is one which no woman can be without, and which must be early taught that it may not take up time when time is more valuable than it is in childhood. A girl of twelve should already be a proficient in all plain needlework and do it rapidly and neatly. The latter is of course indispensable, but the former also is valuable and easily acquired. Quickness and carelessness have been too often classed together, whereas carelessness is often most conspicuous in the slowness that dawdles for an hour over a task, or over business of any kind which an habitually quick person will perform with more ease in half the time. The person who has formed that habit from a sense of its value in saving time, will be the first to feel that *slurring* over work is the slowest thing that can be done, since it will generally require to be done again or to have blunders repaired; but the constant desire to work quickly, induces the habit of thinking rapidly upon all practical matters, of seeing the important points and their bearings and deciding what is best to be done. By excluding dawdling we exclude much space for hesitation and half-measures and half-repentings. Irresolution and uncertainty proceed indeed from other causes besides this; in some fine and acute minds they spring from the habit of looking too deep and too far into cause and consequences, viewing everything on every side till they are unable to make that rough guess at probabilities which after all we are obliged to be content with in most practical affairs; but with the majority of persons the defect would be lessened at any rate in small matters, or checked in its operation, if they had been trained from childhood to be quick in whatever they have to do.

To return however to needlework; there is in general no difficulty in making little girls fond of it. Their dolls offer the first inducement, and then comes in the pleasure of giving their work to others, perhaps the only gift in their power or the only service they are able to render. But whichever way inclination points, needlework must be taught. It is one of the most important branches of household occupation, unfortunately so neglected in modern English education; and it will always be in the mother's power to prevent this necessary accomplishment from degenerating into the frivolity of constant fancy-work, in which so many precious hours are wasted by girls who could not stitch a shirt or make their own clothes.

According to my plan children would have very little brain-work, and some people might think that two hours and a half only of lessons from eleven to twelve years old will leave my pupils idle and difficult to bring in later to the habits of a regular school-room life; but needlework and other household occupations, that a child can learn to attend to, may be made as much use of as any grammar lesson as a means of enforcing system, patience, and perseverance. The effect will entirely depend on the manner in which this homely training is carried on.

A little girl may be told for instance that when she is nine years old she shall, if she seem fit to be trusted, have the charge of her own clothes, to mend and put neatly away, and by which means the first notions of

order and economy are introduced.   Her tenth birth-day might entitle her
as a great privilege to the charge of some younger child's things, or perhaps
to some portion of her mother's, or of the house linen, or she may be
trusted with stores subject to the condition of carefully weighing what is
given out, and entering it accurately and neatly in a book.   These and
many other things of like nature may be made objects of interest and
ambition to the young creature—not from the interest of the occupations
themselves, but from the sense of being trusted and useful.   Once undertaken, however, the charge becomes a duty, and as such never even in its
most trifling details to be willingly neglected.   Thus we may lay the first
foundation of one of the most important principles of life; that of considering our own resolutions—seriously and deliberately made—as sacred
to our own conscience, not to be judged of according to the intrinsic value
of the things concerned, but according to the motives that led us to form
the resolve, and to the value of our own self-respect which wavering and
inconsistency must and ought to impair.   If we desire that seemingly trifling
occupations should be the means of conveying such serious lessons to a
child's mind, they must of course not be treated as trifles; indeed nothing
that serves a purpose of usefulness to others, or conduces to their comfort
or welfare in any degree, should ever be allowed with children to be so
treated.   The hour for attending to duties of this kind must be fixed, as
well as the mode in which it seems best that the thing should be done, and
no capricious change or irregularity allowed. These will however probably
occur, and at first may be passed over with a gentle reprimand, acknowledging the difficulty of getting into new ways, and how hard even grown
up people find it to be quite regular in their occupations ; but if neglect is
repeated or becomes frequent the trust should be withdrawn for a time.
The punishment of mortification in feeling that she is considered unfit for
a charge of any consequence, will have more effect in general on the child's
mind than merely enforcing the punctual discharge of the duty.

Another valuable quality is also trained among these common things,
in preparation for more difficult exercise when serious study begins.   This
is patience; a virtue which deserves a higher place than it holds in most
views of education.   It is remarkable that women who possess so much of
what I would call *moral patience*, that is, of the kind which bears crosses
and disappointments with good humour, and can endure all the trials of a
nursery or sick-room, are eminently defective in *intellectual patience*.   They
are in general soon wearied with the persevering effort required for severe
mental labour, or with the drudgery indispensable as an accompaniment or

preparation for such labour. In consequence their attainments remain imperfect and below the standard of their capacity. Their knowledge is not accurate or complete and their reading is desultory. Nothing great, nothing even tolerably good is to be done without systematic perseverance, and few things require so much patience as that unswerving regularity in all the details of a plan, which method exacts. For instance, while it is very pleasant to read, it is most irksome to make regular notes from our reading, and yet probably the profit derived from a book will very much depend upon our method and regularity in making such notes. So it is with other things which are necessary to make reading anything more than a pleasing way of passing time,—as for instance frequent reference to maps, dictionaries, or chronological tables, laborious search in works of reference to clear up a difficulty or to help to fix an important point on the memory. All these things are severe trials of patience, and of that persevering spirit born of patience and earnestness which is not to be daunted by obstacles, but works steadily, though it may be slowly on, till they are removed or overcome. The often tedious details of household occupations are very fit to train this habit in a child, and thus while the brain has been spared fatigue, no idleness has been encouraged, and time has been turned to the best account by leading the mind to work habitually and among all the common things of life according to those methods which will be most essential for the labour of mental cultivation when intelligence is ripe for it.

Here ends my list of the acquirements I should expect from a child of twelve years old, a mere skeleton preparation for real study. It falls so far short of what is deemed requisite by most mothers and governesses in the present day, that I should expect my opinion to be more popular on the playground than in the school-room. It is particularly important for girls to be as little restricted as possible in play and exercise during childhood, since it early becomes necessary to impose on them restraints which boys never know. I would have them run, leap, ride, play various games with their brothers, in short acquire strength and dexterity of limb, trusting rather for grace of movement to the pliancy and vigour of a healthy, active frame animated by a refined mind, than to a dancing-master's teaching.

But although my list of actual lessons is soon closed, I should be glad to find in my little pupil more information than her tasks have taught her; information of various kinds sought out for herself, or gathered from the conversation of her elders, which gives token of an inquiring mind roused by the love of reading to take keen interest in whatever it hears or sees. Such a child will know the history, if I may so call it, of all the familiar things around her, that is, what countries different productions come from, and the peculiarities of climate or cultivation that make us seek them from afar and not strive to raise them at home. She will know something of the principles of construction of various objects she sees in frequent use, and something of the elementary principles of science by the aid of which other things familiar to her have been effected. The revolutions of day and night and of the seasons with their changes of temperature and of the external appearances of nature—the striking phenomena of chemical forces that so frequently take place around us, the interest of animal and vegetable life,—atmospheric changes, the lightning and the winds, and above all the heavenly bodies in their movements and their beauty which even a child of three years old has been known to watch with rapture,—all these will rouse inquiry and lead to instruction in the first principles of natural history and philosophy, which will stimulate the desire for knowledge and train the habits of observation.

These things will be learned without labour, that is, without wearying the brain, for they will be learned with pleasure under the stimulus of a desire to know. But should it be found that the child has a mere idle curiosity about things, it may be well to disregard it, letting her see that you cannot waste the labour of instruction when there is no earnest intention of deriving profit from it. In laying the foundation of intellectual education in childhood we should be content with the humblest beginnings; but whatever and whenever we teach we cannot be too careful to ensure that all which is learned shall exercise not the memory alone, important as that is, but attention, perseverance, the faculty of observation, often acute in children, but seldom well-directed, and the habit of accuracy. The latter must be cultivated not merely with regard to veracity but to forming accurate and definite notions of things. That is, a child should see *clearly* as far as it sees at all, and be aware when it ceases to have a clear conception. It should know when it does not understand and have learned to seek for help in overcoming the difficulty. At the same time a child should also be aware that many things cannot be made clear to it, and should be satisfied when told ' I cannot explain this now, it is beyond your comprehension, we will return to this when you are able to follow the necessary explanation.' A foolish answer just putting off curiosity never can, and never ought to satisfy an inquiring child; and the more intelligent she is, the sooner she will learn to distrust those who thus treat her honest desire to learn.

At twelve years old a child of moderate abilities is fit to begin study in earnest. At first the period of application should still be very short, lengthening it by degrees, as habit makes the labour of attention and thought less irksome. Subjects can then be studied in good works, not in those milk-and-water dilutions of knowledge which give the skimmings of learning without exercising one of the faculties whose exercise is more precious than learning itself. The continual attempt to reduce the Novum Organon to words of one syllable will never give real knowledge to childish minds; but it may keep minds which ought to be expanding down to childish proportions. Study should be earnest labour of attention, apprehension, and thought; when the mind is capable of these efforts, let it begin without any attempt at disguise; and not till then.

I have spoken in my last chapter of the earliest religious impressions that a child's mind is capable of receiving, but so large a number of persons think that direct teaching of religious doctrines should hold a prominent place in early education, and exercise the strongest influence over its whole course, that I cannot close this chapter without explaining my reasons for not entering into that part of the subject at all.

The numerous and very wide differences of opinion which prevail upon religious, and still more upon theological and ecclesiastical questions, make it impossible to lay down the simplest general system of religious instruction without offending many, and probably raising in the minds of those so offended, a prejudice against every other opinion and principle advocated in the work. Unfortunately, few even earnestly religious minds will judge fairly on these points. Feeling is too strong, and overpowers the truth and uprightness which they may follow in the examination of other questions. Such also is the unreasoning tenacity of bigotry that no one opinion is judged apart or on its own merits, but a notion is quickly taken up concerning the good or evil of a whole system, and even of the character of those who propound it, in proportion as they have chimed in with, or shocked the feelings of the reader on these particular points. Time is not given to examine the moral tendencies of the entire system, or to judge them apart from religious tenets; but it is concluded that an author who believes or does not believe such or such dogmas, or approve of such or such practices or institutions, must be dangerous, and his work likely to lead the unwary into error.

Such is the measure of charity with which different sects and parties treat each other; so do the Evangelical judge the High Church, and the High Church the Evangelical ; so does one section of Dissenters judge another, while they all condemn and are condemned by the Churchman; and Churchmen and Dissenters alike join in suspecting or scorning the philosopher. Each has his own unfailing standard of doctrine and practical truth, and whoever differs from them is not only mistaken, but in dangerous and criminal error. They differ indeed from the Roman Church on the subject of infallibility, but only with regard to *where* it shall be placed, and in what terms it shall be claimed.

It is inevitable that we should hold persons to be in *error* when they differ from us in conclusions of the truth of which we have satisfied ourselves. We cannot believe that we are in the right without thinking our opponents are mistaken, without supposing them to have reasoned ill, to have taken up wrong grounds, or not to have sufficient capacity for seeing the force of the objections against them. But when beyond this, we go on to call their error *morally wrong*, and to look upon them not as mistaken, but as criminal, then we assume that our own views are *the truth*, clear and obvious to all who do not wilfully shut their eyes to it, implying therefore that it is in man's power to come to certain conclusions if he but chooses to do so. These are the fatal opinions which lie at the bottom of all religious intolerance, whatever the form it may take, from the suspicion with which men of different views regard each other, to the bloody trophies of the Inquisition. The difference is in the difference of power and of the state of our civilization, not in the bigoted spirit. If once we hold the moral merit or demerit of opinions, persecution can be condemned only as inexpedient. When such feelings and opinions then are so prevalent, it must be vain to enter upon the subject of religious education, unless controversy were the object, or unless a writer addressed himself solely to his own sect or party. For one who, like myself, wishes to build up a system of instruction without regard to any party, the only safe method is to avoid, as far as possible, all that may occasion my views to be prejudged by those who might find that I attend a different church or admire a different preacher from their own.

There are other reasons also which render it almost useless as well as dangerous to enter upon the subject, for even if we could hope to find tolerance towards others, parents will certainly choose that their children should hold the opinions they hold themselves. On many subjects connected with education, and many studies I might recommend, I might hope to find no settled opinion against me ; many mothers will own that they know little on these matters, and whether their children are taught one branch of knowledge or another, or learn from one author or another, is often a matter of indifference. But not so with regard to religious teaching. All alike hold some religious views and some theological tenets, whether adopted upon examination and conviction, or upon authority and custom ; and these their children must share.

For all these reasons therefore I have decided to omit religious instruction from my plan of study, leaving the omission to be filled up in each family according to the parents' wishes and views. My plan includes the week-days only ; Sunday is therefore left wholly free, to be employed as may be thought fit, without interfering with the studies I recommend; while any time daily apportioned to the same subject must be a matter of home arrangement. At the same time I cannot but enter my protest against the ordinary methods of theological teaching for children. The practical influence of true religion will not flow from reading or catechism, either on week-days or Sundays, but from the whole tenor of the principles inculcated throughout the course of education, and the capacity of the mind for feeling and loving truth, and being governed by a sense of duty. It is not alone among great churchmen of olden times, or ecclesiastical writers in the days of their power, that we see how far theologians may be from Christianity; nor need we go back to history to learn that society might have flourished upon Christian morals better than upon the orthodoxy of the Gregories or the Innocents, or even of Protestant churches. The same sad truth is evident around as daily. Let children, then, at least, first learn to live like Christians, before they are taught to dispute like theologians.

A child has but feeble powers of reasoning, but it will kindle to every lofty motive, and image and take a sublime sentiment to its heart as some simple and familiar thing. This is what we have to work upon in religious education ; let us address the faculties which in the order of nature are developed first. God, the source of life, seems to a child almost visible in his glorious creation—God reading the heart of man, ever present, ever to be found in prayer, is intelligible to the young creature feeling its own helplessness, and accustomed to look upon its parents as almost gifted with that omnipotence he learns from them is the attribute of a higher Being. Nor to him do the thoughts of death come troubled with doubts or fears. He may shrink in physical terror from a mystery which casts gloom and sorrow around, but mental terror belongs not to childhood, unless implanted there by theological teaching. Life is the natural portion of his inheritance, and other worlds are clothed in his mind with forms as familiar as those of his earthly home, only glorified with the nearer presence of that invisible God he believes to dwell in the bright heavens above.

Such is religion to a child, when teaching has only given a form and direction to the dim aspirations of nature. And if it be said that it is like the religion of barbarous nations, a mere sentiment, a vague aspiration, the vision of the fancy governing the unreasoning mind, I can only reply that savage nations are the children of the world, and that in the infancy of reason imagination must be all-powerful. I would add, however, that far better are these workings of the imagination allied to the pure sentiment of religion implanted in the heart of man, than the premature dogmatism of minds still unfit to reason, or to understand the import of what they are made to assert. Besides, the child's religion such as I have described it does not remain a mere sentiment, for on it his mother will early graft the strong notion of duty and the sense of moral responsibility which she hopes to make the guides of his life, and thus the moral action of religion is secured long before the mind is capable of receiving doctrines and opinions except as words to be committed to memory. When reason has acquired strength, then let it do its proper work; let it sift and judge and reject, if it sees grounds for doing so, what before approved itself to sentiment and imagination; but assuredly it will work with all the more vigour and security for not having been early cramped in the fetters of prejudice, nor taught to confound truth and falsehood by maintaining as its own, opinions accepted at the bidding of others.

When I use the word prejudice, as applied to such subjects, I would not have it supposed that I am myself prejudging the question, and using a term of contempt as part of an argument. This indeed is not an uncommon mode of meeting an adversary upon questions of this nature, but it is not mine. I apply the word prejudice to the theological doctrines supposed to be held by children, just as I would apply it to any theories of law, or medicine, or politics, which they might in like manner have been taught to profess. The word opinion belongs to what we have reasoned upon and worked out for ourselves; no borrowed views, no notions taken up without examination can fairly deserve any other name but prejudice. All would agree in thinking it absurd if a child should profess to belong to this or that school of metaphysics, to be a follower of Locke or Hume or Kant; but what is there more ridiculous in this than in the same creature with its feeble reason and scanty knowledge professing theological opinions which involve questions of the deepest metaphysical subtlety, and consequences before which the boldest metaphysician will pause? The great difference between the two is, that in the latter case the absurdity is crowned with intolerance; and what was mere folly when it related to human speculation alone, becomes revolting in its arrogance when it relates to God and to Eternity.

It does not follow from abstaining to teach children theological tenets that they should not be brought up in the profession of Christianity; for the latter contains, by the avowal of all sects, a code of practical morals, no less than a body of doctrines, and that which is practical is comprehensible to the mind of a child as far as it affects his own experience. We have seen how the notion of duty and of obedience to conscience is easily grafted on that religious sentiment which is spontaneous in the human heart. Little by little the child will see that each act that he feels or learns to be right or wrong is brought under the sanction or condemnation of religion. Later, these isolated points of childish morals can be shown to belong to one great system, which we call Christianity; which, besides many things still obscure to him, sets forth the sublime example of the life of Christ,—holds out the promise of immortality,—teaches the necessity of a pure heart and life,—and inculcates active love towards our fellow-creatures, with simple trust in God, whose works of power and goodness are all around us. Later still, the teacher may point to the contrast between Christian precepts and the teaching of heathen moralists,—between the moral condition both of civilized and uncivilized heathen nations, and that to which Christianity would lead us did we not so miserably fall short of the aim and pattern it holds up to us. These things are still within the range of the child's feelings and practical understanding. The grandeur of the doctrine of One God, Creator and Preserver of the world, as contrasted with the polytheism of antiquity,—the sublime conception of that presence in which 'we live and move and have our being;'—the lofty hopes of immortality chiming in with those yearning aspirations of the mind which grow stronger as the sadness and the joys of life become more intense,—these the young mind will grasp and cling to; and truly it will thus be better prepared when the time comes to give earnest attention to the dogmas and opinions of Christian churches, than if religion had been blindly bound up with them from early years.

At that time the course of study will be mostly among works of reasoning and speculation; the nature of opinion, the method of forming it, the caution and accuracy and labour necessary to weigh evidence and establish conclusions will be explained and enforced,*—and the mind thus strengthened and enlightened may turn with fruit to the study of theological opinions, to the examination of Christian evidences, to the reading of Church history, in short, to all that serious consideration which a subject of such magnitude demands, and without which no person has any reasonable grounds for belonging to this or that sect, or for holding this or that doctrine. He may legitimately be content to hold them on authority, but he can have no power to judge the views of others, and no right to maintain the truth of his own.

I am aware that there are difficulties in the mode of religious training which I desire to substitute for that of collects and catechisms. There must always be greater difficulties in acting upon a consistent and philosophical method than in following a blind routine. They are however greatly increased by the common feeling that makes parents shrink from avowing to a child the existence of a doubt or a difficulty in religious subjects; too many unfortunately are afraid of avowing it to themselves. Yet the mother's task would be much simplified if she had courage and candour to own to her child that error and doubt clog the path of man so long as he remains on earth; that while some points will become clearer as his understanding acquires greater power, it may happen that others, on the contrary, will become less clear, since the wider our inquiries, the more often must we expect that they will reach that barrier set to our pursuit of truth by the weakness of our faculties and the littleness of our sphere, compared with the unknown vastness of the universe. Laws of which we catch only a confused glimpse, may be working in clear and simple grandeur beyond our mortal ken. The contradictions that baffle us, the mysteries that make reason dizzy as it vainly seeks to fathom them, all may be full of harmony and beauty,—one great purpose of goodness, the end of all,—while the error and the confusion and the darkness are only in our dim perceptions. Truth, certain and unalterable, may be written in characters of light to higher intelligences, while we, still hemmed in by this ' muddy vesture of decay,' are unable to discern it.

Views such as these, which take from the existence of doubt its bitterness and its terror, can little by little be unfolded to the young mind, and will appeal to it with great force, accustomed as it is to see that

---

* See chap. viii.

many things which, to the child, are dark and evil, seem good and seasonable to his superiors in knowledge. He has been told from his earliest days that the reason for the blind obedience exacted of him now would become plain to him when he had more experience and understanding; it will not therefore, when put in that manner, seem strange to him that the works and purposes of the Creator should in many things appear utterly dark to His ignorant creatures. This admission of doubt as a condition of human life excludes the dogmatism of infallibility, while it saves the mind from the danger of fancying there is no truth, because we cannot see it, from believing that the foundations of the world are unstable because we are tossed up and down in our little barque, and that to our disturbed vision the mountain-tops seem to reel and the fixed stars to forsake their spheres.

There will be no difficulty with regard to the external observances in which parents naturally desire that their children should follow their example. The custom of public worship appeals strongly to the imagination, and if it has not been made wearisome to a child, he easily enters into the feeling which prompts human beings—whether in suffering, in hope, or in ignorant waiting upon the will of a superior being—to give one voice to their common sentiment of trust and praise and love. The nature of his ideas of worship, and of the answer he may expect God will make to prayer, will depend of course on the views held by his mother on these points. And so also with the observance of Sunday and other things connected with religious opinion. The freedom from dogma, in which I am supposing him to be educated, will prevent the condemnation of any views held by others, since condemnation is the expression of a decided opinion, and that is what the child should be carefully taught to feel that he is unfit to assert.

There are persons who hasten to instruct their children in doctrines lest death should overtake them and they perish everlastingly, because their theological education was cut short. I confess I do not hope to convince them. I can only grieve that there should be parents professing Christianity who hold opinions so fitted for the worship of Moloch. When we think that such a miserable superstition has wrung the hearts of mothers as they bent over the death-bed of a child with an agony in which all sense of their own bereavement was lost, our anger is turned against those whose teaching has made such victims. I know no method of reasoning with them. As well might I attempt to argue upon truth with a Jesuit, upon murder with a Thug. We have no common ground to proceed from. The very conception of a God upon which such fears are founded, is so repugnant to every feeling of my nature, to every conviction of my understanding, that, could it be proved true, it would be to me Atheism in its most desolating aspect. Since it would bring the conviction that poor and feeble as are our own conceptions of truth and justice and goodness, they far transcend what we are to expect in the dealings of the Almighty ; that Omnipotence, in a word, was but another name for malignity such as never yet has disgraced human nature in its worst forms. Thanks be to the handwriting of God in our hearts which makes such a belief once fairly stated too revolting a contradiction to disturb us even with a doubt.

CHAPTER V.

STUDIES AND GENERAL MANAGEMENT FROM TWELVE YEARS OF AGE TO FOURTEEN.

§ 1.—In the two first chapters of this work I endeavoured to lay down the fundamental principles of education in general, to point out their special application to the education of women, and to sketch the plan of study which appears to me the most likely to effect what those principles require. Next we have glanced at certain points of moral training and of health as influencing, and influenced by, moral and intellectual peculiarities; and lastly, have considered what the teaching of childhood may fairly be expected to achieve, without that premature forcing of the intellect which is so unfortunately common. In the present chapter we enter upon the serious work of education during those six important years from twelve to eighteen; and the first question that arises is, where and by whom that education is to be conducted?

I should have wished here to enter at some length into my reasons for considering that, except under very peculiar circumstances, home education is alone fit for girls; that many of the things which make school training desirable for boys are precisely what point out its unfitness for those in whose future life ambition and active worldly motives are to have no place. But matter presses, and I am forced to pass over this important subject. The system I propose is arranged with a view to home life, and I shall assume, therefore, that the mother has the real charge of the education, with or without the assistance of a governess, according to her means, position, and capacity for teaching.

We come, then, now to the consideration in detail of the plan of study proposed in the second chapter. For the sake of convenience, this part of the subject will be divided into periods according to the age of the pupils; the present chapter comprising two years, from twelve to fourteen, and each of the following ones an equal period. This will bring us to eighteen years of age, beyond which unfortunately we cannot reckon upon any regular studies being carried on.

In making this division I do not, of course, suppose that two years can be spent altogether in the same manner; indeed, the very progress expected implies change. But some division must be made, and by making it so as to mark tolerably long intervals, more latitude is allowed for the different powers of children. In the course of two years some will just accomplish what is proposed; others though making more rapid progress in a short time may be forced, owing to defective memory, to go often over the same ground; a few may perhaps fall short altogether, and a few, on the other hand, easily pass beyond. The more frequent the division assumed, the more would all these differences tell, and the more difficult therefore would it become for the teacher to avail herself of the general rules which can alone be laid down in a work of this kind.

In examining the plan of study which I have proposed, we find that it falls into three principal divisions: Science, Language, and History,—the first including a short course of mathematics; the second extending to logic, literature, and composition; the third embracing geography and chronology, and leading to some study of ethical and political questions. The reading for each different period will arrange itself easily under those three heads; and with regard to the two years now in consideration, the assigned portions of each division will be: first, arithmetic, secondly, grammar, and thirdly, short general histories, with the study of maps and chronological tables in order to obtain a clear conception of those general outlines. At twelve years old, three hours and a half of lessons may be easily borne, and gradually increased to four hours. This, with the usual needlework in addition, is amply sufficient till fourteen. Let us now see how these hours should be distributed.

The habit of early rising is so valuable that it cannot be acquired too soon; especially as if not established in youth, the exertion is often injurious to health.   None, perhaps, know the full value of the habit but those whose days are at the mercy of claims and interruptions they cannot avoid, and in the midst of which they struggle to carry on their own pursuits.   Those two or three precious hours secured before the turmoil of the day begins are perhaps all they can call their own, and there is a calming effect in this peaceful, solitary time which gives strength and cheerfulness to meet the disquiet of succeeding hours.   Now, as this want of command over their own time is a common trial with women, I consider it most important to give a habit which will secure them against some of its ill effects.   I shall suppose, therefore, that children in good health rise at six, and allowing half-an-hour for dressing, that gives them two hours before their breakfast at half-past eight; * half-an-hour of that time, how- ever, is all I should devote to lessons at the age we are considering; the rest the children should dispose of according to their own pleasure. This freedom, by making them look to that time for anything they are anxious to do, whether in-doors or out, will tend to strengthen the habit of early rising, by associating it with ideas of pleasure.   The lessons to be done before breakfast should be of a kind that requires no superintend- ence, since it would be a cruel exaction to insist at that early hour on the presence of the governess, whose health might suffer from the exertion, and whose habits with regard to early or late hours at night are already formed.   There are always tasks to be done without her, and in the per- formance of which carelessness could not avoid detection ; as for instance, lessons to be learnt by heart, sums or copies to be done; and these can be appointed for that morning hour.

After breakfast, between nine o'clock and dinner-time, we have either four or five hours to dispose of, according as the children dine at one or at two.   But out of this time two hours and a half are all that should be appropriated to lessons at the age I speak of; the remaining hours should be for exercise or recreation—freedom, in short, to relax the brain.   In the course of the afternoon, one or two hours will be given to exercise, according to the quantity that has been taken before dinner; one half hour of lessons remains to be finished, completing the three hours and a half which appear to me sufficient to begin real study with ; and we may

---

* I am not supposing the children to remain without food till that hour.   They should eat directly they are up if they require it.   Rising at six may be found irksome in winter, but the habit is so valuable as to make it worth any effort to make the children wish to do it.   Certain indulgences allowed at that time. and at no other, may prove an incitement, or allowing a portion of lessons to be done if they wish it, so as to reduce the time later.

close the school-room day with an hour and a half of needlework. When an additional half hour is to be given to study, which may, I believe, be safely done at thirteen, it can be deducted from the needlework. I have been thus particular in apportioning the day, in order to show how I should wish study and exercise to alternate, the former never exceeding two hours and a half at a time, and care being taken not to let those tasks which most try the brain immediately succeed each other. For instance, supposing that between breakfast and dinner one hour be devoted to arithmetic and another to grammar, the half hour of pianoforte practice might be placed between them. Neglect of what seems thus trifling will often make the difference, even at a far later period, of work being done easily, or with effort and consequent fatigue to brain and nerves.

I have supposed a child at twelve years old to be familiar with the four first rules of arithmetic; if this should not be the case, that groundwork must be firmly established before anything more is attempted. We then proceed to the rule of three, fractions and decimals. Accuracy and quickness in working them is to be acquired by repeated practice alone, and that of a nature which is seldom attractive to a child; while learning to state an intricate sum, though more difficult and requiring both thought and attention, is often a pleasing exercise. One hour every day will insure a sufficiently rapid progress, but should that length of continued attention be too much at first, it may easily be divided into half an hour before breakfast and the same time in the afternoon.

Many children might at thirteen begin the first book of Euclid; but if there appears to be great labour in following the reasoning, and no firm grasp of the successive steps, it would be better to delay the study another year. It is a most important part of good teaching to prevent the young mind being ever oppressed with a sense of *impotent effort.* Exertion itself is good as mental discipline, when by honest labour and attention clear apprehension can be gained, with that real mastery of a subject which makes us feel that henceforth the fraction of knowledge so laboriously won is our own, not only to be remembered, but to be used when occasion serves; but if it fails to produce that result, confusion and weariness follow, which, if frequently repeated, make the task oppressive and disgusting; and if this is allowed to take place with children, a blow is given to that love of acquiring knowledge which it should be the ceaseless endeavour of education to cherish. It is of course the duty of the teacher to distinguish carefully between the languor of fatigue or disappointed effort, and the languor of indolence. There may also be want of success for a time, and consequent fatigue, which may be overcome by a short rest and a change of subject, after which the mind will return fresh to its work, and see its way clearly through difficulties that seemed insuperable before.

Good books on arithmetic for school use are not wanting. I believe Barnard Smith's, which includes algebra in the same volume, to be among the best; but in this as in other subjects of elementary instruction, the books recommended as the best I am acquainted with, may be superseded by others before these pages are printed. Those I shall mention must therefore be considered rather as indicating the nature of the instruction I should wish to give, than as being really better than others. It is one of those points on which the teacher must exercise her own judgment. For geometry I should recommend the *Euclid* by Potts, which includes exercises and questions, a great assistance to the teacher; but the mode of teaching is more important than the book. Continual attention must be given to ascertain not only that each proposition is understood and can be proved, but that its bearing on other propositions has been clearly apprehended. When reference is made to what has been demonstrated before, the demonstration must frequently be repeated, the pupil constructing the figure for herself. Euclid just committed to memory would answer none of the purposes for which we choose the study. The method of the reasoning, the indisputable certainty with which conclusion follows from conclusion, and the perfect confidence to be placed in that operation of the reason when the premises from which it proceeds have been themselves demonstratively proved,—these are the things to be dwelt upon and made clear to the young mind. If the faculties are not ripe for seizing them, the time is not come for the study to be commenced.

One hour every day I propose giving to grammar and other lessons connected with it. The actual study to be entered upon at this time must depend on what has been previously learnt; whether any foreign language has been taught in early childhood; and whether means and opportunity allow of teaching them now, or require that grammatical studies should be conducted in English alone. I have already said that I consider the latter only as really *essential;* while I have also partly stated the grounds * which make an acquaintance with other languages highly important; I may then here consider the case in which the more extended study is practicable.

---

* See chap. ii., s. 2.

Modern languages are best learnt by ear in childhood; and where the opportunities for so doing have been enjoyed, both French and German may be at twelve years old almost as familiar to a child as her native tongue. When this is the case, the real study of grammar will be best carried on through the medium of Greek or Latin, or both successively if possible. It is the opinion of Dr. Donaldson, and his long experience gives him a right to speak authoritatively, that these two languages may be begun almost together; that if so begun at twelve years old, three years of good teaching will give a tolerable knowledge of them; and that five years of such teaching would make the pupils more fit for college studies and examinations than they usually are when the Latin grammar has been taught from their nursery days. Dr. Donaldson's opinion only concerns us so far as it shows the possibility of acquiring some knowledge of the great languages of antiquity without that exclusive devotion to them which they have usually seemed to require; but as the purpose in introducing them into female education would be mainly for the sake of the more accurate notions of grammar they convey, I believe that one hour every day for the first year, and an additional half hour through the second, would in two years accomplish the desired end. At the same time, enough will have been learnt to make a return to the study hereafter easy, to awaken the desire to know the treasures of ancient literature, and to place them more easily within reach of future labour.

During those two years the modern languages learnt by ear could be kept up by reading, by writing notes or journals alternately in one or the other, and whenever it can be done without sacrificing higher advantages, by the use of lesson-books on other subjects in whichever language requires to be most frequently practised. Thus history and geography, for instance, might be studied in French or German instead of English, supposing that an equally good choice of books was offered. When the two years specially devoted to Greek and Latin are over, they can in like manner be kept up by means which preserve the knowledge gained of words and forms ; as, for instance, by learning poetry, by daily reading a few lines, and by that frequent recurrence to their grammar which the study of modern languages will call for. The labour requisite to keep up the knowledge once gained is less than people seem generally aware of. We are too apt if we have not abundant time for a study to drop it altogether, and then, unless memory is peculiarly tenacious, the knowledge already attained soon fades out of the mind. Ten minutes perseveringly devoted to the purpose *every day* would have preserved for us what perhaps cost long labour to acquire, and will cost almost as much to regain if once forgotten.

We never acquire so thorough a knowledge of the grammar of our modern tongues, founded as they are upon Latin and Greek, without going to the fountain-head. The very construction of Latin, so artificial and seemingly unnatural to us, forces attention to what I may call the anatomy of sentences far more than is done by the simple and to us natural arrangements of words in modern languages. English especially, with its wants of inflexions—its great latitude of construction—its free and unmethodical use of auxiliary verbs in conjugations, is peculiarly unfitted for the study of grammar. French is better, owing to its greater rigidity of construction. Italian, as having retained more of the Latin, gives clearer views of grammar; and German is perhaps the best of all, owing to its inflexions and frequently inverted construction forcing great attention to grammatical rules. It has, moreover, to us this advantage, that being partly the parent of English, partly derived from a kindred origin, our own language seems to be in some measure unfolded to us as we study the foreign one.

Still the greatest advantages with regard to the study of grammar are to be derived from the ancient languages, and in many cases in which neither French nor German could be taught, good teaching in Latin and Greek may be procured. Independently of their value as grammatical studies, we lose too large a portion of the intellectual inheritance of man by remaining ignorant of those languages. It is true that such study of them as I have proposed here will go a very little way: but very little is sufficient to make the student feel the untranslatable beauties of poetry, and to open the mind to the new classes of associations which spring up as we read the thoughts and consider the imagery in which fancy was clothed in bygone times, when the whole of life was different from what we know it, except the feelings and cravings of the human heart and the laws of nature. We must remember also that it is not the pleasure of that contrast alone that we find in ancient literature: that literature has influenced the whole intellect of modern Europe. When society awoke out of that 'sleep of a thousand years' which had fallen like a spell upon the human mind, its infant progress began by the effort to retrace the steps of those mighty men of old. One by one the records of their genius were rescued from darkness and oblivion; and in men's minds, fascinated at this reconquest over time and destruction, the associations of the past became more powerful than those of the present, and coloured every new

production with their peculiar tints. Many generations succeeded each
other, and the spirit of free inquiry was at work in every department of
knowledge, before men dared, in their appreciation of the present and their
hopes of the future, to look back without an almost servile reverence on
the past. It is upon such views of ancient literature that Dr. Whewell
justly founds his defence of classical studies as a part of liberal education
which never can be abandoned without a degree of loss it would be impossible to calculate. 'Even,' he says, 'if the genius and skill shown in
modern poems and orations were as great as that which appears in Homer
or Virgil, Demosthenes or Cicero, the modern works could not supply the
place of the ancient ones in education. No modern works can in men's
minds take their station in the place of the familiar models of poetry and
eloquence which have been recognized as models for two thousand years;
which have for so many generations called forth and unfolded the ideas
of poetry and eloquence, and furnished standard examples and ready illustrations of human powers of thought and expression. The most remarkable
examples of poetry and eloquence in modern times have been the work
of educated men, and have themselves shared in the influence of the ancient
models. We cannot rightly admire the greatest modern poets and orators,
—we cannot admire them as they sought to be admired,—if we read them
in ignorance of the works of their great predecessors in the ancient
world.'*

We cannot hope generally to give girls any instruction in the ancient
languages that will enable them to enter into the spirit of their literature; †
some foundation of grammatical acquaintance with them is as much as we
can hope for; but the views expressed by Dr. Whewell place in a strong
light the value of translations for those who cannot read the originals.
The character of the writings, the cast of thought, may be thus learned,
however the beauty may be destroyed.

I have dwelt at some length upon the value of the study of the ancient
languages, partly because of the unfortunate neglect into which that study
has fallen in female education, and also partly because women are too prone
to join the modern cry against classical education, without pausing to
consider anything beyond the fact that boys who are not destined for

---

* *Of a Liberal Education*, p. 24.

† I may be asked why I would attempt *both* the learned languages, instead of
labouring to give more knowledge of one ? I reply, that my object being grammar
and etymologies, both are necessary, for modern languages are indebted to both.
When help has been given for the early grounding, a girl may take up either at a later
period.

learned professions are not likely to require Latin and Greek in their worldly affairs.

When this advantage cannot be procured for girls, we must turn our attention to making the best use of modern languages. I have said above, that in point of grammar, both German and Italian are in some respects preferable as studies to French, but the latter is of so much practical importance, that if one foreign language only can be taught, it should undoubtedly have the preference. If not learned by ear in early childhood, it should be commenced in a regular manner at twelve years old. The best grammar I believe to be Le Brethone's; the teacher should take care to point out the differences and analogies with English grammar, as soon as sufficient knowledge has been attained to make the comparison clear and profitable. The study of the two languages is then carried on at once by the task of translation. The endeavour to render the French words and forms into pure idiomatic English gives a more thorough comprehension of them than can be acquired by mere reading, or by the method of translating from our own into the foreign tongue, unless under the guidance of a native. It is certainly desirable to have the power of speaking and writing a language, but it is more important to understand it thoroughly ; and we may get into dangerous confusion by the habit of using words or forms of expression in a sense suggested by the practice of the language we are translating from. The teacher should, for the same reason, be very careful about the composition of the translation, since the use of the native tongue must not be corrupted in the process of learning a foreign one. In fact the latter is but half learned if we do not enter into its meaning so as to be able to give the spirit of it in the new form which the idiom of another language requires. The more words of similar derivation are avoided in translation the better, for the mere sound often deceives the scholars, while in truth the apparently similar expressions have acquired in the two modern languages meanings as different from each other as from the Greek or Latin original. How often translations apparently faithful may, owing to this cause, verge upon absolute nonsense, is daily seen in our newspaper renderings of French or Italian speeches or writings. The pupil cannot, therefore, be kept too strictly to Saxon-English, when translating from French, while for a similar reason, when working from a German original, words of Latin derivation may be safely used, and a somewhat French style of composition adhered to; in order to preserve us from the too easy error of imitating German while pretending to translate it, and of coining words which taste and custom reject, though the spirit of our language is sufficiently akin to the German to allow of the freedom. Nine out of ten of the translations from that tongue afford us examples of this deplorable corruption of English.

When some progress has been made, practical facility will be increased and time saved by translating orally instead of in writing. This should, of course, be done out loud, the teacher looking over the original. We may be sure that any person who can take up a French book, and read it off with tolerable ease in pure idiomatic English, has no small knowledge of both languages. When the child has had the advantage of learning to speak French in early childhood, this exercise should be used alternately in the native and the foreign tongue. There ought to be in such a case little or no difference with regard to the facility of expression in one or the other. When this early advantage has not been gained, and when there is no opportunity of learning from a native, the difficulty of acquiring ease or even accuracy of expression is very great. Frequent reading out loud, and likewise listening to reading, tutors the ear, and that is an important point ; both prose and poetry should be learnt by heart, and written from memory ; the prose being selected for its conversational excellence. Nothing can be better for such an exercise than Madame de Sevigné's letters ; fragments from the modern writers can also be chosen— for instance, from Lamartine and Alexandre Dumas. Leclerc's *Proverbes* are excellent in point of language, and generally unobjectionable in other respects. Another mode of acquiring command of language is to take a poem, and write it out in prose, avoiding the poetical expressions and construction ; while we are working in the same language, there is no fear of our falling into a foreign idiom. With a beginner, it is useful when a sentence has been learnt by heart to have it repeated several times, altering each time the tenses of the verbs. For instance, if the sentence describes a thing that has been done, let it next describe the same thing as actually being done at the present moment, next as contemplated in the future. Then introduce an *if*, which forces a change of mood, &c. Thus the proper idiomatic form of the sentence is preserved, and as the exercise should be oral, it gives ready command of the verbs and familiarity with the changes which accompany that of mood or tense.

All these are but poor substitutes for the ease and perfection with which a language is learned by talking with natives ; but I believe that by a diligent use of them the pupil will be brought to that state of forwardness in which she would be able to speak correctly and intelligibly if required, and to make rapid progress should the opportunity be thrown

in her way.   When French has been learned in early childhood, the time
we are now supposing to be given to the study of it may, if not required
for Latin or Greek, be devoted to German without any detriment to the
study of English and French grammar.   For it is certain that the labour
of learning a third language bears no comparison to that of acquiring a
second.   The mind has lost, or—if accustomed to different languages
from childhood—has never known the rigidity which comes from acquaintance with one idiom only, and one form of grammatical construction.
Differences and analogies are both more quickly discerned, and more easily
remembered.

If the studies are altogether restricted to English, there will be less to
do at the period we are considering.   Exercises in English grammar and
correct composition on easy subjects will take up less time, and allow
therefore of some being given to other reading.   Selections from our great
prose writers, and much reading of poetry, may perhaps occupy that time
as usefully as anything, and supply as far as we can, by extensive acquaintance with the different forms of English composition, that knowledge of the
nature and power of language which is best acquired by the comparison of
different languages.   It is not yet time, however, for any study requiring
much reflection.   We are but beginning to draw out the power of reason,
and till that has acquired some strength, teaching addresses itself properly
to the memory.

It must not be supposed, however, that even while learning foreign
languages, the whole time will be absorbed by verbal or grammatical
studies.   Several works or portions of works will have been read in the
language the pupil is acquiring ; and these may most frequently be chosen
with reference to the general plan of education, either for the sake of the
information they impart, or the new ideas they introduce.   Many subjects
which cannot be made to enter into the regular scheme of lessons at the
moment can be touched upon in this manner.   Sketches of natural history,
lives of great men, portions of large works which it is not desirable to
place in the girl's own hands, will easily be made use of, and a good deal
of poetry will also necessarily be read or learnt.   Thus the cultivation of
taste and judgment are really going on while mere French or German
lessons are apparently occupying the time; and be it remembered, the
real work of education is advancing whenever patience, thought, and perseverance are steadily exercised upon any subject.   The acquisition of
knowledge is the *means* even more than the object of education.

One hour only of our lesson-time now remains to be disposed of; and

that belongs to historical reading, or what we may more modestly as well
as more truly call,—preparation for historical reading.   I have assumed
that a girl at twelve years old is tolerably acquainted with scripture
history, and with so much of general history as to know something of the
part the Greeks and Romans played in the ancient world, and of the rise
of modern Europe out of the ruins of the Roman empire.   I suppose also
that she has read an outline of English history.   Any child of that age
whose reading has been well directed will have learned as much as this
without labour.   If she has a love of reading she will probably know more,
as biographies have in that case a great charm, and personal feeling for
the great man whose life is read gives an interest to the times—ancient or
modern—in which he lived which no mere historical lesson can inspire.
It is the fault of the education if that interest does not lead to consulting
maps and to the wish to know more concerning the state and history of
other countries at the same time, or of the same country at other periods.
I may remark here that it is very valuable to give a child who shows any
symptoms of this intelligent interest the habit of noting down at the time
what she most desires to learn or to read upon any point, so that she may
not lose sight of it.   The teacher when consulted must, of course, enter
into the matter with all the care which the child's earnestness deserves,
still pointing to the future for the accomplishment of all that is beyond
present attainment.   Thus the young creature is taught to look forward
to increased knowledge as to one of the privileges of coming years, and
the little note-book stands as a witness against her should her eagerness
slacken, or her perseverance fail.

Two great difficulties in reading history require to be diligently struggled with: these consist in finding out the relative positions of what we
are reading about, both in place and time, geographically and chronologi-
cally.   We must not be content to know simply the date of an event, or
where to find a town upon the map, but we must know how they stand
with relation to other towns or other events.   I have supposed a child of
twelve years old to have already learned something of geography.   She
ought to know generally the position of different countries, whether con-
tinents, islands, &c., their form as depending on chains of mountains or
the sea, their great rivers and principal cities.   The use of outline maps
without names, on which the child is practised to mark from memory the
course of great rivers or of mountain chains, and the position of a few
important towns, affords an admirable exercise of memory and accuracy of
eye.   It should of course be done with a pencil, and carefully compared

with the proper map for correction. When historical reading begins, it must be with the never-failing accompaniment of maps ; and that of the country which is the subject of the day's reading should not merely be laid open ready for reference, but attentively considered with regard to the relative position of the countries that border on it, to its latitude and longitude, &c. &c. For all general geographical views of this kind it is better to use a globe instead of maps ; this avoids the danger of falling into mistakes with regard to relative positions, which often prove sources of great confusion in the reader's mind. When for the sake of detail the globe has been set aside for a map of the individual country or district the day's reading refers to, still the lesson should seldom pass over without a few questions to test that the general knowledge acquired from the globe has been accurately retained. I mentioned above an easy method of leading even young children to a correct knowledge of the course of rivers and position of towns ; such an exercise can be made an amusement to them, and they can as easily be taught, roughly at first and then more accurately, what countries any given line of latitude or longitude will pass through if prolonged north or south, east or west, from a given point. This is mere skeleton knowledge, but it is a valuable foundation, and will save confusion and assist the memory in future reading. There is an excellent elementary work on *Physical Geography*, by Reid, which might be studied at thirteen without difficulty. Principles are clearly explained, and the more attractive parts of the subject given so as to excite interest. The outline of other sciences connected with physical geography, such as astronomy, geology, &c., is also briefly sketched, and the nature of the bearing of the one upon the other pointed out.*

Chronological tables should be no less diligently referred to than maps and globes. Nothing but a mere fragmentary and confused notion of events can be got by reading detached histories, without examining how the events we are occupied with stand in relation to the events passing in other countries at the same time, or which have preceded and perhaps been among the causes that have led to them. When history comes to be really studied for its great and important lessons, we shall find that the very significance of events often lies in this relative position. If, for instance, we read of such mighty changes as the Reformation in Germany, the Commonwealth, Restoration and final expulsion of the Stuarts in England, without reference to the condition of other States at the same period, we

---

* Published by Simpkin and Marshall.

understand but a trifling portion of what those events indicated, with regard to the countries in which they happened, or of the influence they were likely to exercise over the destinies of mankind.

The principal advantage of teaching the early habit of constant reference to contemporaneous events as well as to maps is, that the habit of turning to that relative view of the subject should have become part of the routine of the mind before serious study begins, in order that the latter may be impeded by no collateral difficulties. As a general rule in education, everything which merely requires attention and memory should be taught as far as possible before the time when we wish the whole powers of the pupil's mind to be concentrated on learning to reason, to reflect, to judge of thought and action. The study of words and forms is to the real work of education a mere mechanical routine, and should belong to its earlier stages; and in that study we may include all those elementary processes which are indispensable steps to knowledge, but which, considered in themselves, merely fill the memory without exercising one important faculty of the understanding.

It is advisable to go very slowly to work in the task of mastering contemporaneous chronology. Learning long series of dates is extremely irksome, and when the memory is not strong, the attempt to retain them is almost hopeless. It is much to be regretted that rhyme has not been more employed in teaching this dry preface to history. Much both of chronology and geography would be learned easily by young children in doggrel verse and retained without difficulty; and since this kind of knowledge is addressed to the memory alone, the manner in which it is conveyed is of no importance. To make a mere game of what should be an exercise of thought, is to defeat the purpose of education, but any means must be welcome by which the memory may be furnished with materials for the understanding to work upon.

Good chronological tables are not wanting; the best I am acquainted with are Major James Bell's. They are as easy of reference as Lesage's, and come down to a later period; but with a young reader, reference to a complete table of contemporary events would lead to mere confusion. Let her be satisfied at first with looking out the leading facts. Supposing, for instance, that the day's reading begins with the accession of Queen Elizabeth to the throne of England, let her merely ascertain in a chronological table the contemporary sovereigns of other countries, so as to fix them firmly in her memory; another day she will see what were the marked events which happened in these different countries contemporane-

10

ously, or nearly so, with those which signalised the reign of Elizabeth in England; and a further step yet will be to study the columns which record the great men, or the principal facts of scientific or literary history. Doubtless these are of far more importance than the succession of kings, but the latter must be known, and they serve as landmarks to assist the memory. When we have these divisions distinct and accurate in the mind, it becomes easier to retain whatever else deserves to be remembered within the same period. It is a useful plan with children to collect groups of important dates that fall most nearly together, taking the beginning, middle, and end of each century as the centre point of a group. Suppose, for instance, the most notable event we can discover nearly at the beginning of the sixteenth century to be written down upon a card, and any facts worth remembering within ten or fifteen years of that time, from 1490 perhaps to 1510, to be added from time to time, the dates thus grouped should then be learnt by heart, and habitually considered together, and another group formed towards 1550, and so on. The spaces between may be filled up according to inclination and the power of the memory. The great point is, that what is learned should be firmly rooted. Instead of taking a particular year as the centre of a group, an important event may be taken; but I believe some advantage will result from the former, by leading to a more continuous view of history. By following such methods with perseverance, undaunted by the labour of constant reference, the pupil will be surprised in a short time to find how readily she can discover her bearings on the chart of Time. Supposing her memory to be naturally feeble, she will probably never have that prompt recollection of single dates which is often so much overvalued in society, but she will have laid a clear and systematic foundation of chronology, which is far more valuable. Her mind will have the habit of considering the bearings of many events, instead of looking at each one as an isolated phenomenon, and will be prepared to rise to views of the history of mankind, while another person reading the same book, learns the mere narrative of some national history.

During the two years we are considering, I believe a girl will easily get through some universal ancient history, such as Tytler's or Millot, and general short histories of the different countries in Europe.* Considering the time spent in referring to maps and chronological tables, we may

---

* If the child is familiar with French or German, history will of course be read in the one or the other, according as works fit for the purpose are found in them.

suppose that not more than fifteen pages will be read each day. Taking five days in the week (Sunday and a day for weekly examinations being set apart), we find that a volume of three hundred pages will thus be gone through in a month; and the two years, omitting a month's holidays in each, will allow from eighteen to twenty octavo volumes being read without fatigue or hurry. It is possible, if memory is very bad, that a work, or portions of it, may require to be read more than once; but considering how often, in reading the histories of different nations, we are going over the same ground, and referring to the same facts and persons, while the constant attention to contemporaneous events brings them yet more frequently to remembrance, I believe that by the time those several histories have been perused, there will be a clear and orderly outline of European history firmly fixed in the mind. This is the indispensable preliminary for studying, with profit, the more detailed account of particular periods to which we come later.

The hour spent in historical reading completes the regular lessons for the day. Serious application is required, and must be exacted while they last, but they are short and sufficiently varied not to oppress the pupil's mind. It is very desirable that part of the time spent in needlework should be improved by reading out loud, whether by the governess or by the pupils taking it in turn. This reading should not be of a kind requiring application; its purpose is mostly to lead to conversation; it affords a good opportunity for reading parts of books which are not of a character to leave entirely in a girl's hands, or the account of anything remarkable that is exciting attention at the moment, whether public events or discovery, or perhaps some fine passages of prose or poetry, which the teacher may have met with in the course of her own reading, or about which the interest of her pupils may have been excited by some allusions or quotations they have seen themselves. Critical remarks, comments upon feeling and character, should be freely expressed, and in a manner to lead the children to join in with their own. The habit of taking pleasure in conversation of that nature, and of expressing themselves readily and well, is a most desirable one to give. Young people are seldom sufficiently accustomed to the free expression of their thoughts, and difficulties, and imaginings. It is true that in the present day, when reverence has been nearly scouted out of the world, it is not uncommon to find the most decided opinions held by creatures who are incapable of having meditated the grounds upon which any opinion should be formed; and to hear them expressed with a pert forwardness, prompted by conceit or the prevailing spirit of rebellion

10—2

against authority. But this is not the expression of *thought*, and the best mode of checking it, indeed, is to listen with attention, and simply to desire to have the reasons for the opinions advanced. The shallow dogmatist is thus driven from one point to another till the confession cannot be avoided that the opinions are borrowed without reflection or the means of sound judgment. There will be nothing over-depressing in this process if at the same time a young girl feels that sympathy and attention are always ready for whatever is honestly her own feeling or conviction; that a welcome is given to all her sincere attempts to form an opinion—a ready ear to all her fancies and speculations, whether excited by reading or by what she has witnessed in real life.

Some young persons are impelled by nature to pour out all that passes through their minds; but many are reserved, and a still greater number are timid. Afraid of others, or afraid of themselves, they require to be drawn out—to be led gently on to express themselves freely. The insipid trivial talk of persons whose education and power of mind ought to place them on a higher level often, I believe, results from the habit of never expressing anything of what lies beneath the surface of life. It seems impossible that the general tone of educated society should not be higher than it is, if people showed their better nature to each other with more frankness and simplicity.

There is often more value in an hour's conversation with young people than in many hours' reading. The germ of false notions may thus be checked before it has taken root; imagination and enthusiasm can be met with sympathy while saved from misdirection; singular views may be listened to calmly and reasoned upon gently, obviating at once the chance of their being maintained from mere love of paradox or singularity, or of their producing a sense of moral wrong in timid minds that may honestly hold them, and yet shrink under the feeling of differing widely from commonly received opinions. The more bold and eager require the discipline of open controversy, while the timid and sensitive need the habit of free expression to give them confidence. To all alike, conversation with their superiors in knowledge and experience is highly valuable, as aiding to form judgment upon a great number of points that never come within the bounds of regular study;—and to all alike it presents the further advantage of beginning to form the habit of good and easy speaking so rare in England.

The tone of conversation heard in the drawing-room will, of course, have more influence than anything that passes in the school-room. But

it must often be impossible for very young people to take a part in drawing-room conversation, while the governess will naturally be careful that
her remarks on books or other subjects are of a nature to draw out her
pupils' opinions and lead them to feel and express an interest in matters
they may hereafter hear discussed by others.

§ 2.—Having now completed the course of study and reading for the
first two years of regular education, it will not be amiss to consider a
subject which strangely enough is very generally overlooked, namely,
the art of reading itself. Everbody *gets through* a certain number of
books—in the present day—the number is often considerable—while
comparatively few can be said to know how to read, that is, how to
derive knowledge from a book. Not only with the generality of persons
is the mind passive when reading, receiving impressions and images
which the memory retains or not, according to its native power, but there
is seldom in such readers industry enough to care whether the passing
impression be a clear or confused one, whether the words used by an
author convey a definite meaning or not, and still less, whether his argument or the whole scope of his work have been clearly apprehended.
Reading, in short, is an amusement, a resource against the enemy Time,
that so many people are wearily seeking all their lives to baffle. And
perhaps the very fact that mere amusement so often takes the shape of
reading deceives the mind as to the real fact that the time is virtually
spent in idleness. Even in his day Dr. Butler remarked that the number
of ' books and papers of amusement' favoured habits which were most
opposed to studious reading, ' by this means,' he says, ' time, even in solitude, is happily got rid of without the pain of attention : neither is any
part of it more to be put to the account of idleness, one can scarce forbear
to say, is spent with less thought, than great part of that which is spent in
reading.' * And if that were true more than a century ago, what must it
be now, when for each paper of amusement which existed in Butler's day,
dozens are to be found upon every table, from the boudoir to the back-shop?
Must we not fear that the habits formed upon such materials will be very
unfavourable to earnest attention, and that the mind, accustomed to be
passively entertained, will be hard to rouse to the labour of thought?
Accordingly, how common is it to find that works of real value are read
either for the sake of the narrative they may contain, or because they are

---

* Preface to Sermons.

much talked of, or merely because they come in the way,* without exciting the mind to more labour than it gives to a newspaper article. A clear style is a great snare to such readers; lured on by that, no difficulty is perceived, no new opinion appears startling, no statements strange.

The time actually spent in reading for amusement is a slighter evil than the habit formed of being unable to find anything but amusement in a book, of being apparently engaged in an earnest pursuit while the mind is inert and sunk in indolence. Supposing the books themselves to be unobjectionable, reading is certainly a very innocent form of pleasure. We may even admit more; for the mind is on the way to better things should the desire for them arise; and some casual expression, some statement or allusion in a book may awaken that desire and give the first bend in a new direction, which could scarcely happen in the course of any other kind of amusement, but still it must be remembered that reading without a definite purpose and a studious intention is amusement only. With children indeed it is well to give the love of books at any price. Let them find pleasure in reading, in hopes that we may lead them to find real and serious interest hereafter. It is for this reason that the folly of setting a lesson as a punishment is two-fold, it makes the lesson odious, and it tends to create an unpleasant association with books, while the object of the parent should be to make reading rank high among pleasures, and, if possible, to make the mental exertion necessary for a lesson pleasurable also.

Careless reading arises from indolence, which is satisfied with passive impressions, or from that mental confusion which allows the mind to be satisfied with ill-defined thoughts and images, and does not perceive when a statement is clearly apprehended or not. To guard against this, our great endeavour must be to lead the mind to find delight in the sense of intellectual activity. This should be begun in early childhood by care-

---

* The absence of any idea of the necessity of a systematic purpose in reading is clearly marked by the common way of getting books from a library or book-club. Whatever happens to be sent, or to be recommended as new, is read without reference to any previous reading, or to any acquired knowledge, and without the least intention of following up the subject. To-day a history comes to hand, to-morrow a novel—then a volume of essays, next a biography, or travels, which suppose previous acquaintance with the natural productions, the geology, or the former history of the country, none of which the reader possesses nor thinks of acquiring. Such reading is just a substitute for a series of dioramas or theatrical representations that would keep the mind amused by a constant succession of scenes or images, an amusement harmless in itself, but fraught with mischief if it leads the young mind to believe that it deserves any better name than amusement.

fully applied stimulus and encouragement, and perhaps more than all, by judicious attention to apportioning the task exactly to the powers of the child; it should be just difficult enough to require an effort, and just easy enough to make sure of victory. Then the achievement becomes a matter of congratulation; the child's pride is roused and its ambition awakened. When the understanding is sufficiently developed to be appealed to, then we may venture to expect exertion from a sense of duty or the hope of a more distant reward. Not till then should we set a task which requires the continued attention of several days before the child can perceive its own progress, and feel the pleasant sensation of having conquered.

Every successive lesson, or rather subject on which lessons are given, should be chosen with a view to call forth some additional measure of exertion, both of atttention and comprehension, and a large measure, if possible, of *desire to know*. It little matters *what;* the one important thing is to train that desire, together with the feeling of dissatisfaction in not understanding; the impatience of a confused perception which prompts the mind to seek explanation, and to find pleasure in clearness.

If thus prepared from the early dawn of intelligence, the child will begin studious reading at twelve years old, with habits which will make progress both easy and sure. It will be more or less rapid, according to the measure of natural ability, but the child's own mind will be working with the teacher's, and that mental labour is itself of the highest value. When that early preparation has been neglected, the chief object in studying must be to remedy the defect. Some of the subjects on which the child will be occupied necessarily exact attention, and thus force the right habit without further effort from the teacher. Such is the case with arithmetic and partly with grammatical exercises. Rules of grammar may be committed to memory, but they cannot be applied without some effort of understanding. There must be sufficient exercise of thought to enable the child to distinguish when or why certain rules are to be observed. The lessons on both subjects however may, of course, be made more or less a school for thought according to the method of the teacher; if the latter is satisfied with the mere correctness of a task done, a very good memory in the pupil may carry her through with the help of atten-tion only; but a few questions will soon detect any lurking confusion or any indifference to obtaining a clear apprehension; or a new statement of a rule will force the indolent mind to think and to discover what are the real points which it has to attend to.

But it is in reading that the governess may most readily test her pupil's desire to understand. Unless early broken in to proper habits, the naturally active and intelligent alone will ask questions of their own accord. The lesson is simply a lesson; it is as easy to read what is but half understood as what presents a clear meaning. A long word, strange enough to make a difficulty in pronouncing it, may force a question, but otherwise the indolent will prefer not understanding to the trouble of making inquiries and the chance of lengthening a lesson. On the other hand, the dull do not easily find out that they are particularly in the dark, and are rarely indeed able to ask the right question which would point out the confusion. A child whose questions show that the mind is eager and working upon the subject presented to it, should be met half-way with ready and full information, and that tone of alacrity which marks sympathy and pleasure on the part of the teacher. With the dull every effort should be made to stimulate them; encouragement, an appearance of confidence in their power to apprehend and their wish to do so, an unwearied patience in going over the same ground again and again, so long as the pupil gives earnest attention. With the indolent, on the contrary, it is well to let the lesson owe additional weariness to the effects of their own indolence.

It is not merely the meaning of words that a child will not understand, but that of the sentence which may convey an opinion she never heard before, or an inference from something preceding, the connexion with which has not been clearly apprehended. Or allusions may be made to things or persons she is unacquainted with, but the knowledge of which is indispensable to understanding the author's meaning. Or reflections may occur which are unintelligible, unless the whole scope of perhaps many pages has been clearly grasped and carried in the mind. Now these difficulties are all so many traps into which the indolent fall. If allowed to run on unchallenged they will remain contentedly in the dark, but a few questions will quickly detect the ignorance, and till the latter is fully acknowledged no explanation should ever be offered. Sometimes mental indolence will prompt a child to say she understands when this is far from being true, and that without intentional falsehood, but really because she is too careless to know when she has or has not a clear notion of a subject. In all cases when the question 'do you understand?' is answered in the affirmative, an explanation should be required. 'Why is such or such an allusion made? what does it refer to? what is the inference drawn by the author? why does he say *therefore it follows?*' &c. &c. Questions such as these will expose to a child her own utter carelessness, the complete waste of whatever time has been spent upon the lesson, and the evident necessity of going over it again. For it should be made clear to a child from the first that *getting through* the book is *not* the object of the lesson —not even if its words remain fixed on the memory; that her own earnest endeavour to work and understand is the only satisfactory indication of progress. It is by such a method that an indolent learner may, as I said before, be made to feel additional weariness owing to the effects of her own indolence, and she may perhaps be roused by this means to conquer the fault in order to escape its consequences.

In reading history, which, however briefly treated, touches on so many subjects of deep human interest, the teacher must endeavour to point out the moral bearing of different questions brought forward, the influence of certain courses of action, the tendencies of certain dispositions, the progress resulting from certain great steps in knowledge or discovery. These are the questions for the sake of which alone history will be studied more closely at a later period, but even thus early they should not be passed over. The habit of speculating upon what is read, of exercising thought instead of merely following words, is thus gradually begun. Another important point also is gained, that of exciting interest in something foreign to daily experience and leading the young mind to a large sphere of sympathies. This may be further encouraged by additional information of an interesting nature given by the teacher, such as facts tending to increase admiration for some favourite character, or amusing illustrations of a particular epoch or state of manners. These may be just alluded to during the lesson and the full account given later. The biography may be searched out for the reading of leisure hours, or some fine passages of poetry bearing upon the characters, or the period, or else upon the moral points in question, may be recited or read by the teacher. In this manner the lessons and the leisure hours will be bound together by links of common interest, and the connexion be established in the child's mind between the earnest wish to learn which makes the lessons easier and pleasanter, and the eager interest about many things which gives such zest to the reading for amusement.

In most cases what belongs to human life and action will most readily touch the chord of sympathy, and therefore excite interest, but sometimes the latter will be as quickly aroused upon other subjects, on points connected with natural history, for instance, or even science. Whatever it may be, let the clue be followed up; what we want is to cultivate a habit, and it matters nothing whether it be through the means of one book or another. Such differences of taste should also be carefully watched in another point of view, for the turn of the mind towards facts or speculation affords valuable indications to the teacher. In the one case habits of observation, in the other habits of reasoning, will be the most easily formed, and the general cast of the mind will probably in the one become practical, in the other speculative. These tendencies must, of course, be watched, and the excess or evil of each disposition guarded against in education.

Differences in the mode of dealing with difficulties are among the first intellectual indications which a teacher has to study in her pupils. We may even with grown persons read character in some important respects from their conduct in this particular. Some are impatient of the obstacle put in their path, and attack it with vigour, but are unequal to any continued exertion ; some are overcome at once; they magnify the evil in their own minds, and are often more frightened by the vision they have conjured up themselves than by the real circumstances of the case which they have not calmness and patience to examine. Others again rise with fresh spirit under the sense that fresh exertion is required ; their energy is roused by difficulty, and power grows with the energy. These differences are shown in practical matters no less than in study, and indeed according to the bent of the tastes towards one or the other we may find energy in dealing with practical difficulties and timidity in shrinking from intellectual exertion, or the reverse. The duty of education, therefore, is to excite the active spirit, or to cultivate it if it exist by nature, so that it shall be exerted whenever occasion calls for it, not merely under the circumstances that appeal to strong tastes or feelings, but habitually and from the motive that whatever we have undertaken to do ought to be done with promptitude and resolution : so trained, the young will feel that to waver or turn back, to be daunted by trouble or difficulty, is a form of moral cowardice to be ashamed of.

An indolent child is overwhelmed by difficulties in general without being able to point out any particular thing that requires explanation, and is especially averse to the labour of working alone. If a child desires to plod on and overcome a difficulty by her own exertion, we may be sure the right spirit is in her ; or if when she comes for help, she can point out *where* the difficulty lies, what link in the explanation has failed her, we should be satisfied, for it is evident that she has thought and worked sufficiently to clear up a large portion of the subject. What comes within reach of her previous knowledge is clearly made out, and she discerns the boundary of the new. This is exactly the state the mind should be in to labour with profit; and to this state therefore the governess must try to bring a less willing pupil before she gives her help.

Quick children are very often averse to application, and they require careful watching lest they should deceive both themselves and their teachers. They are often impatient of difficulties and slur them over, being enabled to do so by the quick apprehension with which they seize certain points. The teacher should be merciless in exposing the real confusion which exists under this seeming facility, for the quick child being generally proud of her capacity, will deeply feel the mortification of being thus forced to confess that she was satisfied with half understanding, and she may thereby be spurred to more exertion in future. The lurking insincerity also of such a mode of study, of any want of earnest intention in what we ostensibly undertake to perform, should be pointed out. The first approach to pretension must be carefully watched with girls; for since their knowledge will not in after life be tested practically, like that of men, they will be able to keep up with much better success an appearance of knowing more than they really do, and thereby feed conceit while learning to be satisfied with false pretences. Habits of accurate thought and real love of truth will be their only safeguards against a fault which their intercourse with the world will have no tendency to check.

Idleness, that is a mere disinclination to work, is not so serious a defect as inattention, which trifles with work while appearing to do it. This fault is one which it is very difficult to deal with, because it may be impossible to coerce attention beyond a certain point, and few things are more dangerous than for the teacher to insist on anything which authority is incompetent to enforce. If the pupil be allowed to dawdle over a task, her habit of inattention, of careless working, may be encouraged by it. It is not enough, therefore, to give her a certain task, but the time within which she is required to do it must be also fixed. If it is not finished at the specified hour, then it may be necessary to impose some punishment, but the latter should not include finishing the task, since, if a given time were again appointed for the work, inveterate habit might lead to a second failure, and so on; or the child, if obstinate, may purposely abstain from exertion, and then the teacher may be baffled in a manner very difficult to meet; while on the other hand, if the neglected task is simply ordered to be finished, without fixing the time, the child is at liberty to dawdle, and the very punishment may tend to strengthen the bad habit. It cannot be too often enforced upon teachers that *habits*, not information, constitute the great aim of education. Doubtless we desire to give knowledge, but what we must seek first and above all, is to cultivate in the mind those habits which will make it capable of valuing and acquiring knowledge hereafter.

Inattention is most common with quick and easily excited children. When it is found united with slowness, it requires a degree of patience in the teacher which few can appreciate who have not been so tried. The same management, however, applies to this as to the former case. The only difference being in the extent and difficulty of the task appointed. Provided that it be certainly within the child's power, the performance of it may be as rigidly exacted from her as from the more intelligent. Great discrimination is requisite on this point, in all cases alike ; for if once the teacher can be shown to have imposed conditions which her pupil's honest exertions were not capable of fulfilling, the spell of her authority is broken. The child may feel the necessity of outward obedience, but there will be in her mind a conflict between the feeling of duty and the suspicion that her teacher may be wrong; such a conflict weakens both the moral and the intellectual power of exertion. Great care must be taken in teaching a child of really slow apprehension not to overtax the power of attention. The great point is gained when the child is led to make a determined voluntary effort, say for two minutes only, then relaxation of the weak power should be allowed for a time, till it has recovered energy for another vigorous short grasp of the subject-matter from the point which had been clearly grasped before. It is well to draw attention to the mental power thus exerted, and if some degree of pride and pleasure can be excited in the consciousness of successful exertion, there will be fresh courage for new efforts, and these may be gradually extended to longer periods. At first the child's willingness to make the painful exertion will be greatly owing to the expectation of speedy release, in time the willingness grows into habit.

The most hopeless defect to struggle against in intellectual education is mental indolence, which I have already alluded to in speaking of the difficulty of making children read with profit. But this fault, where it exists, runs through all they do which calls for any degree of mental exertion ; if a game requires a little thought, they will turn from it with as much distaste as from study. It is found in children of various grades of capacity, though seldom probably when the latter is of a high order, unless it be connected with delicate health. In such cases the lassitude of the body seems to cast a torpor over the mind, and it is possible that some highly-wrought natures are saved from injury to the brain by this utter aversion to effort which preserves the mind from over-fatigue while the physical frame is still feeble and immature.

These, however, are exceptional cases.   In general when we find mental indolence in children, it must be vigorously and perseveringly attacked.   It is not so much *what* they do, but how they do it, which needs watching.   For children afflicted with this defect will often go through the routine of their lessons well enough, they are not idle but inert; they enter into the spirit of no one study they are engaged in; they feel the pressure of difficulties, but are insensible to the pleasure of success.   They read without caring to understand.   They hear subjects of interest discussed, and never feel their own interest sufficiently excited to seek an explanation.   They see new or unusual things, and even curiosity cannot stimulate them to seek further knowledge about them.

With a pupil of this description every lesson should as far as possible be given in a form that shall force some degree of thought.   Composition, for instance, is an excellent exercise, especially if the teacher be vigilantly on her guard against imitation and borrowed sentiments, and it may be required in the shape of notes or abstracts of what has been read, or an account of the pupil's own meaning when she has acquiesced in some statement or opinion, which there may be good ground for believing she has never considered at all.   Whenever she is forced to acknowledge that such has been the case, and that she really is ignorant in the matter, it should be always carefully pointed out that it is not the ignorance which is disgraceful, but the being contented with ignorance.   Not to know, is the lot of every one, in different degrees ; all that can be required of us is to be aware of our ignorance and desirous to remove it.

Moral motives may sometimes be successfully appealed to in order to combat this kind of indolence.   The great principle that we are responsible to God and our own conscience for the use of all the capacity we possess should be earnestly enforced; and the duty of usefulness to others which flows as a natural consequence from that principle.   The young mind, while still intellectually feeble, is so often open to the force of moral views, which are more or less connected with feeling, and still more to the action of generous sentiment, that many a child who might resist all mere reasoning about the advantages of knowledge will feel spurred to exertion when made to perceive how the indolent carelessness of one human being inevitably affects others; how the neglect of the means of usefulness we possess, the waste of the time we might have improved, may cause evil and suffering through a circle too wide for us at any given moment to perceive the links that unite us to it. When feeling has been roused on this subject, perhaps some direct office of usefulness or benevolence will stir the indolent mind to exertion better than mere mental labour.

With regard to studies, it is well to try every means of discovering what will excite a taste in the indolent child. Whatever it may be, if not utterly foolish, let her pursue it. The habit of studying some one thing earnestly and with pleasure may influence the mind, and awaken its dormant energies. If the child will learn to love work and seek knowledge by studying and attending to the flowers in her garden, that is more profitable to her than grammar or geography which she commits lazily to memory. Our care must be, however, that the chosen pursuit be followed as closely and methodically as if it were the driest lesson. We may change the subject, but not the *method*, for the latter is education itself.

There are cases, however, where even this fails, where no taste can be discovered, nothing offers sufficient stimulus to rouse the mind to willing exertion; we can then only toil on, hoping for the future. And the future will sometimes—perhaps generally—bring the reward to such persevering effort. Nothing varies so much in different individuals as the period at which the faculties and character develope and assume their right proportions. Thus many a young person who has seemed almost hopelessly inert and indifferent till eighteen or nineteen years of age, and even later, will at twenty-five exhibit a wholly new phase of mental life. Their store of knowledge will of course be very small compared with that of others, and there may never be opportunities of wholly repairing the early defect, but the laborious patience of parents and teachers will be found not to have been in vain. When the mind begins to exert itself, it works upon right principles ; and that habit is more valuable than knowledge without system.

In watching children, the teacher should never lose sight of the important distinction between the original mind and the mere lively retailer of the thoughts of others. This distinction is one of the most striking through life, and more than any other single test decides the intellectual rank the individual deserves to hold in our estimation. Dr. Johnson expressed it admirably when he refused to give an opinion of a man's power of conversation, because he did not yet know whether his talk flowed from a reservoir, or a spring. A person gifted with considerable original power may appear dull in comparison with one who retails with liveliness what a good memory has enabled her to retain. In society this may be very deceptive for a time, but a teacher has too many occasions to test the real capacity to be so deceived; it should be her care to prevent the child deceiving herself. No imitation should be applauded, no borrowed opinion, no statement repeated without examination as if it were made upon personal knowledge, should pass unquestioned; while pleasure should be testified at every instance of simple accuracy, every proof that the thing advanced has been thought over and is a genuine opinion, or even fancy of the speaker's. Liveliness is what makes the want of originality dangerous. Without it no one is deceived. The dull retailer is simply a very tiresome companion. It is the false brilliancy of the lively imitator which encourages conceit, and by the applause of society leads the mind to be satisfied with seeming instead of reality.

Some caution on the mother's part must always be necessary when her children differ very widely in intellectual capacity, lest the interest of the governess should be too exclusively roused for the one who shows most talent. Two evils may result from that kind of partiality. The already active brain may be over-stimulated or conceit may be encouraged ; while on the other hand, the dulness of the less favoured child may be increased by the depressing effect of being made to feel that she is thought less worthy of attention. There is also some difficulty in dealing with the children themselves, in avoiding all deceit without either unduly elating the one or depressing the other.

It is mere nonsense with a clever child to attempt to disparage her powers. Either she is too conscious of them to believe what is said, and then her faith in those she ought to trust is shaken; or else, if nervously sensitive, as gifted natures often are, she will oscillate between low fits of depression and fever-fits of ambitious exertion; alternately believing the voice from within, or the warning from without, according to the condition of her health or animal spirits. With the slow child likewise, it is folly to attempt to disguise the truth. If in the hope of stimulating her feeble powers she is told that she might do as well as her sister would she only take the trouble, she also will be subject to painful alternations of hope and despondency; and finally, in addition to the discouragement of baffled endeavour, she also will lose confidence in those who held up to her a false hope.

It is wiser in every point of view to deal truly and frankly with both children. When they are of an age to understand it, let them be taught that the real object of education is the same for both, not by holding up the same standard of attainment, but by endeavouring to make the most in each of that measure of capacity which God has given. We cannot all learn alike, but we can all give earnest, honest exertion to whatever is set before us, and according to our ability improve ourselves and serve others.

The dull child should see that her mother and governess have unwearied patience in explaining, in going over the ground slowly and repeatedly, so long as she gives unwearied attention; that they are content that she should gain knowledge by very small degrees, so long as they make sure that she is doing her best to form the habit of observing and thinking; that she is willing to sift a question till she understands it thoroughly, never ashamed of the length of time she may be obliged to spend on one point so that she ends with a clear and accurate notion at last. She should be allowed to know,—for sooner or later she must know and feel it,—that she cannot be on a par with the brilliant in intellect; let her see her sister's superiority, and learn to love it. This honest admiration of superior abilities, joined to the calmness and self-possession which belong to knowing our own position, and accepting it as that which God has appointed us to improve, and to be useful in, will be the surest safeguards against any mortification which may await the less gifted in society.

The clever child should be dealt with no less openly. Let her rejoice in her powers, but rejoice only as in the possession of a treasure for the use of which she is responsible. Do not damp her ardour, but give it a higher direction than the whisperings of her young ambition would prompt. Enforce the conviction that in a woman's life there is,—or ought to be,— no place for display, and little for the brilliant exercise of intellect; but a wide field for the usefulness and activity of a well-stored mind, of sound opinions and mature judgment. In accordance with this view let her see that these are the points her mother values most highly; those which she considers the test of real superiority; that she thinks little of the brilliancy which is owing to quick apprehension and retentive memory, but much of the patient labour of thought, of accurate discrimination, of pains taken to form a right opinion, of sound judgment and perseverance whether in study or practical matters. The child will then feel that however much she owes to nature, she will win solid esteem only by the mental habits she must cultivate as assiduously as her less gifted sister. The more she has been favoured the greater she will feel to be the obligation laid upon her.

The cultivation of the memory is a special and important object to be borne in mind throughout the course of study. To learn and to forget is but a melancholy renewal of the toils of Sisyphus—for ever undergoing hard labour, never to attain our object. I believe that when nature has denied the original power of memory, or given it in a very small degree, it is not possible to repair the misfortune, but industry and method will do a great deal to obviate some of its evils ; and this is certain, that few persons of bad memory have given such a degree of persevering attention to the subject as may entitle them to say what is or is not within reach of remedy. The art of treasuring knowledge is too little studied either by those who are, or those who are not, gifted by nature. The former generally trust to their natural power, and the latter give way to despair, feeling their natural infirmity, while both neglect the means which might improve the defect or prevent the gift from being wasted. It is not sufficient in any case to trust to natural power alone ; even methodical reading will scarcely ensure sufficient accuracy without some degree of labour in striving to retain the fruits of our reading in a shape which shall be ready for reference. Notes, which are absolutely indispensable when the memory is weak, are highly valuable whatever be its power, and the very habit of making them helps to keep present in the mind the necessity rather of an accurate than a ready memory, of systematized rather than of varied knowledge.

With children I believe it best to follow the same plan whether the memory be good or bad; to take equal pains to ascertain *what* has been remembered and *how*, and to prevent desultory habits which, though less destructive to a good memory than to a bad one, are equally pernicious to the tone of mind. Of course there will be less need in the former case for the disheartening labour of repetition, and therefore progress will be more rapid, while in the latter, though ground may be gained very slowly, it will be gained surely and permanently. What we have to aim at is that memory should be retentive, accurate, and if possible, ready. Of these qualities the last is least and the second is most within the reach of art. Fortunately the last is also the least valuable, except for the purpose of display in society, where it will win more applause than gifts of far higher character. There are, indeed, occasions in which a prompt recollection of facts is very useful, but in general, time can be afforded for the labour of distinctly recalling what is suggested to the weak memory at first rather as a shadowy phantom than in any definite form. No trouble of reference and repetition should be spared to insure accuracy of recollection; there

11

must be no weariness or impatience in going over the same ground, in looking out for the fiftieth, or if need be the hundredth, time for the date of the fact, or the explanation of the term which has been forgotten.

In order to cultivate the retentive power of a weak memory, or to improve the character of a good one, it is necessary to bear in mind those principles of association according to which knowledge will be combined systematically, not gathered up in a confused mass. We must take care in teaching a new thing that some links should be ready to bind it with former knowledge, and that still, as we work on, it should as far as possible be done as from a centre outwards, order prevailing throughout, and a connecting link being kept up. Systematic study is important in every respect; it influences the mental habits and modes of thought, and is therefore the real matter of intellectual education, but I speak of it here only with reference to its bearing on the cultivation of memory. The latter must be powerful indeed to retain desultory information, which, even if retained, will seldom be reproduced in any useful form.

The character of the memory is greatly influenced by our mode of observation. Attention should, then, be paid to forming right habits of observation in children. At first the object is to make them observe generally, to stimulate the faculty, if not naturally quick, by means both of lessons and games, and gradually to train some discrimination, to turn attention to resemblances and contrasts, then to analogies, and thus by degrees to lead the mind to that mode of viewing things which will give the habit of classing and remembering them according to philosophical instead of mere casual associations. The ground is thus prepared for systematic study, and for a methodical storing up of whatever knowledge is gained. All those first steps in forming correct habits belong to early education. They are part of that hourly mental influence which should be exercised over the child from the moment it is able to compare and remember. It is not a question of books and set lessons, but of constant attention in leading the mind to work on right principles. When we come to the time for real study, the groundwork, as I said before, should be already laid. It is not yet time, however, to explain to the child the principles on which it is unconsciously working; we must still be content to lead without making known the object towards which we are tending.

The actual method of cultivating the memory by means of the lessons at this period, will be first: learning by heart, taking care that no new acquisition drives out the old. This should have been carefully attended to from the earliest time that lessons were committed to memory. Many children learn poetry, or indeed dry lists of words, with extreme facility, but as easily forget them ; and such children generally are fond of learning a new piece, and shrink from the labour of going over the old. Yet this is what must be strictly exacted; and it is still better to force, if possible, the recollection of what has been partially lost than to let it be learnt over again. The latter is no trouble, and is not more likely to make a lasting impression than before. But the exertion of trying to recall the half-faded impression, the working of the mind as it first catches one lost link and then another is beneficial in itself, and tends to impress more deeply what has thus been painfully reconstructed. The practice of learning poetry should continue at the period we are considering, always letting a child choose the lines for herself in the first instance. If the choice should be a bad one, it affords an opportunity of beginning to point out the characteristics of poetry, and what makes one piece more worthy of being studied and remembered than another. There will be other things also to commit to memory ; such as the groups of dates which the child will have partly at least constructed for herself. She should also be made to write down the explanation of any term she was not before acquainted with, and to learn it by heart. In making lists of this kind, some persons have found that their recollection is assisted by using ink of two colours, calling in the help of vision as an auxiliary to the memory. Thus, the term to be explained may be written in red, and the explanation in black ink, in separate columns. The same with the chronological lists; the date may be written in one colour, and the event it refers to in another. Clearness and neatness, which assist in conveying a complete and distinct impression, doubtless assist recollection. Indeed, vividness of impression is so favourable to memory that, other things being equal, we should always expect a person of vivid imagination to remember more distinctly than an unimaginative one. Whatever we can do, therefore, with children to cultivate this valuable property of imagination, to make them take strong and lively impressions of what they hear and see, is highly beneficial. Inertness of mind is no less a foe to memory than to intellectual power.

Besides learning by heart, a girl of twelve years old may begin to acquire the method of storing the fruits of her own reading. The lists above-mentioned belong to this part of the subject, but she may also begin to make notes. This habit is so essential for any profitable study, and the difficulty so great of doing anything of the kind with invariable regularity, that the practice should be early begun. It should be a fixed

11—2

principle in the child's mind, worked in by the daily habit of her life, that what she goes through the labour of reading deserves the labour of being remembered; and that although much must be trusted to memory and much inevitably forgotten, the leading facts, or striking thoughts, and the results of the reading, should be preserved from oblivion, and so arranged as to be ready for reference. Little can be done at the age we now speak of; the habit only can be formed of considering that notes are an essential part of study, and if a child sees that her mother or governess makes it an invarible practice to read with a pencil and piece of paper by her side, she will soon think that she is unduly depressed in the scale of intelligence if she is not thought fit to have a piece of paper and pencil also. When this habit is begun, the teacher must be very careful to lead her pupil to observe and record the right things, and to point out to her the reasons for differing from her on any occasion. She will make her see that of two facts mentioned one leads to greater consequences than the other, or is connected with other facts she has already become acquainted with, and thus supplies a link and forms part of a systematic body of information. The teacher will, perhaps, assist to form the habit of condensing the matter which is to be preserved in notes, if during the first year she dictates them herself, having first questioned the child about the day's reading and ascertained that she feels what are the leading facts which it is desirable to make a note of. The necessity of this preliminary consideration is apparent, when we remember how loosely most people state a fact or an argument which they have heard, and how seldom they can seize at once the important points even of a transaction that has passed before their own eyes. This is not generally from want of memory, but from the want of logical clearness in the mind, from the absence of that sense of the proportional and relative value of different facts or arguments, which belongs to the habit of marshalling our thoughts into order for the sake of accurate reasoning. Children of twelve and thirteen are not yet fit to have their reasoning power directly exercised in study, but the mind may be led to work according to the method which will be necessary when it does begin those severer studies; just as we make little children express themselves grammatically before they are able to understand a rule of grammar, and the habit formed by routine is afterwards explained by philosophy.

Supposing the teacher to dictate the notes, she may accomplish two objects by dictating them in French. Orthography is in that language a test of grammatical accuracy, and to write from dictation is excellent practice. The terminations in verbs and participles being affected by gender and number while they frequently do not sound to the ear, and the rules with regard to participles especially requiring great nicety of application, even educated French people are apt to fall into mistakes in writing their language. Should the pupil however not be sufficiently familiar with French to write with ease from dictation, this double purpose must be abandoned, for the mind must not be diverted from the principal object before it by any collateral difficulties. For the same reason no books in an unfamiliar language should be used as class-books in the study of any other subject but the language itself. Wherever the understanding is to be exercised it must be left unembarrassed in its operations.

The third point I would recommend as assisting the memory is a weekly examination of what has been learned. By the frequency of the examinations the teacher will bear fresh in her mind what were her pupil's difficulties; what are the points that require most attention; where the understanding seemed most to fail, and where the memory. Thus also no large amount of loss can be incurred; the path that must be trodden again will not lead far back. Another and greater advantage is that we avoid going on upon uncertain ground, and teaching new things without being sure that they rest on the solid foundation of the old, in which case the child's mind may be working in that dim state that results from confused recollection, while we vainly believe that we are making real progress. Every week then I would interrupt the onward course and examine into the real state of the acquisitions already made. It should be optional with the teacher to go back to any portion of the former lessons, whether pieces learnt by heart, or notes from reading, or explanations of facts or terms. Week by week it should be ascertained that what information has been gained is accurate,—that what impressions have been made are distinct,—that what thoughts have been suggested, what ideas have been presented to the mind are clear; that, in short, there is no lurking confusion or error to mislead the future efforts of the understanding, or cloud the conceptions of the imagination. The tediousness of this process, involving as it does frequent repetition and frequent enforcing of the same truths, may appear insufferable to some people, while the absence of brilliant results would mortify many; but showy progress is so utterly unimportant, even knowledge itself is so secondary, when compared with the mental habits to be formed by study, that no sacrifice of either should deter us from following the system which promises to cultivate those habits most successfully.

§ 3.—The necessity of economy will not require any great difference to be made in the course of study at this period of education. Girls from twelve to fourteen are too young to be much employed in practical affairs, and under almost any circumstances four hours in the day can well be spared for lessons by a child of this age, although little time perhaps can be spared by the mother to overlook them. Still with the help of the most ordinary governess, or even, if necessary, without any assistance, a mother who can devote even an hour and a half in the day to teaching may accomplish a considerable portion of the course indicated above, and at any rate adhere to its general order. Good instruction in arithmetic is so easily procured that it is hard to suppose any obstacle to that study. Languages whether ancient or modern present more difficulty, but supposing the mother to have any knowledge of French herself, she can begin teaching that most important of the continental languages, and by insisting on much learning by heart, copying, and translating, she may, though unable to speak it, lay the foundation of a thorough knowledge of the language, which will give the key to its rich literature, and be of use in the subsequent study of grammar and composition. It is true that with good native teachers, two foreign languages might perhaps be acquired with less labour in the same period of time, but at least the mental discipline of learning to compare different idioms and forms of expression will not have been lost, and method, patience, and memory have all been exercised. Lastly, the historical reading may also be carried on with little change, though here again there may be slower progress, since it is probable that the mother may not be able to give the same degree of personal attention to it as a governess would. The child will probably read in great measure alone, while the manner of her reading can be tested only by questions. I suppose, of course, that her mother knows each day the portion she has read, and ten minutes will suffice to glance over the pages doubtless already familiar, and to ask such questions both as to the narrative itself,—the geography or contemporary chronology,—and any matter hard to be understood, as will make it quite clear whether the child has read carelessly or with attention. When the pupil is forced to read by herself, it should be an invariable rule that she should write down at the time any word of which she requires an explanation, or make a note of any difficulty. When in the course of examination it becomes apparent that this has not been done, but that points have been slurred over with a confused half-apprehension of their meaning, the indolence or indifference should be earnestly pointed out and reproved. The additional labour of being made to work in this manner will compensate, in great measure, as regards the principal objects of female education, for the greater amount of knowledge to be gained under more favourable circumstances for instruction.

With regard to reading out loud during the afternoon needlework, it is probable that a mother may not be able to spare time from other family duties for such a custom, but she can arrange that the children should work while she is working herself, or one of them can read whether she be present or not; she will of course know what book is read, and by making it the topic of conversation, whenever opportunity offers, she will sufficiently ascertain the degree of attention that has been given to the reading, and of thought that it has suggested.

The education in practical things which may be given under such circumstances ought to be of considerable value. A child of twelve years old cannot do much, but she can acquire some useful notions which it would be more difficult to give if she were surrounded by the means and appliances of wealth, and some habits which in the latter case could be cultivated only by means of study. For instance, the value of time—of money—of punctuality—of order—will be more early and practically learned when a child sees her mother anxiously and carefully attending to and providing for the many wants of her household, and only enabled to do so by working with great regularity and economy. She will learn the value of being useful and active by seeing those qualities daily exhibited among things she understands, and by early feeling the pleasure of giving help herself. So with other habits; she will learn to observe carefully and accurately, for she may perhaps be employed in sundry household matters which require inspection, comparison, and judgment. She will learn attention by having things trusted to her care for which she feels responsible, and her patience may be exercised in the same manner, for sometimes a tiresome task of needlework must be accomplished, sometimes a sick child must be watched while the nurse is busy, or perhaps a little brother or sister taught to read. All these things, which are likely to claim the attention of girls at a very early age under the circumstances we are speaking of, and which undoubtedly are too often mere desultory interruptions to proper school-room studies, may, if properly managed, become direct means of mental discipline. There must necessarily be less study, and therefore less foundation of knowledge, but there will be no hindrance to that important part of education which concerns fitting the various faculties for future work, whether intellectual or among the active duties of life.* If indeed the mother be not equal to this task of directing her children's studies, of giving them instruction, and drawing out their minds in conversation, I know no remedy; but neither, under ordinary conditions of health, do I know any excuse. From the time she had children she knew under what circumstances she would be obliged to educate them, and she had *twelve years* to prepare for the work we are now considering! What would not even two hours of daily systematic reading have done in twelve years? in the name of what other duty can this duty have been neglected?

§ 4.—Many persons object to holidays as too complete an interruption of the accustomed routine, but that very interruption recommends them to me. Such periodical tests of the habits, which routine has striven to enforce, must be useful to those who are watching the real progress of the education. The discipline of education is valuable just so far as it fits the young for self-regulation; but it is well that they should occasionally try their strength, and also taste the joys of freedom, lest when restraint is permanently withdrawn the untried pleasure should leave no room for prudence or moderation. The unfortunate custom of continual superintendence with girls is no doubt one cause that they are seldom allowed holidays; even when the governess is absent to enjoy hers, arrangements are generally made with great solicitude to provide that the lessons shall be interrupted as little as possible during her absence, and especially that the girls should not be left to themselves. Yet this is the very point that would make the holidays desirable. The real tastes and character will then show themselves; the amusements, the occupation, the mode of spending time, whether in activity or indolence,—all afford precious indications to the educator. Errors and follies may be committed, but these may themselves be turned to advantage, by pointing out to the child the faults in disposition or habits whence they have arisen, and by making her feel how much she owes to the habitual restraint which prevents such weakness from being frequently exhibited, and tends by that repression to give strength to opposite habits. This should not be done in the tone of severity or rebuke, or it would lose all its value; but by gently and *privately* talking the matters over, as if assured that the child's understanding and honest desire to do right are sincerely interested in the success of her education.

---

* See remarks on this subject, chap. ii. p. 56.

I would then propose a weekly half-holiday, which may conveniently be fixed for the day on which the weekly examinations have already broken the usual order of occupation, and besides these a fortnight twice in the year of absolute freedom from school-room obligations. The time most convenient for these must vary in different families; an excursion away from home or the absence of the governess offer suitable opportunities; but the circumstance that should mostly determine it, is the period of a brother's holidays from school.

I have always been at a loss to understand upon what principle brothers and sisters are kept so much apart as they are in many families. Nature brought them together under the same rule, the same care, under the influence of the same associations, and sharing the same affections; and at the very period when all these things are beginning to tell most powerfully upon character, those children nursed in the same cradle are separated as though they scarcely belonged to the same family. Accordingly all the good they might do to each other is lost. Girls grow up too exclusively within the circle of feminine interests and pursuits, while boys remain strangers to the gentler influences which should tell upon them, and are wild, selfish, and ill-mannered, without any other check than what the parents' direct authority may give. Unbounded indulgence and little or no tenderness is the strange maxim on which many parents act with their sons; wishing to give them pleasure while they can, and dreading to soften the nature which must be exposed to the hard trials of the world. But what can be better calculated to stifle feeling and cultivate selfishness? Unbounded tenderness rather should be lavished upon the young creature to whom the world will teach hardness enough, and parents might then venture to be more sparing of that indulgence, which would no longer be in the boy's mind the measure of affection. It may seem that these remarks are irrelevant to my subject, but they tend to illustrate the erroneous principles which have been so commonly acted upon in education, and which, though the mode of applying them differs with boys and girls, are yet fundamentally the same. For instance, all parents probably desire to make their children's education a preparation for their future lives; but what is called preparation? Not cultivation of those qualities which will tend to counteract whatever evils may await their future career, but rather of those which will make the evil less felt at the time. Thus boys, who will have to make their own way in a world where all jostle and contend for their own interests, are made to undergo a hardening process from their early childhood, and are sent to school almost out of the nursery, in order that the public opinion of that miniature world should assume the place of conscience and teach them to live without affection. Girls, on the contrary, who will be exposed to the evils of dependence and idleness, are prepared for them by being made dependent in character and frivolous in tastes. It is possible that by such means some degree of suffering may for a short time be avoided; the boy will be less pained by the hardness and selfishness of the world, the girl will not feel so acutely the sufferings of *ennui* and restraint; but is it the object of education to lessen the sensibility of the human creature to the moral evils of his position? Would it be well, had fate doomed us to be born under a despotism, to teach our children to be slaves in soul because the slave will be less galled by the weight of his chain? Yet such is in truth the character of the preparation that anxious parents think it wise to bestow!

I believe it to be a great disadvantage to girls to be brought up apart from father or brothers, and a real misfortune to boys to grow up without the softening and refining influence of women. The mutual action and reaction of the different qualities, tastes, and natural powers of the two sexes is not sufficiently considered either in education or in society. The feelings belonging to one single relation in which they stand to one another have obscured the view of all that fits them, apart from that, to be fellow-workers in the world, to cheer and aid each other, to combine the results of their different experience, and open up their different circles of interests and sympathy. The vulgar opinion that there can be no pure friendship between man and woman, while it is the expression of a coarse feeling, also betrays from what a narrow point of view the subject is considered. Life is twofold, that of the family and that of the world; and although it be true that women belong almost entirely to the former, yet they have a powerful social influence in the latter which they should be fitted to wield; while it is evident that men need to be prepared for the one phase of life no less than for the other. A one-sided education, however, considers the world alone for boys and home only for girls. The boy becomes man, and is more and more engrossed in the selfish ambition or the selfish pleasures for which he has been trained; the girl passes on to womanhood more and more immersed in small cares and trifling pursuits. After a few years of such discordant modes of life, they are too often *jumbled together* in marriage, according as chance, or money, or a fever-fit of passion may determine; can we then wonder that married life, which should be the one type of perfect happiness on earth, is too often a scene of suffering, of jarring unsuitabilities and depressing sacrifice?

The extreme importance of home influence to boys is sufficient to counteract the disadvantages of the very long holidays given by the public schools. Their studies are perhaps too much interrupted, but they are learning to live. I should not however adopt the same course with girls : they are not able to bear so many hours of application as boys do at school, and the period set apart for their education is far shorter, so that time could not be spared for such long holidays even were there no other objections to them. A fortnight or three weeks of complete freedom in the summer, and a fortnight at Christmas, will ensure to the children that full enjoyment of home in common which is so desirable; and beyond that, all the sisters' leisure hours should as far as possible be spent with their brothers; riding, walking, skating, or boating with them, and joining in any games that are suitable to their strength. In the same way the boys may be encouraged to share at other times in their sister's quieter amusements, to sing, dance, or act charades with them in the evening, to read the same books and take interest in the same pursuits.

Under ordinary systems of home management, girls derive more moral benefit from their brothers' holidays than the boys themselves. They generally are ready enough to sacrifice their own pleasure and wishes if they can make the holidays the happier for their brothers. This is as it should be : they are learning the immense pleasure of serving those they love. But if their sacrifices are received as a matter of course, if they are made to feel that because they are girls everything is expected from them, while the selfishness for which *they* would be reproved is in like manner accepted as a matter of course from the boys, they are learning a bad lesson. Whatever tends with the young of either sex to lower their opinion of the other is an evil. When therefore girls have learnt to bend before the ill-temper or selfish habits of their brothers, and to feel that they must expect at their hands a mode of treatment which would revolt them in companions of their own sex, they have laid the foundation for many a painful error in after life.

CHAPTER VI.

STUDIES AND GENERAL MANAGEMENT FROM FOURTEEN TO SIXTEEN.

§ 1.—DURING the two years we have lately been considering, from the age of twelve to fourteen, we have seen our pupil, still a child, brought gradually into habits of application and regular study; and in the two following years we may hope to reap the benefit of that labour, and to see the young girl leaving behind her the faults and weaknesses of childhood, and coming to more laborious tasks with an earnest and willing spirit.

The hours of study may be gradually increased each year; but I believe that in general it will not be judicious to allow of more than five hours and a half of application during this period, when health is often uncertain and rapid growth produces languor. In some cases even five hours may be found too much. These are points which require constant watching, and on which no peremptory rules can be laid down. When health is good, steady work must be exacted; but so long as we guard carefully against frivolity of tastes or pursuits, a period of comparative idleness, if necessary, will prove no injury.

The same general division of the day will continue; the early hour of rising, the early breakfast and mid-day meal, whether dinner or luncheon. If luncheon, and that girls dine late with their parents, the latter will, of course, be careful that it does not lead to late hours at night. At this age there should never be less than eight hours' sleep; consequently girls must be in bed at ten o'clock, for the early morning hours are on no account to be sacrificed. Later, when the claims of society begin to interfere, and it becomes necessary to conform in some measure to the habits of others, it is only too probable that the early rising will be given up to later hours at night; it is expedient therefore to make it as fixed a habit as we can. When the period of growth is over, eight hours' sleep is more than the generality of persons really require for health; some additional time at night may, therefore, be allowed them without altering the morning hours allotted to occupation.

The increased time of study during the two years we are considering, can be taken either before breakfast or in the afternoon, according to circumstances. Three hours' consecutive application is still quite sufficient, and a considerable break should intervene before lessons begin again; while one hour and a half is the utmost that should be given uninterruptedly to one subject. Attention to these apparently trifling regulations enables the mind to bear greater labour at a far less cost of fatigue. Study should never be prolonged till a feeling of settled weariness comes on; for unless there be freshness and alacrity at the close of the lessons, there will be languor and perhaps nervous depression in the whole frame, which will prevent the exercise or recreation that follow from having their due effect in recruiting body and mind.

Needlework ought no longer to be wanted as a daily task, for if a girl has been properly taught she will be as perfect in all its useful branches as any gentlewoman can require, and will have some notion of economical cutting out—a province of the sempstress' art which is too often neglected, even in teaching that class to whom it would be most essential. All that ought to be required now is that the young girl should keep her own wardrobe in perfect order and repair, and occasionally make new things for the sake of keeping up the practice of what she has learnt. Many a rainy day will afford a convenient opportunity for this, while the work that neatness requires may be reserved for one afternoon in the week, when one hour will more than suffice in general for all that ought to be wanted in a wardrobe that is never neglected. Supposing this task to be assigned to the same day fixed for the weekly examinations, the other five days remain undisturbed in their regular course.

With regard to music, as the time is not yet come when the voice can be fairly tried, the daily half hour of practice should still continue, unless there should be that decided indifference or dislike to music which makes it evident that even the power of singing would prove no inducement to cultivate the art. If such be the case, it would be mere waste of time to continue the daily practising. The latter will have done good service at an earlier period, as I explained before; but now we have subjects enough to exercise application and perseverance, and no time to spare for what is to be of no ultimate use. On the other hand, if decided talent and love for music show themselves at this age, another half hour should be given to it, which may be a complete addition to the regular time of study. Music, especially when there is this decided love and facility for it, is no such severe mental exercise as to be prejudicial to health when confined within the limits I propose; and as the pupil will thus be making the voluntary sacrifice of half an hour taken from the time at her own disposal, we have an additional security that real love of the art and not dislike to some drier study prompts the exertion. Undoubted talent or great love for the art afford the only warrant for giving time, when time has become valuable, to either music or drawing. First-rate teaching and very assiduous study will certainly produce a considerable degree of excellence even where no such talent exists, but I doubt if they will ensure real pleasure either to the student herself or to those who judge her performances. The excellence will be purely mechanical, and true expression, which is the life of art, will ever be wanting to it. We listen to the brilliant playing, or look at the finished drawings, and admire; but they touch no chord of feeling ; while our very hearts are stirred by many a simple strain, poured out by one whose fingers obey the impulse of the soul; by many a sketch where a few imperfect touches reveal that the scene had been *felt* before the pencil recorded its features.

When accomplishments of this kind usurp the name of education, it is impossible to denounce them too severely ; but they rank deservedly high among amusements. And in the often lonely and depressed lives of women, the power of music, at once soothing and exhilarating, is far beyond mere amusement. When, therefore, there is real taste for it, it should never be set aside as of no value. Where there is both talent and love for any art, they also afford valuable means of cultivating the imagination. Love of drawing will become the centre of widely-spreading associations; it will reveal the inward poetry of nature, and add very greatly to some of the most healthy and innocent enjoyments of life. Whatever is a spontaneous impulse of the mind becomes one of the forms in which all that is beautiful in thought and feeling will naturally express itself, while it kindles the sense of beauty and delight where other minds remain cold and insensible. The real enthusiast in any pursuit will speak with poetic fervour of what to others is uninviting, even at times repulsive; and whatever will thus touch the inmost chords of intellectual life deserves to be cared for in education.

It will perhaps be said that the utmost time I have allowed for music, —or for drawing, if music be abandoned,—will never enable the student to acquire great perfection. It is possible that she will not on her entrance into society come forward as a finished artist, nor do I think it desirable that she should, since drawing-room display is not the object for which I should wish any art to be acquired. But with real talent there will be proficiency enough to give true pleasure, and that proficiency will increase. When the expense of a governess is no longer needed, there will be more money to spend on good masters if necessary. Parents may regret in some moment of weakness that their daughter's performance is not equal to what more assiduous cultivation might have made it; but if they have resolutely forborne sacrificing any of the real merits of a governess to the temptation of securing a good musical teacher, they will be rewarded by seeing that the innate taste will develope itself even under unfavourable circumstances; and at eighteen there is abundant time before them to cultivate any natural power when earlier studies have come to a close. Of this we may be sure, that any girl of eighteen who without rare genius has attained a high degree of excellence in any art, must have done so at the expense of studies which ought to have occupied the time given to the accomplishment. The education has had for its object the drawing-room display, which secures the triumph of a few hours at the cost of what would have embellished a life. In the same manner a young governess whose capacity as an artist is to be the test of her fitness, is thereby giving the most convincing proof of her *unfitness* for undertaking the charge of education.

For the cultivation of two accomplishments even great talent will seldom be found sufficient without the sacrifice of an unwarrantable amount of time. If a girl shows equal love and aptitude for music and drawing, I would cultivate the former and let the latter be postponed till school-room studies are over. Drawing has this advantage, that it does not require early training, which the mechanical difficulties of music render indispensable; under no circumstances should *both* be admitted.

This long digression, which has kept us from the consideration of the course of study to be pursued at this age, is forced upon us by the blind devotion to accomplishments which must be combated in detail as well as denounced in general terms. If parents would honestly say, 'I do not care for education; I only wish my daughter to play or draw well, for the sake of being admired in society,' the practice would be far less pernicious, for no one would be misled. Parents would not suppose, nor lead others to suppose, that they have laboriously achieved a task they never cared to begin, and girls would have the open acknowledgment of their ignorance to temper the conceit of their success in accomplishments. So long as things are called by their right names they are but half armed for mischief, but when they assume honoured designations to win the respect of the unwary, we cannot too often or too mercilessly expose the mischievous imposition.

The department of historical reading, which occupied a considerable space during the last two years, will now be omitted for a time, or reduced, at least, to very trifling dimensions. The previous course will, it may be hoped, have fixed in the reader's memory a correct outline of ancient history and of the national histories of the principal countries in Europe, with a skeleton map of chronology, such as will afford every facility for the acquisition of fresh knowledge. With this we must be satisfied for the present, taking care only by frequent reference and examination, that what has been learnt be not forgotten, and still as we read upon other subjects adding to the chronological groups, arranged according to the method before suggested, any interesting fact, whether in literature or science or biography, whose date it is important to remember. All such additions will tend to strengthen the links of association which bind the whole in the memory. The more complete this view of contemporary chronology can be rendered without confusing or overloading the memory, the more interesting and profitable will historical reading be hereafter; since the reader will at every step find familiar landmarks, instead of toiling on ignorant of all that spreads far and wide beyond the one track she is following.

The reason for discontinuing regular historical reading at this period is, that the pupil's mind is still too unformed for reading detailed history with profit. Short works devoid of political theory or philosophical speculation were sufficient to give the skeleton knowledge, which for many reasons it is desirable to acquire early; but further historical reading must have a moral and philosophical purpose or it is useless, except as a matter of harmless entertainment. And at the age we speak of, the mind is not ripe for such considerations as these.

The studies of these two years will be divided between grammar and composition, and an elementary course of science, including mathematics; thus two hours and a half daily might be given to each during the first year, and half an hour added during the latter, for whichever branch of reading most required it—taking now and then half an hour from one or the other for geography or chronological tables.

If geometry was begun in the preceding year, some progress will already have been made; if not, it should be commenced at fourteen. I do not propose carrying it further than the three first books of Euclid. Algebra may be begun at the same time or may follow, as the teacher judges most expedient. In this I do not propose going beyond quadratic equations, the whole object being, as I said before, to give some idea of the nature of symbols and the mode of working with them. Let the ground thus traversed be gone over and over again, if necessary, till the knowledge, and more especially the principles thus acquired have become stamped upon the mind; and utterly insignificant as such studies are to the mathematician, they will have done all we can hope to do at that age. They will have exercised the mind through a rigid discipline at the time when its capacity is unfolding and the power of thought and speculation beginning to come into activity, and we may hope that a more vigorous and accurate tone will be due to that influence. Here, however, as I remarked before,* it will depend on the teacher whether that influence

---

* Chap. v. p. 136.

spreads beyond the lesson hours. If loose reasoning, inaccurate statement, hasty inferences, and similar faults of unreasoning minds are
allowed in other matters, whether of study or action, it will be of little
avail to the young mind to have learned the most perfect method of
scientific demonstration, except so far as it may be needed in following
some scientific pursuit. But this is a very small part of the object for
which the magnificent prerogative of human nature, the gift of reason,
claims to be cultivated.

I have stated in the second chapter * what branches of science it
appears most desirable to give some slight knowledge of, and have
explained my reasons for so doing, and the particular benefit I hoped
might accrue from each. I shall here only name the books which appear
to me best fitted for our purpose; but so many are now written with a
view to make the first steps in science easy, that many more, and perhaps
some better, might be pointed out ; this must be left to the judgment
of teachers, who are themselves well versed in these subjects. Very
elementary and inexpensive works will suffice to give as much information
as we can hope to obtain in an early educational course. We may expect
that the pupil will acquire from them clear and accurate conceptions of
the nature and purpose of each science they treat of, knowledge of the
principles on which it is founded, and of the leading facts and laws that
have been ascertained. Works such as I would recommend present the
mere alphabet of science, but if these are not merely read, but studied, till
the fundamental principles are completely mastered and the terms and
definitions rendered familiar, subsequent scientific reading will lose half
its difficulty. The understanding will be free to follow more abstruse
reasoning without the attention being distracted by the half-confused
remembrance of the earlier steps on which it is founded; while the
positive knowledge gained, small as it is, opens the mind to the perception of a whole new range of truths, and can hardly fail to inspire the
wish to know more.

Natural history is perhaps the most generally interesting to the young;
some one of its many branches may then be chosen for a beginning.
Zoology appears to me the most advisable, not only on account of the
interest of animal life, but as being intimately connected with physiology,
which should come next in our course of reading. Patterson's *Zoology for
Schools* is an excellent elementary work, and exactly represents the form
of knowledge which I conceive such a course of reading as I am now

---

* See sect. 2.

12

recommending should give. The matter of the work, the classification and general arrangement of the subject, are such as the great masters have given them, but we have them briefly stated in a clear and simple manner, and facts and results which the young mind can grasp are presented without the abstruse reasoning or detailed research which would only puzzle and make the darkness of ignorance darker still.

After this book has been thoroughly studied I would proceed to the small volume on Animal Physiology in Chambers's Educational Course; which in like manner gives clearly and succinctly the facts and principles which must be the foundation of further knowledge.

When these two works have been completely mastered, the pupil may turn to geology, unless a very decided taste for some further study of natural history should show itself. The pleasure of indulging such a taste is the surest incentive to the pursuit of knowledge; education has, therefore, accomplished one of its chief aims when it has developed the natural bent of the mind. But if this should not be the case, then we may begin Lyell's *Principles of Geology*. I know no work more likely to awaken in the young mind the perception of the vastness of the regions of knowledge, or to give a better view of the spirit in which they should be explored. Some of the subjects closely connected with geology and the alphabet of the science itself will have been made familiar to the pupil by the small work on Physical Geography recommended in the last chapter.* The great use of such compendiums is to give that accurate groundwork which facilitates the reading of larger treatises; certainly, without some such introduction, Lyell's work might be unfit for the beginner; with it, I believe we may safely take it up. All the points taught in Reid, and much that has been learned in zoology, will here be dwelt upon again more widely and deeply; the same kind of knowledge will be constantly referred to, and the more often the same subjects are brought before the student's mind under a different form of connexion, and considered from a different point of view, the more they tend to enlarge the perceptions, while they become at the same time fixed in the memory by so many additional links of association.

I have purposely left astronomy to the last among the sciences I propose to glance at, because it seems best to allow the mind to gain some benefit from mathematical instruction before taking up a subject so built upon mathematical reasoning. I too well know that no study of mathe-

---

* *Elements of Physical Geography.* By Hugo Reid.

matics, which would be practicable in female education, will enable the
pupil to follow that reasoning, but the qualities trained by even a very
slight course of geometry, will make the conditions of an exact science
intelligible, and the grandeur of astronomy is thus unfolded with the conviction of its certainty.

Again, Reid's excellent compendium will be found to have done a
useful work in familiarizing the pupil with some of the primary facts of
the science, and their connexion with the condition of the globe we
inhabit. So prepared, we may proceed to Professor Airy's Lectures on
Astronomy,* which give the simplest and clearest exposition I know, of
the facts and laws of the science he has himself mastered in all its depths.
When this short work has been thoroughly studied, *The Orbs of Heaven*,
by Mitchell, might be read with advantage. The style is both flowery and
diffuse, faults peculiarly objectionable in a work on science; still the subject is presented under an aspect likely to interest the young, and to
kindle imagination and the desire for further knowledge, and these are
qualities which must, for our purpose, be allowed to redeem literary
defects; the more so as this work presents a view of the progress of the
science from the earliest times, and there is no other history of astronomy,
as far as I know, which is at all fit for the young student; yet the lessons
taught by the history of a science are often scarcely less valuable than
those derived from the science itself. It is there that we see the examples
of unwearied patience, of calm untiring love of truth which no failure can
daunt, no prevailing darkness rob of its faith in the coming light. It is
there that we see how in the course of time that which was false falls
away, while the element of truth that was wrapped up in the error and
gave it power to live for a time, expands and becomes clearer and clearer
as knowledge accumulates and is brought to bear from different sources.
There, especially, we have unfolded to us the value of method, when we
see that after men had groped in the dark for generations, or caught now
at one, now at another brilliant conjecture, a new light seems poured in
when the right method of investigation is discovered, and soon ordinary
minds are enabled to reach what before eluded the grasp of genius. These
are the great lessons which make the history of science so valuable a contribution to mental discipline; it must be the task of the teacher to enforce

---

* Originally printed for private circulation only, but since published. *The
Mechanism of the Heavens, or Familiar Illustrations of Astronomy*, by Denison
Olmsted, of Gale College, is also highly spoken of.

them; in this, as in every other department of education, the teacher is of more consequence than the books she makes use of.

It is difficult to lay down any rules about the time that may be required for the careful reading and study of the books I have mentioned. The course of elementary science will be completed with instruction in the principles of mechanics, and the last treatise published by Dr. Lardner will be found well adapted for the purpose. This may, however, be left for a later period, should there be the least apparent risk of producing a sense of hurry or confusion in the young reader's mind; while, on the contrary, should this not be the case, I would recommend reading those parts of Mrs. Marcet's Conversations on Natural Philosophy which refer to subjects closely connected with but not comprised in our course, such as optics and hydrostatics.

Even the subjects I have mentioned, few as they are compared with the range of science, and cursorily as they can be studied, would, if really distinct, or rather isolated one from the other, undoubtedly have an injurious effect on the mind. But the connexion is so intimate of the laws and facts of astronomy with the principles of mechanics, by whose aid some of the greatest of those laws were established, with the history of the earth and its present condition influenced by the other parts of the solar system, and finally with the various forms of animal life developed under the various conditions of climate, geographical and geological formation and atmospheric influences, that the views presented, however various, will rather tend to concentrate than to scatter either attention or interest.

Grammatical studies will begin to assume a new character during the period now under consideration. We have supposed the pupil to have acquired some knowledge and command of one foreign language, at least, whether dead or living; perhaps both Latin and French have been learnt, or under favourable circumstances in early childhood, acquaintance with German may also have been acquired. But whatever number of languages may have been learnt, or in whatever manner, whether by means of books or conversation, mere verbal studies should be at an end now. We cannot, after fourteen, afford time for vocabularies; their work should be finished, and the pupil ready to begin the comparison between the grammar and composition of the different languages she knows, together with some study of their literature. Nothing, therefore, should have been undertaken before which could not be brought to this degree of forwardness by the time I speak of, and the indulgence of any wish to learn other languages should be postponed till school-room studies are over.

The study of language itself is the object now, and English the ground-work of the study, upon which the comparison with other languages and reference particularly to the more rigid grammatical forms of Latin, will throw light.

Trench *On the Study of Words; English, Past and Present,* by the same author; and Archbishop Whately's *English Synonyms,* will be found most useful works at this period, and they may be followed by Dr. Latham's *History of the English Language.* Works, or parts of works, in different departments of literature should now be read with a view to style, and to changes in the language at different periods; and a comparison of English with French writers on the same subjects,—that is, comparing tragedy with tragedy, oratory with oratory,—will unfold differences in the genius and capabilities of the two languages, as well as lead to many interesting remarks on national differences of taste or feeling.

Works of criticism should also be read to help in forming the taste upon some settled principles. Blair's *Lectures,* for instance, with much that is feeble and useless, contain a great deal that is valuable. We are, unfortunately, poor in this class of works, but even when those we read cannot be trusted implicitly, they teach the art of critical reading, and turn attention to a number of points that would otherwise be passed over by the unpractised. Much may be gained in this way, as a mental exercise, from a book in whose individual opinions we may perhaps rarely or never coincide. Addison's papers on Milton * are too well known to require recommendation; they, of course, should be carefully studied. Sir Joshua Reynolds's Discourses on Painting are also of great value; they tend to enlarge the student's conception of the aim of composition, and of the true principles of excellence, by showing how far the standard of real beauty is alike in every department of human effort which speaks to the feelings and imagination. For the same reason, Dubos' *Sur la Poesie et la Peinture* may be consulted with advantage, although selections only from it would be desirable for a school-room course.

In this, more than perhaps in any other study, we depend on the knowledge and taste of the teacher; for we are not only, as I said before, deficient in good works of criticism, but we have no standard history of English literature. Villemain's *Cours de Littérature Française* may be made good use of; his taste is pure, his feeling of the high importance and purpose of literature strong, and his knowledge of English literature

---

* *Spectator.* Saturday Papers, from No. 297, Feb. 9, 1711-12, to No. 369, May 3, 1712.

being considerable, his comparison of the writers of both countries is valuable. It is true that it embraces the eighteenth century only, or throws a mere cursory glance at the preceding period by way of introduction to his main subject; but the view he presents of the English writers since the Restoration may assist the teacher in giving instruction concerning the greater writers of a former period. In the absence of good works, she must herself select portions from our different great writers,* to be read in chronological order, thus presenting to the pupil's view not only the beauties and defects of each, but changes in the language, in the mode of treating subjects, and in the prevailing tone of thought and sentiment at different periods. As an outline, Reed's *Lectures on English Literature* are useful, although his own style is flowery and wordy, and his taste and judgment too much swayed by considerations that do not belong to literary criticism. He falls too frequently, for instance, into that modern error of making the ethical tone of the sentiments expressed the criterion of poetic excellence, dwelling upon theories and opinions, and overlooking the metre, the language, the imagery, which constitute the *form* of poetry, and are the essential embodiment of poetic thought. If we are to be independent of these, let us, at least, have the simplicity of prose. Still, Reed's book is a valuable contribution for educational purposes. Johnson's *Lives of the Poets* will, of course, be consulted; poor and meagre as are his criticisms of Milton, and even of Shakespeare,† they are relieved by some noble passages, and they cannot be omitted. Campbell's *Specimens of the British Poets* will be found occasionally useful, and likewise Lamb's *Specimens of the Dramatic Poets*, since, unfortunately, the works of the latter can be made known to women in fragments only. Craik's *History of English Literature* is more full and complete than Reed's lectures, and might be read after them. It wants the genuine poetic enthusiasm of the American writer, but it is also free from his defects.

If the pupil have the advantage of an acquaintance with several languages, examples of peculiar excellence in each will throw fresh light on the study of English. I have supposed Villemain, for instance, to be read in this view, as much as for the sake of acquaintance with the French writers he examines. In the same manner we may gather from Latin and from German examples to illustrate the fact that the standard of beauty and sublimity in poetry does not depend on the particular forms of any one language, although the expression of poetic thought is moulded and

---

* For this purpose Chambers's *English Literature* will be found useful.
† See Preface to Johnson and Steevens' edition.

may be more or less favoured by them; as we see, for instance, in comparing the language of French poetry with our own, what an incomparably finer instrument we possess for that purpose. Fine poetry in the several languages known to the pupil should be learnt by heart, and fine expressions or single lines dwelt upon and remembered. The pleasure and the real advantage of having the memory so stored can hardly be exaggerated. Many a lonely hour, many an hour of illness when body and mind are too languid for active thought, will pass lightly over as fancy recalls the images which charmed before; and in proportion as these lofty pleasures of the imagination have power over the mind, the hold of the trivial and the mean will be loosened whether in literature or in society.

One great object of studying composition is to acquire the art of writing and speaking well, the latter especially being singularly neglected in this country, even by men, who, owing to our institutions and habits, have such frequent occasion to speak in public.

The tendency of beginners in composition is to aim at eloquence; and if they have much imagination or strength of feeling they are in danger of being carried away by them, and of falling into sentimentality or bombast. The object of the teacher must then be to cultivate the habit of clear, forcible, and appropriate expression, and of logical order in the matter. To possess the power of language in its full form and delicacy, is perhaps as rare as to possess the finer qualities of thought or imagination; these are given to very few; but all may learn to clothe their thoughts in simple, accurate, well-chosen words, and so to express themselves as to run no risk of being misunderstood by others, or what is more important still, of leaving an undetected confusion in their own minds, for want of being able to bring clearly out, what they do and what they do not really think or understand. It is very common with young persons to answer to any question testing their knowledge by saying that they *understand clearly enough, but cannot explain* themselves. This may or may not really be the case, but, at any rate, it points to a defect which is within reach of cure. Either there is a natural slowness or inaptitude in the use of language, and this exercise will undoubtedly remove, at least as far as the purpose of ordinary intercourse requires; or else there is confusion of thought, which lurked perhaps unconsciously till the effort to explain made the existence of some difficulty apparent, or which the indolent mind, indifferent to clearness of apprehension, was content to retain, and which makes the task of explanation irksome and irritating. And in this case also the necessity of finding intelligible expressions will be beneficial.

In conversation, nervous or timid persons may frequently be unable to make a clear statement; or a bad memory may prove an insurmountable obstacle; but there should be no room for these difficulties in the school-room. Ample time can be given there to collect the thoughts, to get over any trepidation, or to consult authorities on any point where memory has failed; and it will be better to give the habit of writing down the statements required before we tax the power of language by demanding *viva voce* answers. Statements of the opinions or facts advanced by a given author on certain subjects or abstracts of the day's reading, are, I believe, better exercises for the kind of composition we desire to cultivate than writing themes. They are directly useful as regards the matter, and they offer no temptation to ill-judged flights of imagination. We want to train the power of language, not to draw out the expression of crude thoughts. It will be time enough for original composition when the mind is some-what better stored and the intellect more vigorous and mature. In this point of view, poetic compositions are more objectionable than prose, for they waste time in spinning out poor materials in a form which is only fit to clothe noble images and conceptions. But as a mere exercise of lan-guage I know nothing better than translating foreign poetry into English verse. The difficulties of the metre force a degree of attention to the language which prose rarely exacts. A variety of words must be sought,* harmony no less than appropriateness must decide the selection, and I believe that a degree of mastery over the instrument of expression will be acquired by this means which will tell very beneficially on prose composition.

I have said that in requiring statements from a young person I would begin with having them written, but when the habit of clear expression and arrangement has been acquired, it is time to practise the same habit in speaking. That men should be content in a country enjoying free institutions to be without the power of speaking in public, content to string commonplaces together which make their best friends dread what they may utter next, is perfectly inconceivable. Women have no public motives for cultivating this noble form of power; but why, because they limit their efforts to private conversation, should that conversation be confused, disjointed, wanting in that order and clearness which are among the surest signs of a really cultivated mind, and wanting also in that grace

---

* A great deal is learnt by searching out words in a large dictionary, especially one rich in quotations like Johnson's. We see the etymology of the word, the manner and sense in which it has been used by good authors, and the period in which it has been used perhaps in a sense now obsolete.

and felicity of expression which give a charm to the trifles of familiar talk ? Without going so low as to speak of those who introduce slang,—the counterfeit wit of coarse and ignorant minds,—into refined society, how often do we find the conversation of educated persons disfigured with unmeaning expletives, empty exclamations, incorrect grammar, inaccurate terms, ludicrously exaggerated epithets, or sayings once grotesque from their very incongruity and now simply stupid as repetitions ? It is a perhaps not very uncommon opinion that great attention to correctness and refinement of language is pedantic ; a charge also brought against the habit of finishing sentences, instead of leaving a portion of them to be understood without the trouble of finding words. No defect is more entirely within the reach of education to correct than this. If young persons are encouraged to express themselves freely and never allowed to express themselves ill ;—if the conversation into which they are drawn to take their part ranges habitually over a variety of subjects ;—and if care is taken to correct exaggerated or inappropriate language, and to give that complete habit of ready expression which overcomes nervousness and timidity, we shall assuredly succeed in forming the power of easy, refined, and simple conversation, though we cannot make brilliant talkers where nature has not bestowed the peculiar gift. Large sums are spent in the course of education upon accomplishments ; but what accomplishment,— to take no higher view of it,—is comparable to that of good conversation? What other *talent de societé* is so independent of exterior advantages, and instead of losing, improves with years and experience ? The matter of our talk depends of course on knowledge and mental power, but the manner and the form are dependent on cultivation. It is not in the matter of their conversation that the French are superior to us, but in their habitual attention to good language. Those even who cannot write grammatically will speak with a correctness and elegance which we rarely give ourselves the trouble to attain. ' *L'art de bien causer* ' is studied as a social accomplishment of a high order, and the slovenly incorrectness and want of finish so common in England, would with them be considered a mark of under breeding and deficient education. It is strange, to say the least of it, that so many parents should spare no trouble or expense to make their daughters sing like angels, while they are content to let them talk like fools !

§ 2.—In the last chapter I said that the practice of making notes from reading should be commenced ; throughout the course now indicated the notes become of great importance, not only as an assistance to the memory, but as helping to methodize knowledge and giving the babit of going back in thought over the matter of the day's reading.

The best method of making notes is a point of considerable difficulty; perhaps among experienced readers each will have in some respects a way of his own which he has found best suited to his memory or to certain purposes he may have in view. In proposing a method for young students, we must bear in mind two principal objects: first, that all which is really important, and that alone, be noted, in a condensed form, with great attention to accuracy, both of statement and reference; and secondly, that the matter so noted shall be arranged in an order that makes reference to it perfectly easy. The copiousness of the notes should depend in some measure on the nature of the reader's memory. If that be retentive, the mere heads of a writer's opinions will be sufficient, with the leading facts or dates that may occur. Others, less fortunate, cannot trust themselves to retain the most important and interesting matter without a clear and somewhat detailed exposition of the writer's views, and of the facts on which they rest: and more than this, their own speculations escape them; the thoughts suggested while reading pass away and are dropped by a treacherous memory, unless they also are recorded at the time. These are differences which must always be known to the teacher. Allowing the pupil at first to note down what she herself believes to be required, let the weekly examinations of her reading be made with her note-book in hand; this will clearly test both her memory and the degree of industry with which she has striven to aid it.

The labour of making notes is also affected by the circumstance of reading our own or borrowed books. In the first case, when making a note, a few words indicating the subject, with a reference to the author, are sufficient; but in the latter case, the passages in question must be copied, and often at considerable length, to make the notes of any value. Under such circumstances, I believe the following method will be found the most effectual. Let one page of the commonplace book be devoted to the actual notes, whether quotations, references to passages, or summary of arguments or facts; and the page opposite be reserved for original remarks, as, for instance, any difficulty that arises in the mind about accepting such or such views—any speculation or reflection that has been suggested. These may perhaps be copious, while a mere reference is all that is needed on the other page. In that case the latter will remain partly blank; or the reverse may happen, long quotations may have to be copied, while few or no original remarks are made. The blank spaces are not without their use, for they facilitate looking over an otherwise closely written book. If, however, this be considered an objection, two note-books may be used, the one for abstracts and quotations, the other for remarks. In either case the books must be paged, since they would be of comparatively little use, unless reference to their contents were made in a detached index. By this means, although matter belonging to one subject may be scattered through different parts perhaps of several books, according to the order of the reading, the index will mark every page in which such matter is to be found. One advantage among others that results from entering the notes and remarks in the same book is, that the matter which has suggested the remark, and the remark itself, are before the eyes at the same moment, without the labour of another reference. The young reader should never fail to note a difficulty,—a passage not clearly understood,—a point that requires clearing up by reference to other books she has not perhaps at hand at the moment. Things of this sort should be written in red ink, so as to catch the eye whenever the book is opened. It should be an essential point in the teacher's examination to ascertain whether all these defects in the full apprehension of a subject have been conscientiously noted down, and to take occasion on every instance of carelessness to enforce again the conviction of the utter futility of reading without caring to obtain a clear and full comprehension of what we read. When points of this kind have been cleared up by subsequent reading, let the memorandum be scratched off; or rather the pen drawn through it, and reference made in the margin to the page where the explanation or further information will be found.

At the age we are speaking of, the original remarks will probably be scanty; the mind is only beginning to work; subjects are all too new to be very suggestive. The teacher must beware of encouraging *much* writing. What we want is not quantity, but evidence of thought; and that may be given in a few short sentences or even words. 'This remark shows observation,' or 'this is a proof that you have reflected on what you had read,' such should be the mode of praise. Everything which denotes love of accuracy should be noted with approbation. When engaged on any science, besides the method of notes recommended above, careful lists, such as I have mentioned before, should be drawn up, consisting of scientific terms with their derivations, heads of classifications, &c., and these should be committed to memory and constantly referred to till the knowledge they contain appears to be indelibly impressed on the mind.   Much of the difficulty that persons who read a little science experience in following reasonings or expositions of a subject, arises from having a more or less confused recollection or apprehension of this primary knowledge.   It is a golden rule of study to grapple with one difficulty at a time; we must not therefore be puzzled with words while trying to understand a theory.

It is possible that some persons may think the system I have indicated needlessly laborious for reading which has no literary purpose in view, and still more for the school-room reading of girls of fourteen or fifteen. But the question is, will a less toilsome method enable the mind to retain more surely and readily the fruits of study ?   Those who read to pass the time require no such labour, for their purpose is accomplished when the hours are passed over; they may turn from one book to another, and read on their journeys, and in their gardens, and in the evenings, and wonder at a friend who can spend an hour in thought, *doing nothing*, as they express it; such readers may spare themselves all the trouble which I have spoken of as necessary.   But those who read to acquire knowledge and to improve their faculties have no other measure of trouble than what best ensures attaining that end.   As a question of labour, therefore, we need not consider it at all, unless some equally or more effectual method can be suggested at a slighter cost of time.

Before leaving this subject, I may remark that the *habit of thinking* is not made as much as it might be a direct object of education. It is, doubt-less, one of the most difficult, but something might be done.   Many persons can attend closely to a book, or even work out their own thoughts tole-rably if obliged to write them down, who are unable to *think out* a subject. Patient, solitary thought is what they never devote any time to, and yet nothing so ripens the mind as this revolving of knowledge and evolving of speculation, which, at first dim and uncertain, gradually clears as attention is fixed upon it, and attains those definite proportions which enable us at least to discern whether it be true or false,—new or merely new-clad,—promising or worthless.   Many a half-formed opinion and views hovering between the uncertain and the false, have gained influence in that cloudy state which they would have lost over any honest mind had they been *thought into decided shape*, till it became clear what stuff they were made of.   Women who often have little time for study, or at any rate for reduc-ing their own speculations to writing, have, in general, much time for thought.   Were it then only as a shield against frivolous desultory wander-ing when the fingers are engaged and the mind unoccupied, it would be a most valuable habit to cultivate in girls. When they are somewhat accustomed to write their own reflections, or what they have gained from a given portion of reading, the teacher may begin to question them in conversation on some point, and then let them think over it at their leisure, and state the result orally. In point of language and method of statement the exercise so carried on from time to time will also be found most useful. Points will frequently occur in the course of the examinations on which the pupil may have no ready answer; they can be left to be thought over, and the result given later or another day. The period considered in this chapter may perhaps be too early for an exercise of this nature, as there can be few beginnings of opinion yet; but of this the teacher must judge. If the exercise of thought leads merely to the detection of confusion, it is, as I said above, of immense benefit.

The difficult lesson of persevering regularity, which is learned by the the habit of doing the same thing daily, has been frequently urged as an excuse for making young people keep journals; but the latter are so apt to degenerate into records of sentiment or of trifling, that I think them in their ordinary form very objectionable. In the still and monotonous life of women, feelings tend so irresistibly to occupy a large place, and to enlist imagination on their side, that I would discourage all allusion to personal feeling in diaries. The latter to be useful should be journals of reading and thought only; if a different tone is allowed, the door is opened to sentiment and sickly fancy, and every subtle enemy of woman's cheerfulness. If it be made a practice to record daily the mere events and occupations of the day, the number of hours spent in study, changes of residence, &c., a few minutes will suffice, and a mere enlargement of this daily plan is required in case of a journey, an interesting conversation, or of any other remarkable circumstance which requires notice. If one or more foreign languages are perfectly familiar, it may be as well to write either notes or diary occasionally in one or the other; the practice keeps up the use of the language without any additional labour. Notes from foreign books naturally suggest the use of the language we are quoting from, but it must be completely familiar, otherwise the pupil might get into a habit of incorrect writing, or being embarrassed with verbal difficulties, lose sight of the main object of keeping the notes.

The plan of study here recommended is so inexpensive compared to the usual labour of acquiring accomplishments, that it still requires but little alteration in any of its important points for persons to whom economy is an object. Foreign languages must perhaps be abandoned, or French be studied, as I remarked in the last chapter, by a less advantageous method. It may likewise be difficult to give as much time to the study of literature and composition. But instruction in elementary mathematics may be obtained very cheaply, and the books I have indicated as introductions to science are all of low price. Five pounds will more than cover the expense of the works here pointed out for the study of two years. If unable to pay a thoroughly instructed governess, the mother will have to undergo great additional labour; and if circumstances of any kind unfit her for undertaking the office of teacher, there will, undoubtedly, be much advantage lost in not studying under good tuition. Still, this may be partly compensated by making the mind put forth its strength in working alone; morally and intellectually it will be braced by the exertion.

§ 3.—At the age we are now considering, the formation of character is going on step by step with the cultivation of the intellect. The earlier stages of teaching, which are addressed almost exclusively to the memory, have a slight and indirect effect only upon the disposition; hence the little that can be effected by schools for the poor, where the children are taken away at an early age, before the influence of improved intelligence begins to tell. But when education has reached that point when all its efforts tend to draw out the reasoning power, to force reflection, and to form opinion, then each change in the intellectual condition of our pupil influences the tone of moral character whether we will or no. A careless, one-sided system of education may thus, by overlooking this fact, produce harm from what should have been productive of unmixed good; for wherever a powerful source of influence exists, it cannot remain inoperative; if not turned into the right channel, it will work mischief in the wrong one. Accordingly, we too often see that increasing knowledge, when not brought by the education to bear upon moral points, appears to stimulate the selfish motives only; it becomes *power* to gratify our own tastes or inclinations, and leads naturally to contempt for qualities which have not that end in view. Duty, left out of sight, sinks in estimation compared with that which is kept prominently forward as an object of ambition and delight, and moral deterioration is the direct consequence. It is the function of education to preserve a right balance between all our faculties, and ensure their harmonious development; thus in proportion as intellectual activity grows more intense, the moral nature must be more strongly stimulated; a higher standard of action and principle must be made to grow out of the new mental capacity unfolding day by day. The more power of observation, or reasoning, or reflection is evinced by the young girl, the more may we require her to give evidence of those qualities in practical things whether great or small, in views of duty and in daily conduct.   Where this direction is given and carefully maintained, we may trust that in all ordinarily well-constituted minds, increased moral power will accompany the expansion of the intellect.

Some points of character that require careful watching at this age, have been spoken of in a former chapter; * but the real work of this period is the conversion of routine into principle, and of the habit of obedience into the power of self-guidance.   The latter is the ultimate object of all education.   Without this power the best disposed are creatures of impulse, or of outward circumstances.   We all feel that human nature is lowered in that being whose own sense of right is not the law of his actions, and yet there is scarcely any consistent effort made in education to cultivate a strong spirit of self-regulation.   Even with little children, where strict obedience is so necessary, it should never, as I have before observed, be enforced in a manner that tends to break down the power of the will; we must respect in the rebellious instinct of the child that element which is the germ of vigour in the man.   Madame Guizot remarks truly, in her letters on Education, that one will only can always govern the human creature, and that will must be his own.†

The neglect of this view in education is doubtless in great measure owing to the indolence or ignorance of teachers, for it is incomparably easier to insist upon submission to rules than to cultivate the spirit which shall frame right rules for itself.   But there has also been a curiously mistaken idea that decision and vigour are out of place in female character, and therefore that in educating girls pliancy and docility are among the first points to aim at.

The old stereotyped complaint that women are 'fond of their own way,' we all have heard, and all women, at least, have laughed at.   And yet it deserves serious attention, as a curious indication not only of the perverted views that result from the possession of irresponsible power, but of the influence of that perversion upon those who suffer under it.   It is analogous to the denunciations of popular rebellion in former times, when a

---

* Chap. iii.
† 'Il n'y a qu'une volonté au monde qui puisse toujours être maîtresse de l'enfant comme de l'homme, c'est la sienne ; il s'agit donc de ne pas soumettre sa volonté, mais de lui en donner une.'—*Lettres de Famille sur l'Education.*   Par Mde. Guizot. Vol. i. p. 56.

feeble attempt was made now and then by the subject classes to resist a wrong or claim a right. When we examine the real meaning of the expression, it amounts to this : that the human creature has a preference for indulging its own tastes, wishes, or inclinations, rather than for seeing them set aside by others ; a proposition whose general truth few, probably, will be inclined to dispute, who know what is meant by having a taste or an inclination. The variety of the instances in which that universal aim is attained by the more dependent half of the human race has, no doubt, attracted attention to the successful; but to those who look a little closer, the really strange point is not the occasional indulgence, but the habitual surrender of will; the habitual sacrifice of self, with all its independent impulses, wishes, and convictions, not merely at the call of affection,— which makes even sacrifice a joy,—but to a vague notion compounded of duty and necessity.

I shall not, I believe, be suspected by any candid reader of seeking to alter the natural and inevitable subordination of women. Here, however, I deal, not with a social, but with an individual question, and I maintain that women, far from erring by too determined a will, err sadly from want of firmness and vigour of character. From that source spring half their mistakes both in opinion and action, more than half their follies, as also of their want of influence, and the slow desponding suffering which is the canker in the lives of so many. They want determination, they want energy and clearness to enable them to see a course, and pursue it. And those for whose pleasure or benefit their nature has been thus mutilated have not failed to revile them for the faults which are the natural result. The satirists and moralists, and all their feeble imitators in society, who rail at female love of power, scoff equally at the featureless character of women in general. Their judgments concern us here, only so far as they approve themselves to our own consciences. When men complain of love of power in women, it is the cry of an interested witness; but when they ridicule our weakness, our incapacity or helplessness—whatever individual injustice there may be in the accusation—we are forced with deep morti- fication to confess that in educating girls to submission we have too often educated them to nullity. In considering certain positions and relations in which woman is necessarily subject, we have too much forgotten the spiritual freedom and dignity of the moral being responsible to God and not to man for the use and exercise of the powers with which He has gifted her.

With regard to education, a system of complete subjection may be necessary, and also quite harmless in schools, while most pernicious at home, for the authority is altogether different in character. Positive and distinct rules are laid down for the government of a school, and punishments incurred if they are disobeyed; but the child is free to disobey, and incur the penalty. The authority enforces that and no more ; it makes no claim to a willing obedience ; it does not meddle with thoughts or feelings, the moral nature is under no subjection. It is in short a conventional system for a given time and purpose, and not a scheme of life ; character developes freely under the empire of such a law ; its great defect is that it has little or no moral influence. In a school the master *teaches* and *commands*, but it is the public opinion of the young community which sways feeling and principle.

It is, and ought to be far different at home. Parental rule is not the sway of a temporarily constituted authority, submitted to for certain purposes and under certain conditions ; it claims the heart and will no less than the outward action; disobedience is a violence done to the child's conscience, from which he cannot recover as from the effects of breaking through school discipline, and which could not be frequently repeated without real injury to the moral nature. If, therefore, this authority, thus deep and far-reaching in itself, be also extended over a long period of life, the young mind will almost certainly suffer both morally and intellectually.

Generally speaking, with daughters that period is not allowed to have any natural limit. They are rarely supposed to have attained the age when they may determine their own course within even the narrow limits which their natural condition allows. An extra demand for frivolous amusement, especially if it holds out any prospect of worldly advantage, is kindly met ; a strong theological bent is generally excused ; but gay or gloomy, wise or foolish, it is all a question of *indulgence,* not the simple exercise of *rational freedom.* And from these nursery trammels, one step places a girl amid the cares and responsibilities of marriage ; never having ruled her own life for a day, she undertakes duties involving the happiness of one she loves, and the comfort of many !

It is not, however, with regard to independence of action only, or to mental activity, that a free spirit of self-regulation is needed ; it is the life of our moral nature.* The feeble and dependent follow mere routine

---

* 'A character,' says Novalis, 'is a completely fashioned will,'—quoted by J. S. Mill. *Logic,* vol. ii. p. 417, fourth edition. Habits, routine, subjection to others, are not *character ;* the latter is the outer manifestation of strong motives and principles of thought and action.

in their religion, in their benevolence, in their daily duties, no less than in their pursuits and occupations. In educating girls, the necessity of freeing them from this dominion of mere habit is increased by the very circumstances of their outward lot which tend so strongly to rivet it; since the more humble and dependent the position, the more need is there, in order that the dignity of the human being be not utterly abandoned, that the inner life should be free, exalted, and vigorous.

It is often said that strength of character renders women less gentle, but those who make this assertion should at least take the trouble to prove some connection between feebleness and gentleness. Undoubtedly they may often co-exist, since there is nothing in feebleness which necessarily fosters any ungentle qualities; but at the same time we must remember that the obstinacy of the fool, the vacillation of the weak and timid, the peevishness of those who have not resolution enough either to do or to forbear, are quite as likely to produce want of gentleness as the more decided forms of pride or self-confidence. On the whole, I am inclined to think that in women—as it certainly is in men—the truest gentleness and tenderness are combined with the greatest force of character. The most helpless are, undoubtedly, the most querulous and exacting in their demands upon others; while the innate strength of self-reliance favours equability of temper, and leaves the mind free to give attention and sympathy to the wants and difficulties of others. Where this is not so, it arises from other moral defects which have nothing to do with vigour or decision. Pride may ape strength for a time, and obstinacy may hope to be called resolution; but in speaking of education, we do not suppose it possible that such disguises can pass undetected. It is true also that really fine-spirited, earnest natures may be more chafed than others at the unnecessary bondage they may be made to feel. But this is the fault of the system, not of the individual; it is the struggle of the full-grown creature trammelled by the leading-strings of the infant.

No doubt one of the great difficulties of education is to know *when* to relax authority; when to sink the absolute ruler in the guide, and the guide in the counsellor and friend; when our opinions and views are to cease to be laws, and the young are to be simply assisted in forming views and opinions for themselves. The difficulty is, however, much lessened whenever parents are willing to consider this change, not as a consequence of the rebellious spirit of youth, but as the real object for which the previous obedience has been exacted. Parents who submit from a sense of necessity to relaxing authority feel every step as an encroachment, but when they have themselves prepared the way for those steps, reverence and respect will only grow with the decline of absolute rule. Children should be made to feel from the earliest time that their parents do not exert authority from love of power ; that they do not demand obedience because they are in a position to enforce it, but because they are wiser, abler, because they know and follow the duty God has laid upon them of nurturing the good and correcting the evil in the weak, ignorant creatures committed to their care. But it is no part of their duty to form mere subjects to their own will; the discipline of early years is imposed only that later years may prove fitness for self-government. This is the real aim of education, and so considered, emancipation from authority is no rebellion, no sad loosening of ties that should have been respected, but the fulfilment of the parent's own purpose. If Bishop Butler's theory of habit* were more studied by those who have the charge of education, there would be less faith in the power of outward subjection, and more consistent effort to make the habits we wish to form emanate from the will and conviction of the young themselves.

The absolute impossibility of keeping young men under constant restraint makes parents early relax authority over sons, while they maintain it over daughters, although superior perhaps in age, character, and ability. But sons know that it is a yielding to necessity, and hence the feeling that they have emancipated themselves, and a sense of triumph in having in some measure conquered their freedom; instead of the wholesome conviction that they are free and trusted just when and how the whole scheme of their education had contemplated their being so. Perhaps *fathers* would never have sunk into *governors* under a different system ! The power of the purse is the last resort of effete authority, and the whole moral and intellectual influence of the highest position one human being can occupy towards another, is degraded into the material yoke of the one possessing and the other needing money ! Daughters who have no way, except marriage, of rendering themselves independent with regard to income, naturally it is said remain under subjection.

But setting aside those who make difficulties by their own undue love of power, I admit, as I said above, that this is one of the delicate points of youthful training. Perhaps one of the best means of preparing the way from the obedience of the child to the willing docility of youth, is to associate the young girl in some measure in our labour by explaining to her

---

* *Analogy of Religion, Natural and Revealed.*   Part i. chap. 5.

gradually the principles on which her education has been conducted, letting her see the aim and intent of the studies and of the rules she has perhaps never considered except as daily necessities; pointing out how they are all parts of one system, embracing the whole of that portion of her life for which her parents are responsible, and tending to fit her for taking that responsibility in her own hands, and fulfilling wider and more arduous duties than have yet fallen to her lot. Let her be frankly told that without her co-operation it is felt that no effort can be successful; while her wish and power to co-operate in working steadily towards a determined purpose, is the surest sign that she has passed the bounds of childhood, and is beginning to act and understand like a reasonable being, accountable to God for the use of its faculties.

The quickness with which the young respond to a high tone of feeling will, I believe, in far the greater number of cases, give great force to such words from the parent, if their mild wisdom be acted upon with entire consistency and frankness. The young mind will expand to this large view opened to it for the first time. A new sense of dignity will spring up as it contemplates those school-room tasks as its own individual share of that great labour of self-improvement and discipline enjoined on all alike. And with this sense of its own dignity, there will spring up also in every generous mind a new feeling of respect and affection for the parent, whose far-reaching wisdom and watchful care it reflects upon for the first time in their true aspect. It will feel that there is something in these so far beyond its own feeble powers, that spontaneous reverence will place the mother higher than ever, at the very moment when she is relaxing authority, and treating her child as a companion and an equal.

From the time the young girl is thus associated in the labour of those who direct her education, every occasion should be taken to accustom her to the exercise of her own discretion. If a new study is to be commenced, she should be consulted about it; if a change of hours is required, let her propose her own scheme and talk it over with you. Let her have the command of her own time as far as may be compatible with regular teaching, so that she may study under a sense of responsibility, not under *surveillance*. This is doubly valuable, since the object of first importance with girls is to give them the desire to work and the habit of doing so without any external obligation or stimulus. When opposition to some expressed wish is inevitable, let the reasons and principle of the opposition be made so clear that she will acknowledge the consistency, and be convinced that there is no love of authority, even when she cannot fully see the wisdom of the measure. In her amusements, in her mode of spending her own money, in her desire to serve others, let there be no sort of interference except when necessary to prevent real mischief. I do not give this name to mere mistakes, though productive of annoyance or temporary suffering. These are the price paid for experience, and which, within certain limits, it is better that we should all pay, because we all prefer incurring the cost to taking the wisdom of others upon trust. The greater the freedom and the more gentle the treatment after blunders of this kind have been made, the more secure will be the future confidence in the parent's advice.

Such, I believe, should be the course gradually adopted at the period we have been considering. Exceptional cases require of course exceptional treatment. There may be difficult circumstances and difficult tempers, violent or sluggish natures, which would make such a course inexpedient, and render the exertion of mere authority still necessary at the age of fourteen or fifteen. But this *ought not to be ;* and the mother, if compelled to that exertion, should let her child see how completely she feels it to be a wrong and a disappointment of all her expectations. The sorrow should be as frankly expressed as the firmness of purpose. Every sign of a better tone of mind should then be watched and earnestly welcomed, while at the same time the child suffers the natural consequence of her own folly in the partial withdrawal of the confidence she has proved herself unworthy of. She must be made to feel that the respect of her superiors for her depends on her own self-respect, of which she is evidently careless, when she can bear to sink back from a reasonable creature to a child. Many a backsliding, many a discouraging symptom of weakness must be expected in all but rare cases; but the mother should labour to prevent discouragement taking hold of the young mind. Her own indulgence and hopeful tone should be in proportion to the signs of mortification at failure shown by the young girl herself, since there is always hope of good where there is sincere suffering caused by the sense of wrongdoing. If the mind be dead to the shame of frequent failure, either through natural insensibility or frivolity, or any other quality indicative of a shallow nature, then the more stringent treatment must be resorted to.

Some minds, it may be feared, are really incapable of self-guidance. A certain grade of mental infirmity may, as we have before remarked, show itself under this aspect no less than under that of direct intellectual deficiency. When such is the case, where the mother's earnest efforts fail to make her child fit to shape her own course under the guidance of conscience, the next resource is to form such habits as will become a routine for the feeble mind to follow, and mark a humble but—under ordinary circumstances—a tolerably safe track through the labyrinth, where she could not be trusted to thread her own way. Habits of constant occupation, of punctual regularity, of attention to the wishes and pursuits of others, and of respect for superior character and intellect, will in a great measure serve as guides, even when the mind is incapable of appreciating their value; and so long as no outward disturbance breaks through the routine, it will preserve its influence. It happens also occasionally that character, like the intellect, develops so tardily, that where at fifteen we had been utterly discouraged by apparently hopeless inertness or wayward-ness, we may some years later find new power unfolded. A new phase of character will appear, and then the routine of habits which have been, as we may say, the cradle in which the feeble moral nature has been nursed and strengthened, will decide the form of the first efforts the enfranchised mind will make towards its own improvement.

Under happier circumstances, when forming in the young the capacity for self-guidance, there is one point of extreme importance to be especially dwelt upon. This is steadfastness in adhering to resolutions; a sense of duty attaching to that which has once been earnestly purposed. From the moment a young person is trusted with the disposal of time, and with some degree of freedom of action, this view of the sacredness of resolutions should be carefully enforced, and we must be sure that the nature of the evil resulting from trifling with them is thoroughly understood. It is not rare to see much confusion on this point, even among persons of thoroughly upright mind. They measure the wrong by the importance of the resolution that has been violated, whereas the violation of conscience involved in the failure is its true and only measure. As a question of expediency, or even of duty to others, breaking one resolution may be a far less blameable act than breaking another; but to the individual, as a question of duty to himself, the evil result is the same.

In order to make a young person understand this point, several other subjects must first be made clear, such as the nature and power of habit; the importance of daily trifling actions towards forming habits; the necessity of ordering life upon a system, of having a distinct aim in view, to attain which certain habits of mind and action are seen to be requisite. Lastly, it must be shown how, in judging of pursuits, actions, or habits of any description, they must be approved or condemned principally according as they tend to forward or to thwart that ruling purpose, with a view to which, one general plan of life is laid out ; since that plan being decided upon under a sense of duty, it is placed thereby under the guardianship of conscience. The young must be made to see that failure in one of these points almost necessarily involves failure in all. He, for instance, who does not consider the force of habit, allows each day's carelessness about little things to rivet its powerful chain upon his mind. One who has thus unconsciously become the slave of habits, his own predetermination had no part in forming, can evidently not act upon system. He who does not act upon system, who has no settled method in his life, has no standard of self-regulation beyond those obvious points which involve questions of duty to others; too often will he fail even in these, from the very waywardness of mood unused to steady control; and as he has no distinct aim in view, resolutions will be made and broken, pursuits taken up and abandoned, time employed or wasted, according to the impulse of the moment, without a thought of evil resulting in any more formidable shape than want of success in the matters in hand. Errors of this nature intimately connected together, and leading to general instability of character, may be joined to such natural goodness and elevation of feeling, that the action which flows from impulse shall have all the appearance of virtue, but can never deserve its praise nor inspire the confidence which steadfastness of mind and systematic obedience to principle command from all who are capable of judging human conduct.

The extreme importance to women of methodical self-regulation, and habitual value for time, is most apparent, not only from the consideration of those temptations to idleness and frivolity which are incidental to their position, but also from the nature of some of their serious duties.* All the small detail of life which falls most legitimately to woman's share, comes in a great measure in so irregular a form, that rigid exactness of occupation would be generally impossible. A child who wants care cannot be made to wait till a leisure moment. A tradesman, on the answer to whose business the comfort of the household may depend, cannot be sent away to return at a more convenient time. The poor person who comes for advice or help in some emergency, cannot be denied. The sick person whose very fancies are a law, cannot be made to submit to the punctual habits so valuable for our own occupations. The old, the sad, the weary, who look to us for comfort or help, or the gladdening of a cheerful hour, must not find their claims set aside for the sake of the systematic regularity so

---

* See chapter on 'Method,' in *Thoughts on Self-Culture,* where the views brought forward in the following pages are more fully dwelt upon.

important to ourselves. Such is the state of things to which women must learn to adapt themselves ; and one of the advantages of home over school education for girls is, that they gradually learn that art under their mother's eye. They do not come from the complete regularity of school hours and arrangements to feel themselves at the same moment free, and yet exposed to the host of small claims which bewilder them, and help to put to flight all notion of regular study or pursuit. At home the freedom has been long prepared, and the habit of occupation rooted in the midst of home interests and engagements.

As a girl becomes old enough to understand these matters, and to feel the danger of letting the daily occurrences of life take the sway of our lives out of our own hands, she can be shown in the first place how far mere regularity and punctuality can assist us in controlling the manner in which these various claims press upon us; how far order and steady adherence to rules can reduce daily interruptions, by enforcing method wherever we have the power of control, and allowing no break in that order except in cases of sudden emergency, or from the claims of the old and the sick. Secondly, this yet more important lesson must be made clear to the young girl from the moment she begins to act for herself—namely, that there must be a system in her life far above all these petty hindrances, embracing all occupations which belong to her social position, whatever their form and whatever the disadvantages attached to them, but making them find their place as parts of a whole : she must feel that women who have no career of worldly activity to force methodical exertion, can never afford to lose sight of those great aims which bind our earthly course with our hopes of eternity through one wide system of usefulness and self-improvement : a sense of responsibility for all our means and faculties governing the mind throughout.

The influence of this high feeling upon the ordinary detail of life is to introduce a different kind of method from that which depends on regularity and punctuality alone. Supposing, for example, that *certain fixed hours* for our own pursuits cannot be secured free from interruption, yet we can generally make sure of doing a *given amount* of work in *the course of the day*. We can acquire the habit of turning attention quickly and readily from one subject to another, so that on returning to our own occupation we may suffer as little as possible from the ill effects of interruption. When time for any regular pursuit is cut down to very scanty limits, we can be careful to preserve the habit and the love of steady mental occupation by doing a little daily, keeping up the thread in expectation of better times. The break will thus be an interruption only, allowed on the plea of superior claims or duty; but while it alters our daily routine, it changes nothing in our settled views of the way our life should be spent and the objects it should aim at.

It is difficult to make any person who is not strongly impressed with the value of method see the importance of the distinction here insisted upon, between a daily life which, though subject to constant interruption, never loses sight of systematic occupation for a given purpose, and the same life subject only to the same trials, but given up without struggle to the shifting rule of circumstance. In the former, although every semblance of regularity be forcibly broken through perhaps for weeks together, the higher system still overrules the whole, and the moment the cause of disturbance ceases, the accustomed order is spontaneously resumed; progress in a given pursuit has been retarded, but the mind has preserved its equability; nothing has been unsettled in the inner life. On the other hand, with persons who have no definite purpose beyond the day's business, even when no unusual interruptions occur, time is frittered away,— occupations daily contemplated and perhaps even begun, can find no place, purposes formed in the morning are neglected ere half the day's flutter of small cares is over; till on looking back over weeks or perhaps months, nothing has been accomplished, though all the while a sense of ceaseless pressure and hurry wearies the nerves and affects the spirits. Nor is the difference one that affects active life or mental occupation only, it tells upon the moral tone of character. In the one case we feel that through whatever eddying currents, under whatever uncertain skies we steer our course, we still hold the helm in our own hands; we are still, in the highest sense, as far as mortal lips can venture on the assertion, the pilots of our own destiny. But in the other case we have yielded the rudder to the fickle waves, and we are borne along day by day as wind and current list. The difference of moral vigour and dignity resulting from these two courses requires no comment.

Many occasions will present themselves of practically enforcing these views during the period of education. Interruptions will occur to break in even upon school-room life, secluded as yet from ordinary social claims; and it is well to lead the young girl to see her own way through difficulties of this nature, to consider for herself what can best be done, what is the relative importance of the different things she is usually engaged with, and what therefore can be omitted from her usual studies or occupations with least injury to the real method of life that includes all duties alike. I would not have occasions of this kind either made or avoided; they occur in every family; and with her mother's example and a firm hold of the principle by which she must be guided, there will be little fear of her going wrong. Illness affords precious opportunities of moral instruction. The sick room falls within woman's natural province, and she must be taught her duty there. The young creature's offer of help in hours of anxiety or sorrow, or when prompted by benevolent feeling only, should if possible never be refused; by accepting it we allow her to cultivate the best sympathies of her nature. Only we must take care that the impulse to seek the new employment is not mixed up with love of change or wish to get rid of lessons, and that it is not carelessly or capriciously discharged as the first impulse dies away. She must feel that it is in the sick room that we expect to see the practical fruits of some of the severest studies she has been engaged in. Observation, judgment, correct inference, accuracy, and method, which are cultivated by means of study forcing the mind to reflection, must here come into action with moral qualities of a high order,—with self-control both as regards temper and the exhibition of feeling which incapacitates the nurse for her duty, with patience, unselfishness in disregarding inconvenience or fatigue, and unvarying gentleness and cheerfulness in bearing with the often querulous humour of the patient; while combined with these must be the sense of responsibility in having undertaken a serious duty, and won a mark of confidence which any fickleness or neglect would make her forfeit. Attendance in a sick room so considered, is an interruption to regular habits and studies, but it is truly no violation of the method of education.

Economy is another point of very serious moment which must come under the control of method. It is a difficult art, and apprenticeship to it should begin early. I think it advisable to give children money as soon as they are able to keep a correct account of what they spend. The next point is to make them understand the first principles of rational expenditure, that is, the difference between the useful and the fanciful, between the more or less useful or important, between a *want* and a *whim;* and also to make them feel the duty and inspire the wish to serve others, which introduces another motive for prudence and self-control in the gratification of our own wants. At fifteen, a girl ought to be fit to be trusted with an allowance for her dress, which, besides enforcing the above lessons, has the further advantage of making her more careful about her wardrobe, and more willing to take some trouble to keep it in order. And care and thrifty management are considerable elements in those branches of economy which commonly fall to a woman's superintendence. There may be no want of good feeling in the carelessness about these things shown by a girl who has everything provided for her; but she does not learn the practical consequences of carelessness as when she is obliged to sacrifice the money she had destined for some pleasurable purchase, because the gloves or stockings that might, by careful mending, have been made to last, must, owing to neglect, be replaced altogether.

Another valuable lesson which a girl can hardly learn till she has money of her own, is how quickly it melts away with sixpenny purchases. So much of the expenditure for women's dress is in trifling and individually cheap things, that no one believes at first that 'only this' and 'only that' can swell into a large bill. There should be in all ordinary cases no sort of interference with the purchases. If she chooses ill to-day, she will be all the more likely to choose better next month for having bought her own experience. Two rules only should be invariable: perfect neatness in the dress, and *no bills*. I mean, of course, by the latter, no long-standing bills, for it often happens, especially when living in the country, that an account must be kept open with one or more shops; but if these be called for at stated times, and if the allowance be paid towards the same period, we ensure regularity in the payment and likewise the immediate penalty for extravagance, when the quarter's allowance, which probably had been reckoned upon for many purposes, is found to melt away in paying for what had seemed such trifling expenses when incurred. It must be expected that the young beginner will get more than once into troubles of this kind, but how slight are they compared with what parents recklessly expose their daughters to, when they have been left till the period of their marriage without the control of any expenditure, and suddenly have a large and complicated one thrown upon their hands. If poor, their ignorance may produce serious discomfort and embarrassment; if rich, it will be a source of folly as regards themselves, and of corruption as regards servants and dependents. In both cases it will be a source of annoyance to their husbands, and too often the cause of the first irritable tones and slighting words which mar the loving peace of their new home.

The mother will, I believe, do well to give no assistance in the small troubles a girl's thoughtlessness or extravagance have involved her in. If a sister or old friend who happens to know her difficulty should wish to save her from the consequences of her mistakes, there is not the same objection, for she never can depend on aid of this kind. But payment of a debt by her mother, or assistance to relieve her from the natural penalty of extravagance, might create an expectation of being so helped again. Whatever the amount of the allowance, there is one rule for every fortune; namely, that *our means*, and not our fancies or even our reasonable wants *must* be the measure of our expenditure. We cannot too soon with young people check any temptation to adopt that disastrous plea of extravagant people, ' I must have, or do so-and-so, for everybody does so.' We must be honest,—that is the one great necessity which is forgotten by every infringement, great or small, of the rule of living within our means.

The question of amusements enters as a very large element into the consideration of the general method of our lives, for nothing needs more to be kept subservient to our serious purposes. It is rather a difficult question in education when the easy pleasures of childhood are given up. Living in the country presents most advantages in this respect; gardening, pet animals, riding, skating, long walks to spend the bright summer day in woods rich with wild flowers, or beside the brawling stream, where bird and tiny insect can be watched enjoying the sunny hours; or again, pic-nics, or family gatherings at Christmas, all afford pleasures as simple as they are delightful to the young elastic spirits untainted by the world's excitements or its vanities. If living in town, we are driven to resort habitually to forms of amusement which are less naturally attractive to the young, and have not the same recommendation of being equally conducive to health as to enjoyment. Still there are many resources without resorting to amusements which tend to feed vanity and love of dress. There are curious and interesting exhibitions, museums, and collections of every kind, illustrative of different branches of study, easy access to books, pleasant society, and every opportunity for cultivating and refining the love of art which sheds so much enjoyment over life. Nor do many people live the whole year round in London, and the pleasure of summer excursions to town-bred children is truly exquisite. It is not easy to surpass the joy of holidays spent by the sea-side, or among the distant hills, where the beauty of scenery will awaken the young heart to a new source of emotion and delight, a source whence will flow soothing for many an hour of depression, forgetfulness of many a weary thought or care, so long as eye or limb retain their power.

No taste, however, is comparable as a lasting fund of enjoyment to a love of reading, which, if fostered by education into real love of know-ledge, becomes a source not of pleasure alone, but of happiness. Unfortunately, common systems do little to inspire that love. The teaching is dry and formal, there is little time left for any reading of the pupil's own choice, and the choice itself is too restricted, the books generally of too trivial a character to excite the imagination, or to rouse a strong feeling of interest or pleasure. It is, perhaps, in general, over-care that so limits the range of reading; and on this subject it appears to me that many mistakes are made both with regard to objectionable matter and also to what is supposed to be above the young reader's comprehension. I believe it is safer to form the taste and love for reading, and then leave the mind to itself; let it learn to cherish the pleasure of freely seeking it and enjoying it in the form it has chosen. The mind is less cramped, less biassed by false notions; it gets more exercised by reading works meant for the public at large, than from being confined to books written expressly for the young. In such books everything is too apt to be toned down to their supposed powers of comprehension;—truths are timidly stated, opinions are modified, society is shown under one aspect only, and there-fore falsely shown, and great principles are dwindled down to small con-ventional moralities. Far from such reading being a benefit, it is enfeebling to heart and intellect. Many things in larger works may be beyond their comprehension; no matter; if our pupils have learnt the art of reading, such things will not be passed over,—necessary explana-tions will be sought in conversation or from other books.

In actual teaching we cannot be too careful to make every subject perfectly clear to the understanding; but when reading for pleasure, it is more healthy for the young mind to be brought frequently to behold the great ocean of knowledge that it can scarcely yet approach, still less explore; to let imagination revel in that poetical dimness of the unknown infinite, than to have everything set forth with a definiteness that belongs to the narrow scope of the work alone. Great things to be done and learnt and hoped for, appeal like generous sentiments to the heart of the young; and it is better for them to see in books the wide world of human action, endeavour, and suffering, than always to have some small section of it cut out and coloured for their own particular use. I would say, therefore, that supposing all really pernicious works to be put out of the way, or simply prohibited, it is best to let girls have in their leisure hours the free range of their parents' library. A governess will, of course, know what her pupils are reading, because their choice is an important indica-tion of character; but let her interfere no further than to talk the books over with them, thus drawing out opinions and modifying impressions, and leading them to see for themselves when their choice has been a bad one.

The dread of letting a girl meet with coarseness of expression or improper narrative is doubtless one chief reason for this great strictness with regard to books; but even this appears to me to be a somewhat exaggerated fear. In the first place, many a passage that would offend an older person passes unheeded by a young girl. How common is it at a much later period of life for a woman to read books without even suspecting the impropriety which she afterwards finds is imputed to them by men? Knowledge of life, with its polluting experience, gives the clue to the slimy labyrinth of coarse writing, while in some sense ' to the pure all things are pure.' I shall hardly be supposed to advocate this style of reading, but I am certain that offensive passages here and there in otherwise desirable works are not likely to be mischievous. The sort of mystery about them that is often made is, I believe, far more objectionable. If certain books are prohibited,—perhaps justly,—or the young reader inconveniently asks for an explanation of expressions she has met with, the tone adopted often conveys the idea of an undue degree of importance attached to the subject, which in some minds may rouse curiosity; while a simple and frank answer might have prevented any willing recurrence to the subject. Explanations cannot, of course, always be given, but it is easy to answer in a manner that satisfies the questioner and does not violate truth; as, for instance, to say in a simple tone and manner, that such or such expressions are coarse words, now utterly banished from decent society and from good writing, used in less refined periods, or as describing a ruder state of society, or alluding to vices which, fortunately, women in the educated classes do not come in contact with, &c. Answers of this kind leave the mind untainted by any needless acquaintance with impurity, and in the very great majority of girls educated with refined and delicate habits, will create a disagreeable association with the subject which will prevent any recurrence to it.

The extreme ignorance of early girlhood is a reason for encouraging the first reading of some of our great poets at that age. I would ask the objectors, at any rate, why reading these in private is more objectionable than listening in public to certain chapters of the Old and even the New Testament, which are read without scruple in our churches? Do they expect when they put the Bible into a girl's hands that those are the portions to which she will revert, and on which she will love to dwell? Neither are the passages of Spenser or Shakspeare, to which we return again and again as to dear familiar friends, those which contain aught that can offend against the most refined modesty.

The same objections would stand, and are often allowed to stand, against reading almost any authors of antiquity; and yet how lifeless must be our notions of those ancient times that have so influenced the course of modern life and thought, if we remain altogether ignorant of their literature! All too poor and faded is the view when we are unable to become acquainted with it in the original languages; but even in translations we get what no modern historian can give us,—namely, the mode of thought, the habitual impressions, the received views of what was familiar to them and is so strange and foreign to us. We read a mere modern narrative of ancient events by the light of our own associations; but when we open an ancient author, we come into a different world of ideas, —into that inner world which was in harmony with the outer events we are reading of. In philosophical and comprehensive views, we, doubtless, gain more from those whom time and generations of research, and means of comparison, have placed on the ' vantage ground' for taking a wide survey of human affairs; but what modern writer can excite the feelings with which we read Herodotus or Thucydides or Plutarch, Livy or Tacitus, or those familiar letters of Cicero, which open home and public life to us at once? Even reading translations of the Greek tragedians, poor as they are, lets us more into the world of Greek thought than the most elaborate of modern dissertations. Yet all this must be cut off if that extreme strictness is to be adhered to.

The real poison to be guarded against is that instilled by licentious sentiment; and on this ground many modern writers in which few, if any, objectionable *words* could be found, are pernicious in the highest degree. The evil here comes in disguise; it is addressed not to a knowledge of degrading facts, but to feelings and emotions which cannot be too carefully guarded from excitement. Writings of this kind do not fall into the hands of the very young, although they would do less harm then than later. The wide circulation of French novels cannot but lower one's estimate of modern refinement, which shrinks with such extreme squeamishness from words that express in a coarse and obsolete form what is certainly not less revolting for being dressed up with all the graces of style, and the veil of high-flown sentiment.

Do what we will, some knowledge of vice and corruption will be forced upon all, and often almost before childhood is passed; and it appears to me unimportant whether the words are also known, by which writers in a coarse state of society openly designated what modern books or gossip more covertly imply. No one will deny that it is an advantage when such expressions are banished from literature and society; for although refinement of language is no certain indication of refinement of mind, any more than polished manners are a test of real kindliness of feeling; yet the tone of public opinion, which exacts the observance of these forms, is one which tends to exalt the estimate of the qualities they simulate. In a state of society, therefore, where the outward indications of coarse and licentious thought and tone of manners are held up as degrading to the reputation of persons in a certain rank of life, the effect must be to heighten contempt for the vices thus compelled to hide themselves, and to establish in a large and increasing number of minds a healthy association on these important subjects. These are reasons for valuing even a fastidious refinement of language, which can easily be made intelligible to the young girl, while we refuse to exclude her from a wide circle of literature, embracing some of the noblest works of human genius, on the petty plea of not letting her read expressions she will become acquainted with in church if nowhere else.

The moral lesson to be taught to the young girl is, that she should value among the highest privileges that exemption from coarse experience and degrading temptation which is ensured to her by her position in society, and which also allows her to remain ignorant of the foul impurities which taint the moral atmosphere of thousands among her fellow-creatures, even of her own sex and tender years. Some of the moral harshness of pure and warm-hearted women, springs from the false views of the world which a timid education has implanted. Had they been gradually accustomed to know what are the temptations and the weakness of our poor human nature, they would have valued the privileges of their own lot in a humbler spirit, and have looked with truer and gentler feeling on the erring and the fallen.

To return from this somewhat lengthy digression on books, to the immediate subject of amusements, we may remark that in general the most desirable forms of amusement for girls are such as lead to out-of-door exercise, and such as can be followed at home with the least expense and the least dependence on others. For women need some inducement to take as much exercise as health requires, and everything is precious to them which can enliven an often monotonous existence without leading them to depend on society which few can command, or on expenditure which they rarely control. The love of exciting pleasures is one of the most unfortunate turns that can be given to the female mind, and it appears to be fostered in one of two ways by most systems of education. Sometimes girls are immured in the frightful dulness of their school-rooms, ignorant of every social enjoyment till they *come out*, as the transition from seclusion to frivolous dissipation is technically called. And it is little to be wondered at if they evince a frantic love for everything opposed to the tedium and restraint they have endured so long. Sometimes, on the other hand,—and this becomes more and more the fashion in the present day,—they are inured so early to exciting pleasures that even they cease to excite. Balls, parties, theatres, concerts, exhibitions of all kinds are thrown open to them, till, when the period arrives for them to go into the world, all ordinary forms of social pleasure have begun to pall upon them. Their early vitiated taste finds still less relish in quieter amusements, and thus in the very freshness of their youth they appear listless,—dead to enjoyment except under the immediate stimulus of some new excitement. Both these systems conspire against happiness; but the truth is, that providing for the happiness of the young is but rarely thought of in education. It is a difficult portion of that wide view of methodizing existence which we have been speaking of above with regard to other matters. It is easier to amuse children as occasion offers, or to deny them all amusement for a time, than to consider the present with relation to the distant future, and to exercise a wise forethought in cultivating to the utmost all those means of real enjoyment which will influence the happiness of years.

I believe that while one class of persons live for pleasure and another are earnestly bent on duty, few perhaps sufficiently consider happiness, and therefore pass it over too lightly in education. Men may perhaps wring theirs from fate, by the strong arm, and the stout heart, and the dauntless will; but women must win theirs by the power of a cheerful, hopeful spirit; knowing they will have more to *bear* than to do; they must have the art of making the means that are thrust upon them minister to their own purposes. When moralists overlook this great question, or treat it with half contempt, they surely forget that happiness is the object of an imperative craving of our nature. When the latter is yet in its young, unbroken strength, it not only seeks for happiness as for any of the indispensable means of existence, but expects it as its birth-right. And when the strength has broken down under the burden of life; when, often deceived, we first refuse to listen to Hope, and then grieve that the voice of the charmer haunts our day-dream no more; when we know how

14

vain it were to expect the twilight to bring the brightness noontide failed
to pour, or

> From the dregs of life think to receive
> What the first sprightly runnings could not give ;—

even in that season of disenchantment, we would rather believe that
it is our own individual fate that has been hard, and that we have been
singled out to be exiled from our inheritance, than admit the dreary belief
that no inheritance of happiness is destined for man. And we only give
it up on earth to cling more earnestly to the hopes of heaven.

If such be the feeling that nature prompts, how can we venture to
overlook it in education which pretends to be the preparation for life.
How can we venture to reason it down in the name of theology or philosophy, or any other system that sets up man's standard against the voice
speaking in his own heart? Many things make happiness unavoidably
difficult of attainment. God gave the craving for it,—but He did not so
frame this world as to ensure the gratification of that craving. This is
one part only of a dark and inscrutable mystery that points eternally to
another life for its solution ; but it does not alter our duty of caring for
the happiness of others, any more than it can alter our own deep thirst
for it. That duty is paramount towards the young who are in our power,
and who may be guided on the right path to find and to bestow this
inestimable boon, or, at least, to feel that they have not wantonly cast it
away. For scanty as the measure is that the majority of men can attain,
who has not felt with sadness how much that reckless waste has lessened
it? not the waste merely caused by vice or direct evil, but by ignorance
or heedlessness of good,—by not knowing how to make the most of what
is in our power, and not respecting that which is or might be a means of
happiness to others.

Education can do much towards remedying these deficiencies. It can
cultivate a cheerful spirit, which shall look out for the means of happiness
and cherish them. It can inspire the feeling that to waste those means
whether for ourselves or others, to spread gloom when we might have
shed light, to rob a heart of one joy we might have bestowed, is a wrong
it may never be in our power to repair. Education* can mould the
associations of young and pliant minds so that their notions and desires
shall be centred on worthy objects. It can so frame their views of life
that their happiness shall depend on the health of the spiritual being,—on

---

* See Chap. iii. p. 61.

what speaks to heart and mind, and not on the supply of artificial wants or material gratifications; that it shall be as far as possible dependent on self-exertion, and consequently be left as little as our earthly condition will allow at the mercy of circumstances.

I have had occasion already to speak of cheerfulness as one of the most valuable qualities we can cultivate in the young; and in the same chapter I have spoken also at some length of the cultivation of that unselfish spirit of activity which seeks out means of usefulness. Both these bear strongly upon the present question. The sense of communion with our fellow-creatures, our social *solidarité*,—to borrow a word for which we have no exact equivalent,—should be strongly impressed on the young. They must feel that no human being can venture to believe himself isolated; that consciously or unconsciously, actively or negatively, we still affect and influence those around us, as we are influenced and affected by them. Our own peace, or comfort, or enjoyment seldom, if ever, come to be considered alone; those of others are more or less involved in the question. We may easily depress or disturb them,—perhaps we may rarely, if ever, be able to give happiness. This conviction of the too common power-lessness of mortal hands to bestow that precious gift, though sad, is a wholesome feeling even for the young, from whom, in general, we would desire to remove all sadness. Who would dare to be reckless in disturbing real enjoyment, in breaking the hush of heartfelt peace, in pouring the gloom of discontent or caprice over sunny hours, in severing the happy intercourse of congenial minds, if they were accustomed to reflect how impossible it is for them to recall the sunshine, how vain the wish to restore the blessings it was so easy to dispel? Or if we dread infusing this taint of sadness into the youthful heart, let us show them, how to have the power of giving happiness is to stand in a position akin to the godlike, and that all we can conceive of the office of guardian angels is to avert suffering, and shield the frail growth of mortal bliss from chill and blight.

It is a trite saying that 'pleasure is not happiness;' but until we live as if we believed in the truism, it is not vain to repeat it. In urging the duty of making youth happy, I consider that an important part of any endeavour we can make towards securing that object, is to enforce the truth of this maxim till the conviction is deeply rooted. Our affections, our spiritual wants and aspirations, are the enduring part of our nature, and to provide for happiness we must provide for that which is lasting. It is not necessary here to enter into the comparison between the

14—2

strength of those wants, and the cravings of physical necessities.   The latter are conditions of *existence*, not of *happiness :* and we daily see how habit triumphs over privations which do not threaten life ; and in the midst of what, to the affluent, seems misery, the human heart seeks and finds happiness when its affections are gratified.   But this fact teaches at least an important lesson to those who have the charge of forming the habits and associations of the young.   They may see there how much it is within their power to place the view of happiness beyond the reach of Fortune, and how every endeavour to preserve to the young their spiritual freedom, unshackled by the chains of artificial wants, which luxurious habits alone convert into necessities, increases their chances of happiness. Every new spiritual aspiration, every want of the soul craving for know-ledge, and truth, and goodness, and affection, is an expansion of the nature, a lifting up of its capacities to seize and enjoy new treasures, and, so far, a direct increase of the means of happiness; but every new want of the body, every habit by which luxury first becomes mere comfort, and ends with being necessary, is a chain tethering us down within a narrower circle of enjoyment, and lessening our capacity for the happiness we might reach.

It is certainly in the power of education to influence the tone of mind in these respects.   No one, it is true, will *say* that luxury is happiness, any more than they would make the same assertion concerning pleasure; but if we look at society, we see how fearfully the influence of both plea-sure and luxury tells against real, elevated views of happiness.   When we see money considerations deciding questions in which all that makes life worth caring for are involved, we may well desire to educate our children to simpler and truer tastes and views.   When we see the influence of amusements over persons whose leisure and wealth leave their time at their own disposal,—when, for instance, we see field sports, racing, and yachting engrossing the lives of men, and when women, emulating the frivolity of the other sex, make a serious business of dress and dissipation, which have not even the excuse of being favourable to health, we may well feel that education has neglected her mission of fitting human beings to seek and enjoy rational happiness.

It is not fair to suppose that girls brought up in seclusion, with the constant prospect of freedom to amuse themselves when their ‘ *education is finished*,’ and then suddenly launched into the gay world, will practise moderation and discern the true from the false forms of happiness.   Their capacity for the latter must be trained slowly and gradually ; it must be the work of years, steadily but unostentatiously creating a different standard of what the heart can desire,—the mind strive to obtain. It is a work not of teaching, but of influence. I believe parents often fail to influence their children because they do not unveil their own minds with sufficient candour before them. They talk *to* them, perhaps, a good deal, on many matters which they think suited to their capacity; but they do not talk freely enough *before* them, so as to let the full influence of their feelings and knowledge, and of that compound of both, the whole tone of thought and opinion, tell upon those young minds, thirsting as they are for impressions. Where this is done, and when children are accustomed to express freely their own feelings, and doubts, and difficulties, there is little need of set discourses by which the stronger minds are to sway the weaker.

We have now glanced at a variety of subjects, occupations, home and social duties, expenditure, amusements, views of happiness, which all require to be brought under the control of a presiding spirit of method. We have seen that it is at the period when parents are beginning to relax their authority, that this systematic regulation of life should be strongly enforced as the basis of self-guidance. The method of our lives must be complete in all its parts and proportions, as far as our endeavours can make it so. At no one point must the rational being be uncertain in his aims, however he may fall short in his attainment of them. He may be baffled by the storm, but never can be as the froth on the waves, or the leaf tossed by the breeze. When this conviction is deeply rooted in the young mind, we may trust that we have kindled a spirit which in some sense will deserve to be called the guardian angel of existence; for it is not too much to say that more than half the follies and vices of the upper classes of society would be starved out of the world, and with them consequently the suffering they entail, if the value of time and a sense of accountability for its use were earnestly felt, and practically influenced conduct.

It is as tending to impress on the young mind a sense of the responsibilities of life, and of the solemn duty to each of us of acting resolutely up to the highest notions of right our reason and conscience approve, that the ceremony of Confirmation,—or of the First Communion, in churches that do not adopt Confirmation—appears to me to be highly valuable. In adherence to the rule I have laid down regarding religious subjects, I shall say nothing of it as a mere ritual observance or as embodying dogmas, but it has a high moral meaning apart from those considerations.

It is the solemn close of childhood, with its irresponsible subjection,—and the opening of the portals of real life, with its accountability, its self-guidance, its self-discipline. The young creature on the threshold of active existence promises before God and man to do henceforth for himself what hitherto has been done for him. Henceforth childish faults and thoughtlessness must be set aside for the earnest purpose of the moral and rational being who has vowed his existence to the service of God, to the cause of truth and virtue, 'in that state of life in which it has pleased God to call him.'

The baptism of infants, whether or no an institution of the primitive church, and whatever the different views held respecting it, is a very touching ceremony. It is one of those occasions that are but too rare, when men are made to feel a tie beyond earthly ties, which links together all who worship the same God, acknowledge the same standard of duty, and live in the same hope of immortality. Round a cradle, as round a grave, we feel this tie pressing on our hearts. This brotherhood so bound together, opens its arms to receive the unconscious infant who is destined to share the same perils, the same toils, the same everlasting hopes. But if this be a touching ceremony, that of the solemn admission of the adult into the congregation of Christians is more touching and impressive still. There they stand in all the fresh purity and vigour of their youth; the past all fair to most, or but chequered with quick forgotten sorrows,—the future full of light and promise; and ere the curtain drops upon that childish past, ere they spring forward to meet that future to their eyes so bright, to ours so full of peril, they pause to consecrate themselves, their bodies and souls, to a holy purpose, by renewing the vow made for them in their infancy; to promise to eschew evil and follow good, to seek truth and obey it, to study the will of God and make it the rule of their lives. Such is the purport of the vow, and such the solemn time for making it; and I believe that early education cannot be closed in a manner more likely to impress its highest lessons firmly upon the young mind.

CHAPTER VII.

STUDIES AND GENERAL MANAGEMENT FROM SIXTEEN TO EIGHTEEN YEARS OF AGE.

§ 1.—At sixteen, it is not too much to require six hours a day of real work,—music, which should now be optional and depending on the pupil's own taste, being a thing apart. The amount of study, however, must always be regulated by the state of health ; no other objects can be allowed to overrule that consideration. I shall presently give the reasons which make it difficult to draw up a programme of the day's occupations; but taking a general view we may distribute the twelve hours now at our disposal, between rising at six in the morning and dressing for tea or dinner at six in the evening, as follows:—Six hours for study—half-an-hour each for dressing in the morning, breakfast, and luncheon,—leaving four hours and a half for exercise and any chosen recreation or pursuit, such as music or drawing. The shorter the time that girls can be accustomed to give to their toilet, the better on every account. No school allows more than half-an-hour, and that appears to me as much as any active young person can require for bathing and dressing in the morning. The dawdling that is so common in these matters is injurious in every respect. It is a habit of slow movement where quickness is just as easy and effectual, and it moreover encourages that lingering over personal effect which is only too likely to become a habit at that age. Perfect neatness, cleanliness, and independence of all assistance, are the points to be insisted on from childhood. At the age we are now speaking of some attention to fashion is unavoidable, but must not encroach upon good habits. With a little trouble for a day or two, a new or more elaborate style of *coiffure* will be executed quickly and without help, and the additional time required for learning the art may be gained by leaving the drawing-room half-an-hour earlier in the evening,—certainly not by dawdling over the looking-glass in the precious morning hours. These seem very trifling details to dwell upon ; but when we see the time spent on dressing, three, and not seldom four times in the day, and the dependence on servants which diminishes the pleasure and increases the cost of every absence from home, it is not unworthy of a work on education to enter into these points. The constant habit of waiting on oneself will often give a positive dislike to receiving help; and we may venture to hope that a more rational style of dress will, in time, make women as independent in this respect as men now are. The fine gentleman was quite as helpless seventy or eighty years ago, perhaps even later, as ladies in our day; we may hope that the latter will in their turn grow ashamed of this prolonged state of childhood. Attention to dress and expenditure on dress are both increased by girls having a maid to attend upon them, and perpetually to remind them of what in her estimation is naturally the one important thing in life. This consideration alone seems to me sufficient to decide the question.

With regard to the distribution of the day, I would only remark that there should on no account be more than four hours of consecutive study, and this time never to be given undivided to one subject. The time for study and for exercise must be regulated according to circumstances; but it would seem best to give the morning to the former, so as to reserve the afternoon free, and thus guard against the possible irregularity caused by the interruptions of society, which I must suppose will become more frequent at this age. A mother will naturally wish to have her daughter with her in her walks or visits, or to let her enjoy the society of friends who may be staying in the house; or she may wish her to ride or walk with her father, and school-room hours could not always be attended to. As far as possible, therefore, I would leave the afternoon free, as it is very desirable at this time to fall into the sort of habits which it will be most easy to adhere to when the quiet school-room life is at an end.

It is certainly to be wished that girls of sixteen should dine at table whether there be company or not. The complete seclusion of a school-room has many disadvantages : it forms a dangerous association between the anticipation of enjoyment and the cessation of study; and it occasions much of that shyness and awkwardness of manner so common in England. I may perhaps be told that these uncomfortable symptoms are more rare in the present day, and certainly the perfect assurance of which we see not a few specimens, might almost make one regret the absence of shyness. If we were forced to choose between a timid, retiring girl, fearful of doing wrong or of being ridiculous at every turn, and a self-confident woman of the world at eighteen, to whom nothing seems new, nothing either alarming or admirable, with little of youth except its ignorance, we could hardly hesitate to prefer the former. But I cannot believe that any such melancholy result would follow from a rational education. Both extremes mark a defect of early training : the one springs from moral or intellectual shallowness, perhaps both; the other in great measure from want of early familiarity with the forms of society.

There lurks, however, in shyness, also some degree of moral weakness; there is too constant a habit of self-contemplation in shy persons; they go into society without that genial spirit which simply seeks to give and receive pleasure, and are occupied with the effect they produce, instead of attending to others. Shyness is commonly the fault of languid and unsympathetic persons; the lively and imaginative, if occasionally afflicted with it, may bring their *mauvaise honte*—as the French so aptly term it—to the door; but once within it, they are too easily roused, they too easily catch the tone and interest of what is going on, to remember themselves or their fancied deficiencies any more. Apart from real shyness, however, there is a degree of nervousness at being called upon to do anything unusual,—to tell a story, for instance, or sing before company,—which has no connection with any mental qualities, and which habit alone will lessen. Persons with this feeling dread attracting particular attention, but the ordinary forms of society, which are formidable to the really shy, are too insignificant and habitual to awaken any emotion. Timidity to this extent is not necessarily suffering, but shyness is, and to a high degree; I would, therefore, take every precaution to save a young girl from it, and to let her come into society able to enjoy conversation, and to take such a part in it as befits her age.

The plan of studies I should propose for these two years will differ essentially from that of the former period. Science and mathematics, which together took up two-thirds of the time then, will now be reduced to narrow limits, rather with a view to keeping our ground than to making much progress. The study of style and composition, which occupied the other third, will give way to a new class of reading; while history, which had been laid aside, will now be resumed.

The first tendency of the young, as they acquire some little knowledge and begin to join in conversation, is towards precipitancy in forming opinions; they are in a hurry to 'make up their bundle;' they are afraid of appearing ignorant if they have not a settled view upon whatever comes before them. It is the man of mature thought and knowledge who ventures to say not only 'I do not know,' but 'I *cannot* know.' Education must then, at the period now under consideration, direct its chief efforts towards counteracting this tendency, towards teaching the nature of sound opinions, and the method of forming them.

This method requires a combination of intellectual and moral qualities; not only knowledge, sound judgment, and accurate reasoning, but also freedom from prejudice, a simple desire to know the truth, and to decide accordingly. Now is the time to enforce upon the pupil, what a careful education will throughout have held up as a principle, even before the young mind was fully capable of appreciating it,—namely, that love of truth should be the ruling, as it will be our most lasting motive for seeking knowledge. Mere information may gratify curiosity, or may become a means of advancement to the ambitious, or a refuge against time to the idle; but the earnest desire to know *what is true*, alone leads to that knowledge which satisfies the mind of man and enlarges its power. Real knowledge is truth,—truth certain or probable, truth of fact, or truth of principles or laws; truth demonstrated, or within the possibility of demonstration; or truth which cannot be demonstrated, but which comes home to our hearts with such an irresistible conviction, that we feel the principles on which it rests belong to a higher region than that within which the ordinary powers of the understanding are exercised. As truth in word and action is the life of life in morals, so is love of truth, mentally considered, the informing spirit of our intellectual existence. And just as perfect integrity demands the sacrifice of all private and selfish considerations that might warp the judgment and bias action, so love of intellectual truth requires the expulsion of every prejudice, of every motive that tends to sway the mind from the one object of ascertaining what is true. Our *power of discovering truth* must depend on the extent of our knowledge and the vigour of our faculties; but *sincerity* in our *love* and search for truth is subject to no such conditions; it may be possessed by all, and so far as it is possessed, our opinions will have some essential characters of soundness, for they will be the genuine product of our own minds, of our own reason working upon the knowledge it was able to compass. There will be in them neither conceit, nor pretension, nor party spirit. Many a false opinion may lurk undetected or be held in ignorance, but they will only await a ray of better knowledge to be abandoned without hesitation.

When real love of truth is the governing principle with parents or teachers, it will exercise a strong influence over the whole process of forming the young mind. The habitual accuracy, the careful discrimination, the dispassionate examination of any subject on which an expression of opinion was necessary, the tolerance for opposite views, and candid admission of doubt and ignorance in the elder mind, will have wrought almost unconsciously into the younger the conviction that a different mode of judging is unworthy either of an upright or a reasoning being. The natural precipitancy of youth, the unreasoning prepossessions or quickness to attach moral censure to opinions which appear erroneous, will have been repeatedly shamed by contrast with the different views expressed and acted upon by those who are held in highest reverence. Even before they are capable of accurate reasoning themselves, children brought up under such influence will have learnt what is the basis on which better instructed minds form opinions, and they will not dignify with that name their own crude notions or prejudices. We shall find few precocious politicians or theologians among such children; but the last and crowning labour of education will have been rendered an easy task.

Throughout the studies of the last two years many opportunities will have occurred to exercise the pupil in the right method of judging on any subject brought under consideration,—to explain the nature and value of evidence, and the care necessary in drawing inferences. Scientific reading is especially valuable in exhibiting frequent examples of the manner in which some of the finest minds have proceeded in this important operation. Moral training previous to this time has also called judgment into action, and the mind at the age we are speaking of has attained that degree of development when, rightly or wrongly, it will begin to work for itself. Now, then, it is time that it should gain a clear view of the principles on which it ought to act, and should know exactly what are the lines of demarcation between opinion, and maxims received from authority; between views influenced by feeling or association, and convictions that satisfy the understanding.

Foremost among the lessons to be inculcated is the folly of attributing moral merit or demerit to opinions.* The person holding or rejecting them may deserve praise or blame, but this will be for the purity or the corruption of their motives, for their diligence in seeking, or their indolence in neglecting to seek, evidence of the truth; these are grounds on which to pass a moral judgment, though we rarely have that knowledge of another's heart which entitles us to do so; but the opinion itself, a conclusion of the understanding, never can come under that judgment. The reason may have erred, knowledge may have been wanting, the inferences may be utterly inconclusive; but no such operations include an act of the will, and therefore are not amenable to the moral sense. We do not

---

See for a more full discussion of these points, *Thoughts on Self-Culture.* Second edition, chap. v. sect. 3.

think so or so, because we *choose* or because we *wish* it, but because *we cannot help it ;* because to our perception the balance of truth is on that side, and not on any other. The reason may be obscured by ignorance or prejudiced feeling, but once cleared of those obstructions, it can no more be influenced by the will to perceive truth in a certain direction than the body can be made to feel heat or cold unless placed under the right conditions for receiving those impressions, in which case it cannot refuse to feel them. Again I repeat, the one moral condition is sincerity of purpose; and concerning this we can always be rigid in self-scrutiny, but can seldom venture to pronounce judgment upon another. Unless this principle be firmly rooted in the mind, we shall neither judge fairly of the opinions of others, nor be ourselves in that calm condition so requisite for the impartial formation of our own.

In the next place, the young must learn what are the degrees of knowledge necessary for forming opinion. We do not say we have an *opinion* concerning geometrical propositions, for we see their truth completely and beyond dispute, if our understanding is able to apprehend the conditions of the proof; but on other subjects we feel that we are far from that simple and single impression of absolute certainty. Sometimes, as in a law of nature, we know the truth of the facts to have been proved ; but the process was long and difficult, and the evidence such as we are ourselves incapable of appreciating. Again, on some subjects that touch us most nearly, as in religious or metaphysical speculation, we never can attain proof at all; the evidence is of every different degree of probability, and of such a nature that different minds receive different impressions of it, according to their various habits and associations, knowledge and modes of thought. The difference, then, between truth which admits of proof, and that which rests on probability, must be carefully explained; for if there be any confusion on this point, there is necessarily confusion in our mode of viewing the subjects, in our attempts to reason upon them, and in our expectations of the result. If we expect *certainty* either in ourselves or others, when we are only able to attain *probability*, we shall be miserable in the consciousness of our own failure, and unjust in our condemnation of the failure of others.

A want of fairly estimating the value of probability is the source at once of much intolerance and of much painful scepticism. Some persons are not aware that their most cherished convictions rest on this ground of probability only, and have no right, therefore, to be received as proved conclusions; and these are the intolerant. Others are quite aware of the ground, on which opinions rest, but they under-estimate that ground, and do not therefore give to the opinions the weight they deserve; they forget that in every important action of their lives they decide upon probability, and would think it madness to remain vacillating until the points on which they have to determine could be absolutely proved. Again, when they reject an opinion or doctrine because it cannot be proved, because it belongs to that class of subjects on which the human mind is incapable of attaining certainty, they forget that by that act of absolute rejection they are proceeding as if they had attained it. They overlook the fact that the negative side does not admit of proof any more than the affirmative. These persons form that most offensive class, dogmatic scep- tics. Truth there is,—clear, undoubted truth,—on one side or the other, but we are not able to discern it. Probabilities, however, we can trace and weigh, and if we are content to give them due weight, we can form a judgment, subject indeed to error, and which we must always remember is so subject, but such as will save the mind from the restlessness of an ever-renewed, ever-unsatisfied search, and from the suffering of extreme scepticism.

Truly does it behove parents to shield their children now against that form of suffering. Both those who deprecate and those who hail the spread of free enquiry into every region of knowledge and speculation, must agree that the time is gone by when enquiry could be arrested or evaded. The young of the present generation must be ready to ' give a reason for the faith that is in them;' they must know *why* as well as *what* they believe; they must be prepared to see the conflict of opinions without losing the balance of their own minds; to know that points which hitherto the scoffer alone has ventured to attack, will be examined and sifted and called in question now, by men as earnest as those who uphold the other side; while their only chance of mental peace is in knowing the real grounds of their own opinions, and in the determination to abide by the truth as far as they are able to discern it, without judging their fellow- creatures. More often than we think, perhaps, a lurking consciousness of the unsoundness of opinions, or of the real uncertainty of the grounds on which they were formed, is the cause of the fiercest blustering against those who venture to think differently. When we are quite sure that our assertions are true, and that their truth ought to be evident to others, or when we are certain that we have done our best, and know that others can only do the same, we can afford to be calm and tolerant in discussion. Impatience or fear of doubt creates irritation against those who assume to

222 INTELLECTUAL EDUCATION.

have escaped from the condition that torments ourselves; and then passion, not reason, takes the lead.

It is essential also that the young mind should be led to distinguish some important differences between truths which are alike incapable of demonstration. Some—such as most of the great metaphysical questions that have divided men in all ages,—belong entirely to the region of speculation. An impenetrable veil hides the truth on such questions from minds hemmed in by mortal sense. So much mystery in what touches us so nearly, brings to the heart an irresistible conviction that we yet *shall be* satisfied, that a period of light and knowledge will succeed this probation time of darkness and ignorance; but except for the consolation of this belief to those who are able to receive it, generation after generation, age after age, have asked these mighty questions in vain.

There is, however, another class of truths, which, although not based on demonstration, admit of positive conclusions in practice. These are moral questions which lead to action, and come under the dominion of conscience. We rarely, perhaps, enter speculatively into these questions, and if we did so might often come to wrong conclusions; but we know what, according to our means of judging, our own conscience pronounces to be right or wrong. If we err, it is our knowledge that is at fault, our knowledge of the circumstances or conditions of the case, not any speculation upon the grounds of the moral question involved in them. We do not go wrong because we do not know whether truth or mercy are virtues or not, but because we have not been able to discern what was the particular exercise of mercy or of truth that was called for in that instance.

Nor, fortunately, is this element of certainty in such important questions left to individual judgment alone. On these points the immense variety of human minds exhibit a general similarity of feeling which does not exist upon merely speculative questions. The great principles of morals appeal with almost equal force to the hearts and conscience of mankind generally, however much the influence of passion may stifle that appeal for a time. Men commit crime indeed, but they will not assert that to inflict an injury is right in itself. They will continue in a long course of injustice, cruelty, or ingratitude, while some will strive to show how, in that particular case, circumstances extenuate the evil; others, again, plead the violence of the passion that blinded them for a time; and a few may glory in their vices and boast of their contempt for virtue;— but even these will not deliberately attempt to prove that ingratitude, injustice, and cruelty are not wrong, are not violations of some law written in deeper characters than the legislator's code. Accordingly, we hear the thief complain of dishonesty among his comrades, and tyrants reproach their minions for selfishness. So convinced are we of truths of this nature, that we do not hesitate to doubt the sanity of the man who, without strong misleading motives, acts in violation of them; we conclude that his understanding must be either blinded by passion, or infirm by nature, if he does not acknowledge the ordinary distinctions between right and wrong action, recognised in the social world of which he is a member.

Some things there are which the bulk of mankind hold as truths, which rest on intuitive convictions that the understanding cannot reach to establish or deny. Setting aside the question of a revelation which must be established on other grounds, it is upon such convictions that we accept the belief in immortality, and certain other points beyond the domain of experience or strict reasoning. Beyond these again there is the wide range of truths to which I have already alluded in speaking of the value of probability, principles in great measure deduced from a few fundamental convictions, but liable to error in proportion to the complexity of the subject, as in social and political questions, or to the uncertainty arising from imperfect knowledge and ill-disciplined reasoning power.

When practical points involving right and wrong action become difficult to decide, it is because they are partly mixed with speculative doctrines,—as, for instance, in the questions above alluded to,—and then they are liable to error from the same sources. That is, the judgment is perplexed by complex relations, by the variety of conflicting or seemingly conflicting interests, and by the extent of knowledge and experience required to be capable of coming to a sound conclusion; while the difficulty is greatly increased in the majority of cases by want of the habit of weighing evidence, and also in questions that touch human life by allowing the feelings to disturb the operations of the reason.

When the young mind has been thoroughly impressed with the nature and extent of the difficulties in forming opinions, and of the value of probability as our only guide in so many momentous questions, it is time to inculcate a sad, perhaps, but necessary lesson, namely, acquiescence in doubt as the inevitable condition of our earthly existence. All that has gone before has led to this conclusion; now it must be brought forward in plain, unvarnished guise, till the mind learns to contemplate it without dismay. We may make to ourselves if we please a panoply of prejudices, and say we are satisfied and certain, but we cannot, even when we wish it, be always proof against reason; and once let our artificial defence be overthrown, we are cast into a sea of perplexities, and rendered miserable because we have lost the certainty we had deemed a virtue. There is but one true refuge. We must learn to bear doubt, that our own ignorance may not impose upon us ; we must learn to bear doubt in order to exclude despair.

A desperate determination to escape from doubt is but too common,— and naturally most so with the young, who are terrified at their own boldness in doubting when they have been led to fancy that all besides themselves see clearly and rest in certainty. But this rash impulse of a suffering mind that has been cramped in the use of its reason leads to more extreme views, violent changes, intolerance, and mental anguish, than those who have the charge of the young are apparently willing to believe; since there are few points more neglected in education. Parents impose opinions, discussion is pronounced irreverent, doubt an indication of moral evil, yet the doubt *will* perhaps intrude; the young then feel under a sense of reprobation, they bear the anguish in silence because they dare not expect help or sympathy, and the struggle is but too likely to end either in abject superstition under the shelter of an infallible church ; or in utter scepticism, bearing away perhaps at the same time the practical principles of morals which had been rooted only in the weak ground of speculative belief.

How often this has been the case with young men carefully nurtured upon the Church Catechism and Thirty-nine Articles, we need not pause to inquire. Hitherto parents may have thought that their daughters were safe from such dangers; but, as I said above, they can indulge that flattering idea no more. Even were not sceptical opinions making themselves loudly heard on all sides in England, the literature of other countries would bring them before us. In history, in philosophical speculation, in the very pages of fiction, we find them ; if then women are to read at all, they must be prepared to see a diversity of opinion upon every subject that cannot be brought to the test of demonstration or experience. A wild confusion of views may exist with regard to practical points also, as we see in the political speculations and in the light literature that touches upon social and domestic duties, especially in countries where opinions and institutions are less settled than in our own. Unfortunate, however, as this undoubtedly is, experience will recall men from any serious error of this kind. The suffering and disorganization following from any false views of action, brings us back again to agreement upon practical principles. To attempt to educate girls in ignorance that such diversities of speculative opinion exist, or to persuade them that they exist only among the careless or the unprincipled, is a fruitless and absurd attempt to work good by evil means; to root what we believe to be truth, in what we ought to know is a falsehood.

Borrowed opinions,—that is, opinions received on the authority of others,—we all of us, within different degrees, must hold; and in youth nothing can be more legitimate, or more fitting the modesty of ignorance, than to rest satisfied with that foundation even on most important subjects. But what is essential to a right state of mind is, that the young should never forget that such is the foundation; that they cannot call such opinions really *their own*, since their own reason has never examined whether they are true or not, and that they must always in candour be ready to avow that they have accepted them on the warrant of knowledge and capacity they feel to be superior to their own ; whence it follows that they are utterly unfit to pronounce any judgment on the different conclusions to which others may have been led by the exercise of their own understanding. Wherever there is the pretension of original thought, when a bold assertion is made of opinions we know to be borrowed, and, above all, when the slightest blame of others for difference of opinion is uttered or implied, then the teacher cannot be too severe in exposing the unstable ground on which this dogmatism is reared. She cannot point out too strongly how contemptibly feeble is the attempt to oppose as error what we have not examined,—what we cannot even be sure, therefore, that we are able to understand,—while we do not even know the real grounds of that which we would set up in opposition.

Parents naturally desire that their children should embrace their opinions; and I believe perfect candour will also be the best means of attaining that object. The young would spontaneously expose all their difficulties, lay bare their mental as they would their bodily discomfort, if they felt sure of the same sympathy in the one case as in the other ; if their speculations, or their enthusiasm, or their mistaken, ignorant views had never from the dawn of intelligence known the chilling rebuff of a laugh, or a sneer, a shocked look, or an authoritative word putting down discussion. Parents have little opposition to dread, when they have themselves drawn out and fostered their children's powers of mind, instead, as is more commonly the case, of merely witnessing their development, standing on the defensive against any inconvenient display of them. When their own care has prepared the way, there is little fear of their guidance being rejected. The young are glad to shake off mere authority, but their

15

self-confidence is really of very slender growth; they want to walk alone, for they instinctively feel that the dignity of the rational being is in self-dependence; but they gladly seek the help of those who will teach them *how* to walk alone; they are easily amenable to the influence which they know is working in the same direction towards which their own desires tend. If, then, parents are content never to check discussion unless it arises from love of paradox, they will find their superior knowledge and power of reasoning have its full weight. When obliged to give a check on that account, the reason should be simply stated. ' It is useless to argue that point,' a mother may say, ' because you are not in earnest just now; that mode of bringing forward extreme views is adopted by many feeble-minded people for the sake of startling others, and they do so for a time till it is found out that such is their custom, and then no one attends to what they may say,' &c. &c. Such a reproof, accompanied with the perfect conviction in the young mind that sincere endeavours to get at truth, however wild or mistaken, will be met with patient sympathy, will not fail to check the spirit of mere paradox or love of opposition. Indeed the latter dies away from want of food when the parent's desire is clearly felt to be that their children should learn to distinguish truth, not simply learn to assert that certain opinions are true. If parents would but remember what a fund of clinging, affectionate trust there is in the young mind, they would not so often destroy it or fling it away to strangers by the exercise of authority, or the deadly influence of ridicule.

With regard to books that may give some assistance at this period, Bailey *On the Formation and Publication of Opinions* will be found very useful; it sets some of the points we have been considering in a very clear and simple light.* Sir James Mackintosh's *Essay on Ethical Philosophy* might also be read. There the young student will see the different theories of morals, and of the origin of moral sentiments, that have been held by the best thinkers. The most important thing to be learnt from this survey will be knowledge of the limits within which earnest doubt and discussion upon such points have ranged, and the nature of the evidence, and of the reasoning on which the conclusions rest. The teacher must judge how far her pupil is fit at seventeen to read the whole of a work of this kind, or whether it is better to give instruction based on

---

* Sir Cornewall Lewis's *Essay on the Influence of Authority in Matters of Opinion* is also valuable. In some respects it may even be preferred to Bailey's, owing to the lucidity of the style and the numerous illustrations, calculated to produce greater effect on the young mind.

some portions of it, or to select parts to be read. Those referring to Butler's sermons, to Paley, and the examination of the utilitarian theory of Bentham and his followers, will perhaps be the most valuable to study.

When the mind has no natural bent towards speculation, and therefore that there is little danger of disturbance or suffering from doubt and fluctuating opinions, it is unwise to force this kind of reading. It is enough, then, if we destroy the foundations of intolerance by clearly teaching the difference between the moral and intellectual preparation needed to investigate truth; the perfect honesty of intention which all can secure for themselves, and none can judge of in another; and the sound knowledge without which accurate reasoning is impossible. Let us be careful to leave the timid mind to the trust which gives it strength, the practical mind to its devotion to that which it can grasp and understand; we have done enough if we make it impossible that they should fancy that their indifference or their submissive trust can be a rule whereby to condemn bolder or less happy minds.

Apart from the difficulties which arise from the very nature of many subjects of speculation, we have also to contend with the difficulties of language. In mathematics, axioms and definitions allow no room for confusion; in physical science, terms may be, and generally are, rigorously defined; but in moral and social questions we are liable to the confusion of ignorance and the confusion of sophistry—to the erroneous impressions given by a bad style, and to fallacies of reasoning cloaked by the ambiguities of words; and thence the necessity of guarding ourselves by a careful study of language, and of the logical method of language, against ceaseless contention and error. It is only by a frequent examination of the terms we use ourselves that we guard even against self-deception. None of us perhaps are aware to what extent our use of language is unconsciously swayed by a host of associations, the gathering of years, which have been woven into our minds, and have coloured our views, so that it becomes next to impossible to ascertain that even two persons apply exactly the same meaning to the same word.

Through this, to a certain degree, inevitable confusion, Logic is our surest guide. Supposing the utmost pains to have been taken to limit and define the terms, Logic teaches us the art of strict reasoning by means of words, as Geometry taught it by means of the relations of figure and space. It teaches us how to frame a correct argument, and thus how to detect a false one; how to place the members of a proposition so that a double meaning or any other ambiguity of expression shall be exposed by

15—2

the very form of the argument, and therefore rendered nugatory ; it shows us how incorrect inferences may be drawn from true premises, as likewise how a true inference may be drawn from unsound premises. There is a small work that will be found useful as an introduction to this study, namely, *Early Lessons in Reasoning* ; * its admirable clearness and felicitous illustration make it particularly apt for its purpose, and betray the master's hand in that unpretending form. Archbishop Whately's *Logic*, on which the former is founded, may be read afterwards ; the close attention required, and the necessity of frequent repetition, tend to work the subject thoroughly into the mind. The chapter on Fallacies should be studied with peculiar attention, as showing the source of much unconscious as well as intentional sophistry.

The short treatise on Rhetoric, also by Archbishop Whately, will very fitly follow. It will serve to connect in the young reader's mind these severe studies of language considered as the instrument of reasoning, with the lighter studies of the past year ; proving to her how intimate is the connexion between logical clearness and precision, and excellence of style.

This slight course of study of the art of reasoning may be followed up with advantage by reading Sir John Herschel's Discourse on the Study of Natural Philosophy. Here we have set forth the method by which the subject-matter of knowledge variously gathered must be arranged so as to facilitate and secure the right operation of the reason respecting it; the different modes of investigation by observation and experiment, and the slow and cautious steps by which accurate reasoning proceeds in the midst of difficulties or uncertainties. In a work of this kind, which draws its illustrations from such a wide range of knowledge, there may be many things that will not be immediately understood,—allusions and references made to many subjects of which the reader is ignorant; but, assuming that points of this kind will be noted down for enquiry and explanation, they need be no hindrance to reading a work so pregnant with valuable lessons. What we want is to learn the method of scientific investigation and reasoning, and these are set forth with a clearness and force equal to the author's thorough grasp of his subject. We want especially to learn them, because the same principles, although not precisely the same method, must be borne in mind when considering the subjects we daily and necessarily deal with. That is, although we cannot use experiment to ascertain truth in moral or social questions, nor obtain the same accurate

---

* Published by John W. Parker and Son.

observation, nor make the same analysis of phenomena, nor venture to generalize so boldly from ascertained facts, yet the principles are alike; the same caution is required, the same close reasoning, the same freedom from any motives apart from the wish to discern the truth, the same patience and accurate observation, the same constant recollection of what are the real conditions of proof, of what can warrant us in concluding the connexion of cause and effect between separate phenomena.

But more than this do we learn from this work of a real philosopher; we learn not merely by what methods, but in what spirit we may venture to approach the lofty regions of science; we find repeated that lesson which we cannot con too often,—that the value of knowledge is not alone to foster the pride, or the power, or the material enjoyments of man; but beyond all these, to feed the insatiable aspirations of his immortal soul.

Now, also, after the preparation afforded by the course indicated above, the time is come to introduce the young reader to the study of the evidences of Christianity. With some labour and attention, I believe Butler's *Analogy* might be profitably read; or Paley's *Horæ Paulinæ*, if the mind is yet ripe for following Butler's close argument and great condensation of thought. The history of the Bible is so important an element in the external evidences of Christianity, that it also requires to be carefully studied. Every day, new researches in history and philology are throwing new light upon the distant antiquity to which the Old Testament refers, as well as upon the-period of social disorganization and conflict in the midst of which the Christian Church was founded, and rose to power. The choice of works will here so much depend on the opinion of the parents and the section of Christians that they belong to, that I shall content myself with pointing out the importance of the subject. I am unacquainted with any work of real value upon what is more essential still,—namely, the moral evidences of Christianity. Perhaps when men have ceased to wrangle about words confessedly beyond all clear definition, about the dates and authority of Councils, about the particular epoch which is entitled to hand down its traditions as sacred, and that when they merge into the profane, about Churches claiming infallibility, and Churches acting as if they possessed it; when men have ceased from such contentions, they may have leisure to dwell upon the moral grandeur, the lofty spiritualism of Christianity; and to examine what means its prin‧ciples open or facilitate, for some higher purpose of social development and happiness than the dominion of one or another Church, of one or another settled form of doctrines relating to that unknown world to which we so earnestly look for the solution of all mystery, the lifting away the weary burden of ignorance and error and suffering.

The course of reading marked out above will require copious notes,—frequently, also, abstracts or summaries of opinions or theories. After what has been said before, it seems almost needless to repeat the caution about care and accuracy in making the notes, and frequent examination by the teacher of the extent to which the understanding has grasped and the memory retained the matter studied. This reading will accordingly occupy the largest share of time. Study of physical science may continue, either by taking up, according to the pupil's choice, one of the subjects before glanced at and reading some larger treatise upon it,—as, for instance, Herschel's *Astronomy*, or Lyell's *Elements of Geology*, or Mrs. Somerville's *Physical Geography*; or else by reading some general sketch of natural philosophy,—Whewell's *Bridgewater Treatise*, or Humboldt's *Aspects of Nature*. But we could not spare now more than one hour in the day to this branch of reading, and once in the week that hour should be given to keep up the slight knowledge of mathematics that has been acquired. It is possible that so decided a taste for mathematics or for some branch of science may manifest itself, as to make the pupil desirous to devote herself in great measure to that; but I conceive that this could not be done without injury. The course recommended above, which, as a part of mental discipline, is more essential than any accession of knowledge, will try the power of thought and attention considerably, and, together with the requisite notes, will not take up less than two hours daily throughout the two years under consideration. When we add to this the historical reading which we have presently to consider, and which having also an educational point in view, cannot be set aside, I think it would be unadvisable to admit of another close and arduous study.

The motives for adhering to the original plan can be explained to the young girl. Far from discouraging or slighting her own tastes, every wish of the kind should be warmly welcomed, and she should feel that the gratification of them is only delayed till a certain school-room course is over. She will then be free to follow the bent of her own mind, and, in the meantime, may feel assured that the studies which tend to enlarge and strengthen her general capacity, and to give her more ready power over the operations of her intellect, are increasing the facility with which she will hereafter follow any pursuit of her own. Thankful should the mother be when education has roused in her daughter some decided studious taste to the gratification of which she looks forward; she has thus discovered for her the armour she needs against that idleness which is sure to be her worst foe. One strong intellectual taste, one incentive to mental activity, and the young girl is rescued from more than half the perils that await her in the world.

With regard to historical reading, little more can be done during the time we have to dispose of, than to learn the proper method of studying history, to make some acquaintance with subjects which are essential to a comprehension of it, and to glance at the most important periods to which future study should be devoted. Should there be a taste for historical reading, the field is abundantly ample ; and it may be hoped that to a really cultivated mind the ease of reading narrative will not be, as it too often is, the principal inducement. History so considered is little more valuable than fiction, and it is not to provide a mere pastime that I have postponed historical reading till the mind was somewhat ripened by other studies.

All women will probably, at some period of their lives, be more or less engaged in the labour of education. With rare exceptions, this essential part of their natural vocation falls to their share directly or indirectly ; often, indeed, does it happen that the labour is only the more varied, and in some respects the more arduous, because she has no children of her own. It is this which gives so much importance in female education to the study of ethical, and partly also to purely metaphysical questions. In order to influence other minds, and especially to be enabled to draw out their powers for certain determinate purposes, we must know something of the nature of those powers, of the feelings and motives of action, and of the laws which regulate intellectual development. It is also with a view to this branch of female duty that the study of history is important. Debarred from large practical experience and knowledge of the world, it is, as I have had occasion to notice before, by this yet wider survey of human action that women must study the application of philosophical truths, and from the consideration of the principles, which have led on a large scale to happiness or misery, to success or failure, to the discovery of truth or the cherishing of error, that they must learn what are the principles, the aims, the convictions and motives, which the educator should nourish or condemn. I am aware that I am in part repeating what has been said before, but I am led to do so, because the great difficulty of persuading the world that women can have a serious and extensive view in their studies, is what keeps the latter at so low a standard, and makes women so listless about them. The soul cannot put forth her strength and fervour for what is the mere fashion of the day, what has no connexion with earnest life, and its interests; but let it be proved that such a connexion does exist, that it is intimate and strong, reaching to what is dear and sacred to all, and the apathy will vanish from every mind that has imagination enough to conceive a great purpose, and sufficient energy to work up to it.   Nor are such minds uncommon; I speak of no rare gifts of intellect, but only of such powers, moral and intellectual, as are daily wasted in the listless, objectless inactivity of woman's life, till at some call of duty they are often roused to noble exertion.

There is one subject of such immense importance in its bearing upon the study of history, and the intelligent comprehension of the political and social questions agitated under our own eyes, that it cannot be passed over :—I allude to political economy, some acquaintance with which must preface the regular course of historical reading.   In many respects even practically this subject is of great importance in female education. Women to whom the detail of charities is so constantly trusted, who sway expenditure through so many channels, who have so much influence over the ignorant both through domestic servants and the poor whom they visit in their own homes,—women are miserably unprovided for this wide circle of duties if they are ignorant of the principles of that science which deals with so large a portion of our social relations.   So likewise in reading history, this knowledge is requisite to give us the key to some of its most valuable lessons, while in their turn historical events afford the clearest illustrations of the principles of political economy.

I cannot pause here to argue with those who contend that women have no concern with politics, and therefore that an attempt to introduce such questions into their education is absurd.   I must be allowed to refer to what I have already said on that subject in a former work.*   It will be time to give a further answer to the objection when it shall have been proved that ignorance of all connected with political and social questions prevents women from exercising a mischievous influence on the public conduct of men.   It must, however, be admitted that in introducing either logic or political economy into an early educational course, we are forcing a somewhat premature consideration of wide and abstruse subjects.   But circumstances allow no choice.   At the age when young men are beginning these studies at college, girls are already in the world; some have even taken upon themselves the grave duties of life; at any rate, for all

---

* *Thoughts on Self-Culture,* p. 295, &c., second edition.

alike regular tuition is over. Once more, we must teach them early or not at all. We may, however, hope that the systematic education I have supposed girls to receive, the efforts made to draw out their powers of thought and reasoning, will have brought their minds to an earlier maturity than we could expect to find in boys who have had mere class-teaching in classics and mathematics.

In our slight study of physical science we were forced to restrict ourselves to the most elementary works, partly on account of the age and unexercised faculties of the pupil, but in still greater measure owing to the mass of other knowledge, often of a deep and abstruse nature, required to read the best works on those subjects; as, for instance, knowledge of mathematics, if we would read any large treatise on astronomy, of physiology if natural history be our object. But in political economy this difficulty does not exist. No wide range of knowledge is necessary to make the best treatises as intelligible to a careful reader as the most elementary sketch. And this is no small advantage; for wherever the works of great writers can be studied, we gain not only the pleasure of contemplating a subject in the light in which a man of genius has placed it, but we also, by that means, enlarge our acquaintance with literature of a high order.

In political economy we will then go boldly to the fountain-head at once, and read Adam Smith's *Wealth of Nations*. In no mere manual shall we find the principles of the science unfolded with the clearness, the power of illustration, and the thorough grasp of the subject that mark the work of the great master himself. The omissions or errors, or points only partially developed, that subsequent writers have corrected or exposed, will be of no consequence to us; on this, as on all other subjects educational studies have glanced over, a wide field for labour remains, if the young student should have the wish to return to it later; a conscientious study of this one great work is sufficient for the present.

We next come to consider the proper method of reading history itself. The early course our pupil has gone through has been some initiation into this art; she has learnt the value of geography as an accessory to history; and of chronology, not as giving the succession of dates merely, but far more as keeping before the mind the contemporaneous condition of different countries. Smyth's *Lectures on Modern History* will afford help for what remains to be learnt of the right method of historical study.

It is not that the actual course of reading suggested by Smyth should be followed; for, in general, the minuteness of research he recommends, and the books of difficult access which he marks as important to be read, make his scheme as a whole inapplicable, and in some respects undesirable for our purpose. The real value of his work to us is in the soundness and liberality of his political views, alien from all extremes, and the opinions given on books and writers which the young reader cannot form a judgment of herself. These lectures also afford admirable lessons in the mere art of reading, which, as I have before remarked, is less easy than is commonly imagined. The examples that he gives of inferences of wide import to be drawn from passages which appear at first sight to be of little moment,—the importance which he shows must sometimes be attached rather to the silence of an historian on some particular point, than to pages of narrative on which he has spent all the graces of style,—these are of real instruction to the inexperienced reader. She will see how true is that saying of Montaigne, quoted with reference to historical reading by Bolingbroke:—'I read in *Livy*,' he remarks, 'what another man does not, and Plutarch read there what I do not.'*

The field of historical reading is so wide, that with so little time as we now have before us, the great difficulty will be to choose the periods which it is most essential to dwell upon; and that mostly for the sake of an apprenticeship in historical study, leaving all else for future reading.

In our early course, Tytler's or Millot's *Universal Histories* were all that was read of ancient history. Every imaginative child will also, no doubt, have read Pope's *Homer* and Dryden's *Virgil* for her own pleasure; and if her taste for reading has been carefully directed, and her childhood was saved from stories of good little boys and girls, she will have read in like manner many of Plutarch's lives, and have had her favourites and her aversions among the heroes of Greece and Rome. If time presses much, this must suffice for the present, since modern history is more important as a lesson, and the future will afford ample leisure for making acquaintance with the great historians of antiquity, in translations at least if not in the originals, and for reading the works of real research which the labour of the moderns upon that ancient field has produced. If, however, we find that no such pressure of hurry exists, it would be well to take some rapid survey of ancient history before beginning the modern, which has been so incalculably influenced by the tone of thought and association inherited from antiquity.

The plan I would suggest in this case is to take as the text-book

* Bolingbroke, *Letters on History*, p. 32, ed. 1770.

Dr. Smith's *History of Greece**—a perfect model of an historical compendium—and as we come to the most interesting portions, whether as regards political events, or great men, or literature, then to refer to other books, such as biographies, portions of the ancient historians, and of the great writers both in prose and verse. For instance, besides reading the lives of some of the great leaders in Plutarch,† if these have not been read before, we may take the account of the Persian war in parts of 'the four last books of Herodotus, which will give us the interest of contemporary narrative. We gain the same advantage by reading the war against Syracuse, in the sixth and seventh books of Thucydides, and thus make acquaintance in some slight measure with the style and manner of the most *naïf* and of the most philosophical historian of antiquity. If time allows, and the pupil shows sufficient interest in the subject, portions of Xenophon's Retreat of the Ten Thousand might be read in his third, fourth, fifth, and sixth books; or this most romantic episode of military history may be read in Grote's admirable sketch from Xenophon, in the ninth volume of his *History of Greece*. With regard to other writers, although it may be yet more vain to read Plato than Homer in the feeble transcript of a modern language, yet, rather than remain altogether ignorant of what his genius bequeathed to all future generations, we must be content with translation, and make our pupil read at least the *Apology of Socrates*, the *Crito*, and the *Phædo*. The actual mode of thought will be better known thus than by any mere modern comment upon Plato's works, however eloquent. So with the great dramatists. When the chapter concerning them in the history has been read, turn to the translations of Æschylus and Sophocles, and read two or three of the great masterpieces of each.‡ No young reader with any touch of poetic feeling will lay down even a translation of the *Agamemnon* or the *Antigone*, without longing for the time when she may read more. This is the feeling which we should lose no opportunity of encouraging.

---

* *A History of Greece from the Earliest Times to the Roman Conquest.* By William Smith, LL.D., Editor of the *Dictionary of Greek and Roman Antiquities*, &c.

† Plutarch should, if possible, be read in the French translation of Amyot, since that work is highly prized for the purity and force of the old French language, before it was *smoothed down* by the writers of the seventeenth century. The translations of Herodotus and of Thucydides, in the *Classical Series* published by Bohn, are, I believe, as good as any we have, and are very cheap and accessible. Plato is also in the same series, but the French translation by Cousin is better than any we have in English.

‡ The extremely interesting account of the Dramatic Literature in the 8th volume of Grote's *History of Greece* might be read at this time. There is a German translation

When the history of Greece is brought to a close, we then turn to that of Rome, premising always that the old caution of following the contemporary chronology of the two has been borne in mind throughout. Here we may take Dr. Schmitz's history as our text-book, to be used as we used Smith's before.

If the pupil can read Latin easily, she should enjoy the pleasure of reading at least the early legends of Rome in *Livy*. Beyond this we have not time to linger over the rise of this wonderful people, who unfortunately began to influence the rest of the world when the era of their truest strength and noblest patriotism had passed away. The real modern interest of Roman history begins when gigantic conquests, blinding the people to the loss of freedom, first brought Western Europe to view, and were followed by the Augustan age, whose powerful intellects, bequeathing to us an immortal inheritance, console us in some measure for the existence of its warriors.

Here, as we did before with Greek writers, we may select some portions to give life to history and inspire an interest in the literature. One or two of Cicero's orations should be read, if possible in the original; as well as some of his familiar letters, which carry us to the very heart of a life so unlike our own, with all its human sameness of hopes, fears, passions, and ambitions. Virgil I suppose to be already known, and probably also some odes of Horace, if any Latin has been learnt. If time allowed, we might now take Tacitus for the history of the early emperors, and obtain some idea of what the feelings of a true Roman were, while Rome was sinking deeper in corruption and servility at home, in proportion as she extended her empire afar. The history of the Roman Empire through five centuries is a fine study, if we wish to learn what luxury can do for the happiness of individuals, and love of glory for the well-being of nations; but we cannot dwell upon these topics now, and may therefore be content with the information to be gained from Dr. Schmitz, and after him from Niebuhr's last ten lectures on Roman history, which brings the rapid sketch down to the final overthrow of the Western Empire, late in the fifth century.*

---

of Æschylus and of Sophocles, by Minckwiz, which is better than anything we have in English; but even through the medium of Potter's version, the mind is opened to a new range of images and of impressions of life and thought, which otherwise remain sealed up for ever to those who cannot read these magnificent poems in the original.

* If there be any turn for political or philosophical speculation in the pupil's mind, she might add to this course Montesquieu's *Grandeur et Décadence des Romains*.

We must now pass hastily over the dawn of the modern world, with its new religion triumphantly rising to reign over the crumbling civilization of antiquity; the birth of Mahomedanism, and its wild career of victory; and the gradual ripening of the rude energies of those northern hordes, so despised by Greek intellect and Roman pride, and yet destined to outstrip both Greece and Rome in knowledge and in power. Sources of information about this period are pointed out in Smyth's lectures, and to them the young student can refer at some future time. Our educational course of history must be restricted to epochs of more completely modern interest, the right comprehension of which bears more immediately on the great questions of civil and religious liberty, such as we now understand them, and on social life and commercial enterprise under those forms from which our own directly spring.

The history of the sixteenth and seventeenth centuries is that which deserves to concentrate attention. The former slight study of the histories of the different countries of Europe, and the careful comparison of their chronology, will enable the pupil to take up a detached portion in the manner now proposed without fear of confusion. In order to give, however, some notion of subjects which those slight general histories will have passed over, such as the feudal system, the rise of chivalry, the influence of the Crusades, &c., it will be advisable to read Robertson's 'View of the State of Europe,' prefixed to his *Life of Charles the Fifth*, which embraces precisely that period 'from the subversion of the Roman Empire to the beginning of the sixteenth century,' which we do not propose to study in detail. To this might be added the chapters referring to the twelfth, thirteenth, and two following centuries, in Sismondi's English abridgment of his *History of the Italian Republics*. The wealth and power to which those small States rose, their enlightened attention to commerce, and the love of the fine arts among them,—to which we owe so much, not only for the efforts of modern genius but for the preservation of the antique,—the rise of the first great modern literature, to which Dante's name alone would suffice to give imperishable glory, the ardour for the study of Greek which saved inestimable treasures of ancient literature and contributed to revive the love of letters throughout Europe,— all these things give to that portion of Italian history an interest we seek for in vain elsewhere at that period; an interest apart from that of a sadder cast afforded by its political vicissitudes and the usurpations of ecclesiastical dominion. The study of Italian does not enter into my plan. The language is easily mastered without help for the purposes of reading, and few educated persons who have time would fail to acquire it for that object.   Lives of the great writers and artists, among whom so many— as Dante, Petrarch, Leonardo da Vinci, and Michael Angelo—took a part in public affairs, are to be found in English ; they will give additional interest to the narrative of the period, and, we may trust, kindle a strong desire to study the language at some future time.

I should wish, in considering the sixteenth and seventeenth centuries, to take England as the centre point, turning to other countries as one or another plays an important part.   I take the history of England as the basis, because it is that which the young reader necessarily requires to be most familiar with; but the whole course of reading should refer to Europe generally, as acted upon to a certain extent by the same causes. It is the history of opinion, and of the progress of society as influenced by the gradual enfranchisement of opinion, that gives such importance to those two centuries, during which so powerful an impetus was received, and so many striking changes manifested.   It is this view which the teacher should keep before her pupil's mind.

For example : the first great phenomenon of that time is the Reforma-tion ; but if we simply read a narrative of what was done and said by the Reformers or their royal patrons in Germany, England, France, or Switzer-land, we get little idea of the real nature and importance of the move-ment.   The young reader must be led to see that this apparently sudden rebellion against the corruption of long unquestioned authority was the effect not of the outraged feelings of one man, but of slowly working changes.   It should be pointed out that light had gradually been stealing over long-benighted Europe; that here and there, in all quarters, men who thought most had been the foremost to hail the dawn ; that many had begun to see that the fetters they had worn in the dark were ropes of sand; that the ramparts which had hemmed them in, and made inquiry into all beyond seem a daring impiety, were shadowy and unreal.   It will be seen that as the few learnt to think thus and act by this light, public opinion was gradually influenced, till the spirit of opposition waxed strong, and the boldest rebels formed a sympathizing audience; that in literature, in science, as in theology, that same spirit showed itself; and thus that revolt against mere authority began, which crowned with so many victo-ries, has been the ceaseless struggle of every subsequent generation.

It should be noticed how the great instrument of intellectual freedom, the press, was looked upon with prudent suspicion from the beginning by those whose power was based on popular ignorance.   Thus in 1515, less than a century after the invention of printing, and before Luther had raised his voice, Leo X. laid severe restrictions on the liberty of the press; knowledge was felt to be the future enemy, daily gathering strength for the contest. A glance at science will show the same spirit and the same opposition. In 1530, the very year the Protestant party signed the declaration of Augsburg, Copernicus ventured to teach that scientific doctrines which had been held as most sacred, and rested on the apparent testimony of the senses as well as on the authority of the Church, must be abandoned. And although, even a century later, Galileo suffered persecution for maintaining the bold theories thus enounced, they continued to gain ground till the labours of Kepler and Newton established their truth and put a glorious close to the contest. It will be seen that in other sciences besides astronomy giant strides were also made; while, guided by the same free spirit, history, jurisprudence, and politics were studied in a different manner from that in which they had ever been studied before. Then also literature, which had previously shown little life north of the Alps, as though inspired with the mighty promise now held forth to future generations, shone in full splendour during those two eventful centuries,—centuries which in Germany began with Luther and ended with Leibnitz; in France, beginning and ending with two of the most powerful satirists the world has known, including all the writers, except Voltaire, whose works rank as standard models in the language; which gave birth to all the literature of real genius Spain has ever possessed; and which in England boast the long list of glorious names, from Spenser to Locke and Dryden, of which the nation may well be proud. Again, let it be noticed that midway in that career of intellectual progress—at the beginning of the seventeenth century—Bacon shed the light of philosophical method upon the daily enlarging field of knowledge. Men began to hold closer communication with each other in different countries, although at the same time the more frequent use of national languages by great writers—as, for instance, Bacon and Descartes, who both used the vulgar tongue for some of their works—indicates a wider public at home. Finally, let it be shown that wherever the spirit of freedom, struggling for utterance in every country of Europe, was stifled, as in Italy and Spain, the glory hath departed from the nations; where it triumphed, as in England, a succession of fearful struggles ended in peace, stability, and national greatness; the Revolution of 1688 being as fit a crowning act to the political history of these centuries as the poetry of Milton and the discoveries of Newton were fitted to seal their glory in other paths of progress.

It is almost beyond the limits of this section to enter even so far into subjects of this nature; it might seem that I should have been contented on this, as on other branches of this course, to recommend books, but not to enter upon the matter of the studies; I felt it necessary, however, to indicate at least in a few words what are the points, what the views and reflections which make one period more important to be studied than another, and to draw attention once more to the essential office the teacher must perform in conducting studies of this nature. If we simply put books into a young person's hands, we do little more than give an impulse to self-education; the real educator prepares the way for what those books are to teach, brings principles to view, sifts out the trivial and concentrates attention on what deserves labour and thought, giving prominence to those relations of facts often so much more important than the facts themselves, but which are not seen by the inexperienced student. To read through a given number of volumes of Hume's *History of England* in ordinary school-room fashion, is doubtless a pleasant pastime, and will accustom the ear to the charm of an admirable style,—so admirable that the falsehood embalmed in it will assuredly descend to the latest generations that speak our language; but for all that makes the study of history useful, such reading were better left alone ; since we know not which is most likely to mislead—Hume's honest prejudices or his dishonest party spirit. And truly, value for no one thing that

> Makes men glorious and a place divine,

is like to grow in the young mind, from blindly following one who upholds the integrity of the Stuarts and contemns the assertors of civil and religious liberty; who decries Bacon and places Shakespeare below Racine.*

Nevertheless, for the history of England during this period I recommend taking Hume. In a mere literary point of view his work is one which cannot be passed over, and it is better read when the teacher's warning is at hand. But according to the plan I propose it will be the text-book only, correctives will be duly resorted to, and whenever events of importance bring some other nation prominently forward foreign works must be consulted, and if possible read in their own language. Ranke's *History of the Popes* gives the best view of the rise and progress of the Reformation, and of the efforts made to oppose it, especially of the establishment of the Jesuits, that master-work of the opponents of spiritual freedom. If

---

* This opinion is expressed more than once in his private letters. See Burton's *Life of Hume.*

the pupil be not acquainted with German, she can read this work in one of the few good translations we possess from that language.* But the whole work may not be necessary, portions relating to the dissension among the petty princes of Germany, and perhaps some theological discussions may be omitted. Lacretelle's *Guerres de Religion* presents a striking picture of some of the consequences of the Reformation in France, and Blunt's *History of the Reformation in England*, scanty and imperfect as it is, will in some respects correct Hume's account, which betrays in every line the writer's indifference to the principles which were brought into conflict. The chapters in Hallam's *Literature of the Middle Ages* which relate to the sixteenth century should now be read, to follow the progress of intellect in other fields, and as we proceed with the reign of Queen Elizabeth it will be well to turn to Hallam's *Constitutional History*, and read at least his account of Hooker and of the first promulgation of views both on Church and State hitherto unknown, or at least shunning open discussion.

We may now pass rapidly on, satisfied with Hume's narrative and keeping in view the contemporary history of other nations,† till we come to the Fronde in France and to the Great Rebellion in England, movements as unlike in character as in their results, but both indicating the progress of the spirit of freedom. The history of the Fronde to be carefully studied has to be sought in a mass of memoirs and other writings unfit for a course such as I am indicating; we must be satisfied with reading the account in a general history of France,‡ and portions of Madame de Motteville's memoirs will afford an amusing comment on the historian's narrative, and also show what was the feeling excited by the first news of the successes of the popular party in England and the distress and danger of the royal family.

In considering this momentous period in England, it will be well to turn from Hume to Clarendon. The open honest fervour of the partisan is a relief after the mock candour of the historian; and the style of the two works affords also a curious contrast well worth studying, marking

---

* By Mrs. Austen.

† Hénault's *Abrégé Chronologique de l'Histoire de France*, is a valuable book of reference for this purpose.

‡ For a short history, that by La Vallée is very good, but portions of Sismondi's large work might now be read. The best history of the Fronde is that by M. de Saint-Aulaire ; but, perhaps, such a course as I am recommending can hardly afford to comprise two volumes on one short period.

16

the distance of a century in our literature. Foster's *Lives of the Great Men of the Commonwealth* will show the opposite views of the same events and the same characters, and are full of interest. A higher interest still attaches to the contemporary memoirs of Mrs. Hutchinson, which surely no woman will read without being moved. For a course so slight as this must inevitably be, it is not perhaps advisable to attempt more in elucidation of this period than the works named above.* When Hume—whose history closes with the Revolution of 1688—is finished—Macaulay will be our best guide to the end of the century. His masterly sketch of the state of England in early times and down to the Restoration, and the vivid manner in which he brings men and events before the mind of the reader, will not fail to make a strong impression on the young student; some of the discussions and reflections on constitutional questions in the third volume might perhaps be passed over as too long and detailed for our purpose; but the tone of political opinion, liberal yet moderate, based so firmly on principles important to national life, will, it may be hoped, be no less impressive even to a young mind, if somewhat trained to consider these things, than the picturesque descriptions of men and manners.

In looking over the contemporary history of Europe during the latter half of the seventeenth century, nothing requires close attention except the reign of Louis XIV. in France. This, the *grand siècle* of French literature, and the period which by its military madness, its extravagance and errors of government, became the seedtime of after miseries and ultimately of the Revolution, is always full of interest. Voltaire's *Siècle de Louis XIV.* will perhaps be the best work for our purpose; it is short, it sums up in his admirable manner the characteristic points of political, social, and literary history, and it is a good specimen of that great writer's best style, with which it is advisable that the young reader should become acquainted. Most of the eminent French writers of that epoch I suppose her to have been introduced to in the course of her previous studies in literature. Some of Bossuet's masterpieces of eloquence would be fitly read here,

---

* I suppose some acquaintance to have been made during the reading of the previous two years with the great writers in different departments of our own literature; but when reading the political history, frequent reference should again be made to them and to the general literary character of the period, as well as to the history of scientific discovery in England and abroad. Unfortunately, we are not rich in works throwing light on manners and the condition of the people; and those we have, including almost the whole dramatic literature of the period referred to, except Shakespeare, are seldom fit to be placed in the hands of the young.

funeral orations over those whom the historian presents in their glory or their courtly splendour. Labruyère gives an inimitable portraiture of manners, and Madame de Sevigné's *Letters* also let one into the intimate life of the age; besides that, no one studying French can omit to read them for the sake of their unequalled grace and charm of language.

I have so far entered with some detail into the course of reading which I propose should lead the young student to appreciate those two eventful centuries. Abundant sources of further information exist within easy reach, but it seemed necessary that I should mark out what I believe might suffice for the purpose we have in view; it must be for the teacher to judge, according to the time she can command and to the capacity of her pupil, how far she might be forced to contract, or might afford to enlarge it.

Other periods there are which ought to be better studied than through the medium of a general history,—such as the rise of our colonies in North America, and the war which ended in their independence; the history of British India, concerning which the ignorance of the public generally is truly singular; and the French Revolution, with its wide-spreading consequences working even now in different nations of Europe; —but of these I shall say little, leaving it to the teacher to apply to these portions of history the same method employed before. The early part of the eighteenth century may be passed lightly over, the latter half is only too full of stirring interest. Here, as before, some narrative must be taken as the text-book, and portions of other works, biographies more especially, must be consulted. Lives of Washington and of Franklin, for instance, should be read; Burke's speeches on the American War, with his letter to the Sheriffs of Bristol, should be studied, and not for their historical interest or political wisdom alone, but as masterpieces of English writing.

There is a short history of British India by Mr. Gleig, originally published in the *Family Library*, which will serve our purpose better than works of more research and detail. Macaulay's two brilliant sketches of the lives of Clive and of Hastings, in his Essays, should not be omitted. With regard to the French Revolution, so much has been written that the only difficulty is to choose; the sixth volume of Lacretelle's *Histoire de France pendant le dix-huitième Siècle* contains a *Tableau de l'Etat de la France avant la Révolution* which is worth reading. M. de Barante gives deeper views of the causes of the Revolution in his *Tableau de la Littérature du dix-huitième Siècle*, a short but admirable sketch. For the narrative of events, Thiers's, as being a work of some reputation and well written, is perhaps the best to select, but with a careful recollection of his unfairness, both nationally and as a political partisan. These are faults not perhaps to be avoided in studying times so near our own, and which stirred up passions not yet set at rest. It is difficult to select, as I said, among so many histories and biographies; but there is one which I must name to be avoided, lest the reputation of the writer, and the beauty of his style, should make the choice fall upon him. I allude to Lamartine's *Histoire des Girondins,* in which the name of history is desecrated to the mere dramatizing of human passions and emotions. The good and the bad— heroism and infamy—philosophic patriotism, and the most debasing ambition, all come in one sense alike before the author; all serve to dress up the hero of the hour. No one to whom political or private principle is dear would put into young hands so melancholy a perversion of the great lessons of history. The fact that such a work is from the pen of M. de Lamartine, from the man whose own steady moral courage contributed more perhaps than anything to save France in 1848, only makes it the more sad.

If Thiers's history be read to the end, embracing the whole of Napoleon's wonderful career, the teacher must not fail to administer the necessary antidotes to what is most false or exaggerated in the estimation of this idol of national vanity. After reading the brilliant campaigns in Italy, a few chapters of Botta* will show all the suffering caused by hopes of freedom raised only to be dashed to the ground. When Thiers leaves the issue of the battle of Trafalgar doubtful, it may be well to read Southey's *Life of Nelson.*† When the victories in Germany, and the preparations for yet more extended conquest have been passed in review, let us turn to Segur's account of the Russian campaign, and to Niebuhr's letters referring to that period, or to the extracts from different biographies collected by Mrs. Austen in her volume upon Germany in the nineteenth century, and thus lead the young mind, which is but too easily fascinated even by the errors of genius, to contemplate the reverse of the medal that is struck to commemorate the glory of conquest.

Between two and three hours daily have been set apart for this course of reading with the requisite making of notes. But the proper study of Adam Smith alone will take up a considerable time, and his work should

---

* *Storia d'Italia continuata da quella di Guicciardini sino, al* 1814. Da Carlo Botta.

† As one of the most simple and admirable prose narratives in our language, this short work should at any rate be read.

be read again when the historical course is finished, and when, therefore, the student's mind is more impressed with the growing importance, as modern civilization advances, of all those questions which political economy deals with. Such being the case, it is possible that the entire course indicated above may be found too long. It can be materially reduced by omitting either the ancient history, or else the latter portion relating to the eighteenth century; this must be regulated by the pupil's tastes or the teacher's judgment. If the young girl have a love for historical reading, it is safe to let her make a choice now, since she is sure enough to return later to the ground she has thus left unexplored; if she does not possess that taste, and especially if indolent in general about reading, it is best to leave her no option, but to make her read while in the school-room what it is really requisite that she should know—namely, the modern history brought down to the peace of 1815. In no case would I omit the study of the sixteenth and seventeenth centuries, nor abridge it unless there were really not intelligence enough, not the capacity of being roused to sufficient interest to make the lessons we wish to teach instructive and impressive. If the mind is of that calibre which cannot be awakened to philosophical speculation at all, if after due pains have been taken to draw out its powers and lead it to some independent exercise of them, we find that it can only grasp facts, that it follows the succession of events, without ever caring to look for a cause, it may perhaps be as well to shorten the course in some degree. Yet let us hesitate long before we give up any portion of knowledge we have desired for good reasons to impart; since that inert mind may yet wake up to activity, that tardy intelligence may be quickened by those very appeals to it that seem so hopelessly fruitless. If a generally indolent unintelligent mind showed a decided taste for one subject, undoubtedly that should be made use of; we cannot do in this case as with the better endowed, follow steadily our own method of instruction, leaving them to cultivate their chosen pursuits later. In the latter case, the question is simply between adhering to well considered principles or gratifying a taste; in the former, it may be a question of giving the only possible form of development to an intellect that has seemed hitherto dormant. I would not, then, with such a one insist on the study of history which is to her without meaning or interest when there is a promise that her soul might be awakened by the study of plants or crystals. But we must bear in mind that social and moral questions are what the most unintelligent of women will have to deal with, and through which they must affect the welfare of others, and therefore that if possible it is upon such subjects, and not upon botany or crystalography, that we desire to create a habit of reflection, and some capacity of forming accurate opinions.

§ 2.—Throughout the course of study of various subjects which we have now brought to a close, there will remain room for the exercise of the teacher's judgment in questions of this kind. Moderate average abilities have been alone taken into consideration in framing the plan, great talents and very tardy or defective intelligence would render it necessary either to enlarge or curtail it. These exceptional cases cannot be provided for in a work intended for general use. One caution only I would give,—when the powers of the pupil are such as to admit of more study than I have indicated, let it be deeper, not more varied. These are the cases in which concentration is necessary. The love of knowledge is keen and active, but we must beware lest by feeding it over too wide a range we allow a habit of intellectual dissipation, if I may use such an expression, and neglect the severer exercise through which the mind matures its vigour. If, then, we have a pupil of more than ordinary intelligence, let her read more and think more upon those subjects which for various reasons have been chosen for her. If the elementary works are rapidly mastered, let other and deeper treatises be read, and let us especially be careful that her own mind works upon what she reads; that she strives to methodize her knowledge.

This is truly the aim of all intellectual culture; we begin to give instruction to minds that are yet passive, but it is because that very instruction is, we trust, to be the means of rousing them from the passive to the active state. It is only when that change is effected that the knowledge really becomes mental nurture. There is in Newman's lectures on University Education, a passage on that subject that exactly expresses this difference. 'It is not,' he says, 'mere application, however exemplary which introduces the mind to truth, nor the reading many books, nor the getting up many subjects, nor the witnessing many experiments, nor the attending many lectures. All this is short enough; a man may have done it all, yet be lingering in the vestibule of knowledge; he may not realize what his mouth utters; he may not see with his mental eye what confronts him; he may have no grasp of things as they are, or at least he may have no power of advancing one step forward of himself in consequence of what he has already acquired, no power of discriminating between truth and falsehood, of sifting out the grains of truth from the mass, of arranging them according to their true value, and, if I may use the phrase, of building up ideas. Such a power is the result of a scientific formation of mind; it is an acquired faculty of judgment, of clear-sightedness, of sagacity, of wisdom, of philosophical reach of mind, and of intellectual self-possession and repose, qualities that do not come of mere acquirement. The bodily eye, the organ for apprehending material objects is provided by nature; the eye of the mind of which the object is truth, is the work of discipline and habit.'

Such, then, as I said, is the object of intellectual education; and the greater the power of the young mind we have to form, the more anxious must we be to aim early and steadily at attaining that object, rather than at heaping up the materials of knowledge; lest the real use and purpose of those powerful faculties be forgotten; set aside in the very eagerness of the search after fresh knowledge. With minds of a wholly different order we may proceed differently. With them the passive state will last longer,— we must be content to be longer occupied in instilling first principles; it may be years before anything will awaken the intellect to any further exertion than that of receiving, and more or less retaining impressions. Our long labour of years upon years may produce no further result, may only have stored up impressions, and somewhat cleared the understanding, leaving us to hope that the future may yet bring some vivifying influence, when the crop that springs up will witness to the care with which the soil was prepared, and the seed cast in.

A difference must be made between the dull, slow understanding that learns with labour and difficulty, and the inert mind, or defective intelligence. With the former, few subjects should be attempted, and those few thoroughly mastered; that labour is itself the means of rendering the faculties more supple, just as exercise would produce suppleness and agility in the limbs. The perceptions become quicker, the apprehension more rapidly clear; such minds are often tenacious of what they have learnt, and this power is increased by the efforts so laboriously made. In modifying the general course of study I have proposed for young persons of this turn of mind, I should adhere to the geometry, but omit the algebra; they would not have time for both; and the lessons to be derived from the former are much needed to give them some clear perceptions of the nature and method of reasoning, which will help further efforts. The less we can trust to liveliness of apprehension, the more careful must we be to give the student the means of clearing each step as she advances. In continuing the study of reasoning, the logic should be carefully worked, but speculative opinions may be passed over. The studies of language must be assiduous : the more completely we can give the use of the instrument of thought, the more we help the slow understanding in becoming clear to itself, and able to follow clearly the thoughts of others. But as we are supposing slowness and difficulty of learning, not more than one foreign language certainly should be attempted, and even that must be according to the power of memory and the circumstances under which it can be taught. The reasons for studying more than one form of language are so potent that we must not, if possible, forego the advantage, but all consideration of the literature may be postponed. French may be used, for instance, as a means of mastering English more completely by the help of translation and comparison, while time cannot be spared for reading any of the great authors. With regard to the slight course of science, it may be curtailed according to the same principles; we may restrict ourselves to the mere elements of mechanics and astronomy, leaving the other subjects I have mentioned for future study. In short, our great object must be to *work* the mind rather than to *enrich* it,—while in extenuation of this severer labour, we do all we can to make reading agreeable by the help of history, poetry, biography, anything that may prevent the weariness which will perhaps attend the *lessons*, from growing into disgust for books in general.

With the other class of backward minds, or rather two classes—the feebly intelligent and the inert—a different system should be followed. With them it is desirable to appeal to the imagination, to stimulate curiosity, to resort to all means that promise to excite some degree of intellectual activity, it matters little in what direction. I have already had occasion to speak of this,* but it was necessary to mention it again with reference to the alterations in the course of study which such a case might make requisite. Let us try to give a taste for literature, to let the charm of poetry be felt, before we attempt grammar; let us store the memory, give a knowledge of two or three languages as the instruments of future knowledge, but studying them conversationally if possible, or at least through the medium of light literature that may give a taste for reading as an occupation, before the time comes when it may grow into an earnest pursuit. In science, let first the curious or the amusing, next the great results, be placed before the mind; labouring less anxiously to work in the first principles, appealing first to the imagination, while the reasoning power is yet wrapt in its tardy infancy. A considerable amount

---

* See chap. v. sect. 2.

of information possessed by the teacher herself, is an incalculable advantage under these circumstances. The dormant faculties may often be roused by oral and incidental teaching, when books are utterly distasteful. Natural objects, effects and changes produced by the powers of nature, simple experiments, &c., may be used by a well-instructed person to draw attention to what otherwise would pass unobserved,—to lead the young mind almost imperceptibly to draw inferences,—to perceive relations to reason, in short, and above all, to wish to see and know more. In choosing the subjects for actual teaching, it would be well to be guided in some measure with reference to the power of commanding means of ocular demonstration, in order not to depend on books alone. For instance, to select natural history, if placed near museums or zoological collections; or mechanics, if opportunities of seeing machinery can be easily found. Geography may be made a study of great interest, and travels might take the place of part of the historical course before recommended. If we can rouse the indolent or feeble mind to take an interest first in travellers' adventures, next in descriptions of scenery and natural productions, then in the account of the social condition of the inhabitants, we have advanced some steps towards kindling a wish to penetrate into their past history; and we have prepared the way for some of the lessons that study should teach.

Such are the alterations I would suggest under these peculiar circumstances, but in doing so it is merely as pointing out the principle upon which a method adapted to average abilities may be departed from when necessary. They are hints, not rules.

There are some objects which I trust, with every variety of intelligence, may be attained by such a system of education as I have proposed. These are—a certain degree of enlargement of the natural powers of the understanding shown in love of truth, in candour, in practical judgment, in wider views of duty embracing the exercise of mental as well as moral influence, in clearness of ideas, so that the mind shall be able to discern distinctly what it does from what it does not understand; and lastly, some love of knowledge and appreciation of the objects that affect the real interests of mankind. These are what the least gifted by nature may surely be endowed with by education, and these, though in a higher degree, are all we expect the latter to do for those to whom nature has been most lavish. The young will be thoroughly aware that it is a labour commenced only, a labour methodically prepared, not a finished work, that education bequeaths to them when their school studies are over. The miserably false association created by the terms ' finishing schools,' 'finishing governess,' will not mislead them. If they have one notion more clear than another in their minds, it will be that of their own ignorance, as they catch faint glimpses of the vast regions of knowledge that spread out on all sides of them.

With regard to expense, I have throughout endeavoured to regulate my plan to suit average means as well as average abilities; and to justify what I laid down at the outset,—that the serious cost so often complained of is for the accessories, not the essentials of education. At the same time it must be confessed that even when other expenses are lavished, there is often a strange dislike to spending money on books. It is not uncommon to hear it said in a school-room, 'I use what books I can; so-and-so would be far better, but it is not to be expected that they will be bought,' &c. Yet in the same family one or two reviews or magazines are taken in, shilling or half-crown novels bought at the railway station before every journey of a few hours, while useful works are wanted for serious instruction. It may be said that such purchases are trifles, and so as to price are many of the works I have recommended, while all are easily accessible; the old can be borrowed from any gentleman's library or found on any book-stall, the new at every circulating library. It is undoubtedly better to purchase books than to borrow them; for purely educational books, as well as works of reference, it is necessary to do so, and the cost will at most be very inferior to that which more fashionable systems lavish upon accomplishments.* Even where economy is strictly necessary, till there is no luxury of show or dress that can be given up, parents must surely be ashamed to own that they will not incur the yearly expense of a few pounds for the essential means of their daughters' education.

When the parents' circumstances are so narrow as to require the time

---

* Good works of reference are extremely important. The following will be found most useful:—Brand's *Dictionary of Arts, Science, and Literature.* The new and abridged edition of the *Biographie Universelle*, which is hardly a third of the price of the large edition, and comes down to a later period. Good maps are essential. Johnson's *Physical Atlas* is invaluable, placing before the eye at once, in different plates, the results of laborious investigations, which few memories will retain if presented in the form of ordinary reading. Bell's *Chronological Tables* I have spoken of before. The *Penny Cyclopedia* is very useful when no larger work of that kind is at hand. Dictionaries of the different languages taught are of course indispensable; and for English, either a large Johnson, or one of the newer works that have in some measure superseded his, though none, I believe, are equal to it for the variety of the quotations, which afford so admirable a study of the language.

of their daughters to be given to household matters rather than to books, it must then rest with the mother, as I have before said, to turn that practical education to the purposes of mental discipline also.* Under such circumstances, whatever small portions of time can be devoted to books, should be employed on solid systematic reading within a very small range of subjects. We know how much has been often achieved by self-educated men in the intervals of laborious occupation; the same determination and careful husbandry of time will produce equally good results in the case we are now considering. It must be the ceaseless effort of the parents to stir up that spirit; and when they have done so, I feel convinced that no poverty likely to occur in a class removed above the necessity of manual labour will prevent a mother giving to her daughters an education which, for solidity and true refinement, shall surpass that of the most expensive schools. And however small the scale of attainment, love of knowledge, at least, is no growth of a wealthy soil alone. It can preserve an elevated mental condition amidst the homeliest cares. It can animate the minds of those who are tied down to manual drudgery no less than the favoured student with all 'the means and appliances' of learning around him. It can open glimpses of a higher life to cheer the flagging spirit, and save it from seeking its home among the things that minister to bodily necessities.

§ 3.—It may have been remarked that I have hitherto, in speaking of a parent's influence and control, confined myself to the mother only; the father stands more apart from the education of his children, and in very early life his influence is far inferior to hers. Men seldom possess that quick perception of character and feeling, that delicate observation and ready sympathy which are requisite to understand children, and which afford the key to their management. Neither is it common to find in fathers that unselfish, untiring love which in the mother makes it impossible that any amount of care a child may require,—whether physically or morally,—should weary or disgust her. The instinctive feeling for the young is mercifully given in greater strength to the female mind, and is roused by the care of children in almost all women, whether themselves mothers or not. When this is strengthened by all the moral associations connected with the mother's office, with the hopes and fears for the future, the pride, the joy, the new life she lives in that young existence, it is

* See pp. 55, 167.

no wonder that maternal love becomes to most women the strongest feeling of their nature.

And this love, from which she is not diverted by the worldly business or ambition which take a man's heart as well as his thoughts from home, —this love is the source of her power. Women may choose to abdicate the latter, or make themselves unfit to exercise it, but it is an unlawful abdication. Nature gave the influence, and Nature will exact the penalty if it be not wielded for good. These considerations make it essential in a work on Education, especially on the education of girls, who are not even partially withdrawn as boys are from the influence of their mother, to address the latter as the exclusive directress of all that is done. But far from undervaluing the father's influence for good, I am convinced that it cannot be too highly prized, especially at the age we have been lately considering. Throughout the period of education, indeed, if a man be not too much engrossed in his own pursuits or in the labour of a profession to give attention to such detail, he may materially assist the mother's endeavours.

The influence of a man's mind in directing a girl's later studies, and in forming her views of the world, is inestimable. Men whose knowledge is practically tested are forced to acquire a thorough grasp of it,—a completeness which women, owing partly to the absence of that very test, rarely attain. The mental discipline of working up to the expectations of one who views knowledge in this light, is excellent. But it is still more in conversation that I should expect a father's beneficial influence to tell. Men and women necessarily look upon the world in some respects from a different point of view. Woman's is the moral and individual view ; and it is advantageous to a girl to be forced beyond that to see the wide and bold views of men, to look into some of the workings of society which cannot come within her narrow ken, to get the benefit of that wide and deep observation upon men and things which the habit of dealing with large questions gives to a man of any thought and knowledge.

Knowledge of the world in women, means, for the most part, insight into character, into peculiarities of sets or individuals, and into the deep mysteries of feeling giving the key to action and motives ; in men, it is rather a knowledge of classes than of individuals ; shades of character often escape them ; their observation is wider and less delicate ; they discern less of the hidden springs of action, and yet are more suspicious from their general knowledge of human depravity. Women are more confident in the prevalence of goodness, and more intolerant of in dividua error; men are indulgent to the latter, and severe in their general estimate of mankind. It is evident, from a mere glance at these differences, how beneficial it must be to young girls to have their views early directed in the broader channel, and trained to that vigour and boldness which will make them dare to look at the world as it is when seen from a wider sphere than their own.

The very tone of a man's conversation,—his manner of treating a subject,—the more precise, sometimes technical, language that he uses, owing to habits of business and of dealing with those who are as well versed as himself in the subject he is speaking of,—all these are highly useful to a young girl who will never herself be brought under the same necessity for precision and accuracy. The intellectual power, the variety of subjects, that instinctive superiority which belongs to a man of any ability, captivates the young mind and opens it to feel the charm of real companionship and of mental sympathy with a mind of a higher order than her own. A father's influence is often enhanced by the very fact of his having kept apart from the detail of education. His daughter forms probably a somewhat exaggerated estimate of his wisdom and of the importance of his avocations, and is deeply sensible of the honour that is conferred upon her when her father seeks her as a companion. That he should talk freely to her, draw her out and wish to help her in forming her own opinions, raises her in her own esteem, and gives what is the only elevating form of vanity,—the joy of feeling of some value in the eyes of one who is reverenced as well as loved. It will be seen from the very words I use that I am not supposing the father to descend from his pedestal of dignity, to *condescend* to converse with his daughter, to dictate his opinions to her and make her feel that she must be terribly in fault if their truth or wisdom is not apparent to her. I am supposing that he habitually and freely enters into conversation on the tone of an equal, and the less stress he lays on his superiority the more will she feel and remember it. I suppose that he takes an interest in her pursuits and amusements,—in her wild, girlish fancies and visions of delight; that he tries to draw out that half-formed mind; that he leads her to express thought and opinion freely; that he helps her to give definiteness and vigour to the conceptions that are but just taking shape in her imagination; that he tries to show her the nature of any error she holds, encouraging her to seek and examine, and giving the sanction of his warm, loving approval to every earnest endeavour to judge correctly or to act uprightly.

In the present day, the ignorant or the shallow-hearted among men alone deride woman's education or overlook the importance of their duties and influence; from such a man as I have spoken of above, his daughter will hear neither ridicule of her sex for their tardy endeavours to improve their condition, nor any of the commonplace sarcasms that commonplace men have been content to echo from generation to generation. She will see what a lofty standard is before him as he cheers her on to more and more exertion; she will know that her happiness, her dignity, her intellectual worth, are all sacred in his eyes; she will feel that when he remembers woman's inferiority, it is only to think with more exquisite tenderness of all that may best shield that inferior position from sorrow or wrong.

Such companionship may have a lasting influence upon a girl's destiny far beyond what was contemplated in a mere educational point of view. If it is important to man's true happiness that he should cherish a lofty ideal of female purity and worth, it is no less essential to women to have a high conception of the manly character. Not that unreasoning reverence for man as enjoying the higher position and right of command, that family deification of the right of the strongest, which is only too common, but an appreciation of what man ought to be to claim as an *individual* the respect and deference which his sex, as a whole, receives from those who, also considered as a whole, are inferior to him. The girl who has learnt by her father's side what it is that really entitles a man to command, who has instinctively *felt* his natural superiority, the greater vigour,—the greater power of will as well as of intellect,—she who has felt the influence of that power over her own mind, and known all the aid and support that it gives, and who, joined to all this, has learnt the real pleasure of mental companionship,—she will not be easily fascinated by the homage of empty-headed coxcombs or mere agreeable men of the world. I do not mean that she will be proof against some unfortunate delusion; we know too well how fancy will dress up its idols in the virtues they have never even sought to assume; but she will have one invaluable shield in that high standard of manly worth, and she will not carelessly or readily give her affection where she cannot give her highest esteem. She has known what the relation between the weak and the strong ought truly to be; and with her sense of the superiority man *ought* to possess, she will shrink from that moral degradation so many women fall into, of bowing down and giving up their existence to a nature inferior to their own, of accepting life-long subjection to one whom neither nature nor education have formed for command.

I shall have occasion to return to the subject of marriage in the concluding chapter. I would only say here, that everything which tends to raise women's spiritual standard in their views of marriage, is of incalculable benefit as regards their own happiness and the true interests of society. For the higher that standard, so much is the probability increased that those indissoluble ties will be formed only where real union of mind and character, as well as heart, is the basis of deep and earnest affections; affections which so based can no more be altered or swayed by the changes and chances of outward circumstance, than the full river can be arrested in its flow by the leaves which the autumn blast flings upon its waters.

CHAPTER VIII.

SOME PECULIARITIES OF WOMAN'S SOCIAL POSITION.

I CANNOT close these remarks on Education without pausing to consider what that education is to lead to. School-room studies are over;—if they had any purpose at all, it must have been to prepare the young creature for real life in the world where she now must take her part. What, then, is that life to be? If the eighteenth birthday and the dismissal of the governess are to be the signals for closing books, giving up regular study, for spending the mornings over music or carpet-work, the rest of the day in frivolous society or more frivolous reading, what was the object of so much labour spent before on things so different? * In a word, if ' coming out ' in the fashionable sense is life, what is the value of all that has been so painfully acquired? And if there be no discoverable relation between a careful education and the mode of life that succeeds it, what relation does the latter bear to the serious duties

---

* Among the generally accepted forms of idle pastime is that of novel-reading, yet few are more pernicious at the age when girls eagerly indulge in it. The excitement of feeling, when everything should tend to keep their lives free from emotion, is but one evil. Novels give false views of life, from the very necessity the writer is under of making a love-story the centre of interest, thereby representing that passion which, indeed, with few exceptions, exercises *some* influence over every life, as the ruling motive and sole arbiter of human destiny. It need hardly be pointed out how mischievous such an error may be to girls, in their ignorance of the world. On the different influence exercised on the imagination by novels and poetry, see *Thoughts on Self-Culture*, p. 335 to 338. Second edition.

and responsibilities of marriage, which may speedily follow, or to the lonely self-dependence of single life?

Viewed in this aspect, how disjointed is the course of a girl's life,—how evidently betraying the want of any ruling purpose! Fashion dictating the education, custom governing the subsequent career.

In the early part of this work,* I have founded the plea for a higher education for women upon the very fact that life makes upon them no demand for intellectual exertion; so that the spring of mental activity must be altogether from within, and independent of all worldly motive. I endeavoured thus to show that women are placed in a far more difficult position than men, the majority of whom are saved by the necessities of life from the perils of leisure and the consequences of their own feeble power of self-regulation. And now it is that these difficulties and dangers begin,—now when the school-room course is over, and the world is offering its untried pleasures. The test of education is here.

Accordingly, throughout the system I have endeavoured to unfold in these pages, the one unvarying aim has been to prepare for this time of trial; every study, every effort to cultivate tastes and habits, has had reference to the period when riper faculties might be exercised upon a wider field. The notion that education could have finished its work for girls, at the very age when young men are just beginning their serious studies, has never been contemplated for a moment. Every pursuit will have been so directed as to carry the mind forward to contemplate the fathomless resources of knowledge. So many things begun, while nothing is perfected beyond the foundation, point ceaselessly to future work. Languages that have not been learned for lack of time,—literature that has been merely glanced at,—science of which the alphabet only has been conned,—history whose lessons have been just shadowed forth,—all these have looked to future completion, and tended to associate coming years with fresh labours, and labour with animation and enjoyment.

To create that association, to inspire the love of knowledge for its own sake, is the crowning work of intellectual education. Henceforth life can never be either idle or barren. For that love growing with what it feeds upon, and finding food everywhere, opens a source of unalloyed pleasure which never while the mind retains its power can satiate or fail. It is not merely the amount of information which an educated person possesses that gives such animation to life, but the various sources of interest that knowledge opens. Nature and the world are veiled to the ignorant,—their

---

* See chaps. i. and ii. pp. 10-31.

souls respond to a few loud calls alone; while to the lover of knowledge, voices speak from all things animate and inanimate,—from the heavens and the earth, and the waters below the earth,—and there is scarcely a familiar scene or obscure position that does not open some field of thought or observation. He has not to seek occupation; his mind is never unoccupied.

Minds in which a really careful education fails to excite the taste for purely intellectual pursuits, are of two classes: the homely, who are strangers to all the higher forms of excitement; and those who are exclusively fond of action, and possess very often a great fund of practical ability. This cast of mind among men is very valuable. Those who possess it often stand highest in the world's esteem; they carry into execution what the thinkers have elaborated in their studies; they stand foremost in an hour of peril, and win the race of ambition. But for women this cast of mind is the one that gives the least promise of happiness, and more especially if they remain unmarried; since, with an active, energetic spirit stirring within, they are shut out by circumstances from one sphere of activity, and by their own mental peculiarities from another. Thus the same qualities which would have made a man a leader in society, which even to a woman with a large family or a position of much influence might have produced great benefits, turn too often in single life to restless meddling, to fussy excitement about trifling matters, to eager anxiety about many plans which may end at last in bitter discontent. A watchful mother will be aware of this tendency of her daughter's mind; and it must be her care to make the most of all the resources home life affords to cultivate that power of active usefulness, and give it a steady, thoughtful direction. Education may fail to excite love of knowledge, but never with fairly well-constituted minds will it fail to establish the conviction that life has an earnest purpose to each and all,—a purpose of self-improvement and usefulness; that if to-day in a position where we cannot apparently serve others, the time may yet come, and we must prepare for it. These moral views bearing directly on the intellectual condition, and investing it with a new interest, will save the mind from that silly contempt for intellectual pursuits which we see too often in those who boast of being practical. They will lead them to respect knowledge, and to regret their own want of capacity for seeking it,—a regret which may, when the practical activity finds little vent, lead to more earnest endeavours to enter into that wide field of interests which study opens to all who desire to share in it. There will, at any rate, be no entrance for that low

17

view of mental cultivation so unfortunately common, which represents it as a mere matter of taste whether a woman embroider muslin and a man keep a pack of hounds, or whether they cultivate literary tastes and store their minds with knowledge.

No forms of practical usefulness are to be despised which can save a girl who has no love of study from sinking into mere trifling the moment her school-room studies are over, or feeling that she has nothing to do. The management of a household, the care of children, teaching, nursing the sick, accounts, gardening, or farming, may excite the interest that cannot be roused for books; and not seldom interest in some practical matter will lead to a serious study of it, in the course of which the mind may begin to feel the pleasure of intellectual exertion. I should desire a girl, under these circumstances, to undertake the responsibility, and enter into the details of anything for which she felt any wish or aptitude; but every such occupation must be followed steadily and methodically. This the mother should use all her influence to enforce.

All young girls should go through a certain course of this practical training. They should be taught cooking for a sick room, if no other; and all the minute detail of domestic work and management should be made familiar to them, which can be done by practice alone. There would be less blundering among young housekeepers, and less discontent among their husbands, if this apprenticeship were carried on under a mother's eye. Those who have no taste for mental occupation might likewise be initiated into other kinds of business as occasion offers. It often happens that a man's occupations, whether literary or scientific, or even professional, makes him require help, which he may reasonably hope to find in his daughters, and which, if not claimed as a right, but asked for and accepted kindly, will be given in glad earnest and be a benefit to both parties. Work done as a willing service, which wins thanks and gives pleasure, has a very different effect upon the mind from work done to avoid incurring displeasure; just as every generous mind knows the delight of giving, while pleasure in paying a tax no Quixotism of liberality has yet pretended to feel. It would often be most valuable to women to be taught the forms and method of business; for many who have no property of their own requiring this kind of knowledge, are deeply concerned in the management of charities and schools,—sometimes on a large scale, —involving considerable expenditure, and requiring business correspondence and much arrangement with others. Knowledge and habits of business, besides giving the sense of increased usefulness, would certainly tend to raise the estimation in which women are held as capable of system and management beyond the details of a household, and would entitle the individual possessing them to that degree of consideration that society seldom refuses to successful labour.

With regard to the other class of minds I mentioned above, in whom it seems impossible to create any taste for intellectual pursuits, it is some consolation to know they are of that order to which a confined position is essentially congenial, and therefore that they will neither feel the sufferings nor the temptations against which it is needful to protect higher natures. Routine is not wearisome to them; small cares and amusements absorb them ; their sensibilities, less highly wrought, will not prey upon themselves; thought will not wear, nor doubt torture them; they have not the same capacity for either happiness or misery. Women who belong to this class are generally cheerful and contented in single life, unless defects of temper interfere, or some peculiar cause of bitterness has soured their feelings ; and if they marry, they remain happily ignorant that they are without influence, and incapable of fulfilling the sacred trust of educating their children.

This is a very common tone of feeling and character, from which society suffers, while the individual escapes some evils which press heavily on minds of a higher cast. But it must be remembered that the more a higher education spreads, the more it tends to cultivate the understandings of women, to refine their imagination, to elevate and widen the circle of their sympathies, the more will it tend to lessen the number of those who just vegetate on the earth,—who are content with anything which does not bring actual pain or privation, and who aspire to nothing beyond household and domestic cares. We cannot aim at a higher condition, without taking its penalties with its advantages.

Supposing a girl to marry young, a little judicious management obviates all difficulties during the few years that intervene between her introduction into society and her entrance upon a career of definite and important duties. But it is when a woman remains single, either altogether or till late in life, that her position becomes exposed to those peculiar trials which education should have prepared her to meet. It is then that women feel the narrow bounds of their sphere of activity,—it is then that, forgetting the true value of leisure, and all that its possessors owe to society, they are tempted to rate the social value of the influence of refined minds, of noble hearts, of cultivated tastes and pursuits, below that of money-making professions, and utter too often the melancholy cry

17—2

that their lives are useless to others, their knowledge and their faculties valueless to themselves, because the world offers them no task-work to perform. It is then that they need that spirit loftier than ambition, which will keep the mind active and aspiring without the spur of worldly motive; and that true appreciation of life which maintains, against all false associations, the conviction how superior what we *are* is to what we *do.*

Still, it must be remembered that what is thus required of women is no easy attainment. The instincts of activity and the yearnings of the social spirit are so strong, that when education has done its best, there will be many causes of depression in the social position of single women. Success and hope are two indispensable elements in human happiness; they are absent from the lives of those who have no positive occupations in the present, and no definite object to look forward to as the reward of exertion. Before we condemn women who sink in listless depression under the burden of years so spent, let us try to fancy for a moment what would have been the mental condition of the great body of men who are now acquitting themselves honourably in different active careers, if they had been confined within these narrow and sterile bounds,—let us consider what is the condition of the generality of those who are free from professions, and see how few of them are able to make a noble use of their freedom. We may thus form a juster notion of trials that have been too lightly regarded, or the weight of which has been unjustly attributed to other causes.

No doubt, men also must often mourn over the flight of youth, with its bright dreams and glorious visions; but in the midst of active employments, the long years that follow bring much to compensate for the fading of early hopes. A man's social position is more or less improved; he has won honour, or money, or professional distinction; his character and abilities have been made known,—they have given him weight, and he holds a place in public esteem which never can belong to the young. Even to the many who are baffled in their long struggle, hope at least is not short-lived as it is to a woman. It cheers his path twenty, even thirty years after its rainbow tints have faded from hers, unless she lives again in a husband's ambition or the future of her children. And during those years he is looking forward to possible good to be attained by his own exertions; she with folded arms is contemplating inevitable decline.

I need hardly say that I do not mean, in pointing this contrast, to put out of sight all the bitter sufferings that a life of toil and ambition is subject to; my only object is to draw more earnest attention to the absence of active objects and interests as a source of real depression, which the spur of mental activity,—a high and earnest love of knowledge,—is alone effectual to counteract.

It is true that some women do not apparently feel these evils,—they are content within their circle of trivial interests and occupation,—but this is owing to the homeliness of their own character, as I said before; they are in a congenial position, and therefore have nothing to complain of. It often happens also that the unmarried find much to do in their natural woman's vocation. Age and sickness, widowed homes and orphan childhood, make too many claims on those who are not wrapped up in ties of their own, to let single women feel that they are excluded from those charities of life which appeal most strongly to a woman's heart. Beyond these, the influence of mind and character tells in its appropriate female form through the various channels of intercourse, from the cottage of the poor to the confidential intercourse with the many who are prone to confide their difficulties, their hopes, and their sorrows to those who are supposed to have few interests of their own to divert their sympathy from others; and all these things prevent the causes of depression mentioned above being severely felt. But, after all, let us remember that when single women thus find occupation thrown upon them, it comes through the gates of sorrow or of death;—it is the burden of another that has fallen to the ground, and must be raised and carried; and perhaps we may own that we can hardly paint a condition in more dreary colours than to say that such a burden becomes a relief.

Yet the difficulties of this condition must be met. Without considering whether the time may come when different social arrangements may produce a change, certain it is that, at present, a large number of women in the classes we are speaking of remain single, and a great proportion of the rest marry late, and therefore for some years are exposed to these trials. In other countries, *mariages de convenance* diminish the number, and the sufferings of the remainder are hidden in nunneries, under whose 'funereal shelter *ennui* may silently consume them.' * We shall hardly wish to resort to either expedient. More than enough is the ridicule and disgrace which matrimonial manœuvring has brought upon our sex, and the grief which the attempted revival of conventual establishments has

---

* ' Ces vastes abris mortuaires où l'ennui les tuera sans bruit.'—Michelet: *Hist. de France*, vol. xi.

caused to many families. What, then, remains to be done? What pre-
servative against these evils are girls likely to find in the resources of a
common education, or in the course of reckless frivolity and idleness
which hails the close of their school-room studies?

I would not have it supposed for an instant that I write in a spirit of
ascetic opposition to pleasure and amusement. Far from it. I do not, as
I have said before,* think the capacity of youth for enjoyment is even
sufficiently considered. Let us cherish every joyous impulse,—every
innocent manifestation of the light-hearted, careless spirit, which with our
tenderest fostering will droop too soon in a world like this; and therefore
would I not let those young lives be so barren of joy that they should have
leisure to be engrossed for weeks and months in the fripperies of a milliner,
in the busy idleness of shopping, in the listless vanities of crowded rooms.
These will never satisfy the minds that have felt the animation of higher
enjoyments. Pleasure, be it remembered, always borrows intensity from
the mind that feels it; and truly youth, when all its rich gifts are drawn
out, is far different, considered under the aspect of pleasure alone, from
that half-developed existence which the sound of a fiddle galvanizes into
momentary animation.

It is not, then, against pleasure that I write, but against living for
pleasure;—against that systematic frivolity, that laborious idleness, that
solemn consecration of existence to amusement, which girls do not seek,
but which is thrust upon them; which is as much a part of the business
of life as the confirmation which went before, and the wedding which it is
hoped will follow after. I would not urge mothers to refuse to introduce
their daughters in London society, but I would desire to see them so
educated that a regular London season would be an impossibility,—a
weary violation of their own wishes and tastes. Bolingbroke says of the
frivolous that they are 'forced to trifle away their age, because they have
trifled away their youth;' and we may truly say of the nightly frequenters
of balls and assemblies, that they are forced to waste their days because
the previous nights have been wasted. Neither study nor social duties
can without risk to health be attended to in the morning, if the sun has
risen upon the night's amusement. As an occasional thing, nothing of
that sort can injure a young and strong person; but if persevered in,
mind and body are both too much jaded even to give to rational employment the three or four hours in the morning which the claims of society

---

* See chap. vii. sec. 2.

have not yet interfered with.* The afternoon brings its necessary trifling, —the shopping, the round of visits, the gossip, the arrangements for future pleasure,—varied occasionally by an equestrian assembly in Rotten Row, morning concerts, breakfasts, afternoon tea-parties, polka parties or flower-shows, one or other of which will be found effectual to prevent the intrusion of a leisure hour till the time for the dinner toilette arrives, and is followed by the usual course of evening gaieties.

When it is remembered that such is the routine of London life for three months, that foreign capitals or watering-places often continue the same round for some weeks longer, while scattered over the remaining months of the year there are country balls, races, and race balls, archery meetings, and gatherings in country houses, during which the joint endeavours of fifteen or twenty people are spent in getting rid of time, it is only wonderful that so much that is good and estimable should have survived in that portion of society where this exuberance of folly is found. Strong affections, and the high view of a wife's duties, which no imitation of foreign fashions has yet been able to alter, are, I believe, what save us in great measure from the natural consequences of such reckless neglect of all that is earnest and elevating in human life.

Nor let us suppose that the fashionable have a monopoly of frivolity. It is true that wealth and station alone can enable women to get rid of their better selves in so thorough and systematic a manner as that above described; but without speaking of the heart-burnings of those who look on and are not allowed to join in the race,—of 'the cark and care' with which numbers, who think they have a claim to mix in the fashionable throng that unjustly excludes them, embitter their lives, toiling with a perseverance such as few great causes have witnessed,—without, I say, speaking of these things, we may see at a glance that frivolity can wear more than one garb, and that the cap and bells can be made of foil as well as gold. Thus, while envying those whom wealth allows to sink unchecked below the level of rational humanity, parents are still saved from the necessity of condemning their daughters to any useful or elevating mode of spending their time. If London is too expensive, a hunting neighbourhood offers some resource;—if they cannot afford to travel, there are watering-places at home. If girls cannot spend their mornings

---

* Accordingly we find that riding in the forenoon is becoming more and more the custom, thereby cutting off one more chance of quiet occupation. It is good for health is the plea, and doubtless it is so; but why first endanger health by nightly folly, in order to sacrifice the next morning to retrieving the mischief?

in shopping, they can spend them in the careful revision of such finery as they already possess, to see what amount of time and trouble will suffice to make them appear, at least, to dress beyond their means. If they cannot attend the great marts of gossip, they can gossip over the neighbourhood and the village; if forced to stay at home, still useful occupations may be avoided; embroidery, with its sham title of *work*, will afford ladylike means of getting rid of the obnoxious hours, and night will come, if not to summon them to haunts of amusement, at least to mark that they have succeeded in drawing a day nearer to the grave, without running the risk of leaving one mark of their flitting through life.

That a welcome should be given to any form of pleasure or novelty is most natural, when the mind is unoccupied, and time hangs heavy as a curse upon the idle hands. Many girls, fit for better things, are reckless in the search of amusement for want of something else to do. Their lives are so devoid of real interest and animating pursuit, that in their utter weariness the hard toil even of other classes often seems enviable.* In many a noble dwelling the daughters of the house are feeling that all the luxury to which habit has made them insensible would be well bartered for anything that promised some change or excitement. Let those reproach them for being excited about a ball or an archery-meeting, who feel that they could themselves live in cheerful content with nothing to look forward to, and nothing to do. Truly there is less promise in the mind that sinks down satisfied with such an existence, than in the restless and discontented.

What but the vacuity of life I have been complaining of makes so many young women fall a prey to superstitious devotion? Marriage is their only hope of change, and some years pass away without any prospect of marriage that suits their wishes or their ambition; the world affords them no mental stimulus or active occupation, and they sink back disappointed and sick at heart, often without knowing why. Then the Church steps in and claims them. If they happen to 'sit under' an evangelical preacher, he sends them to distribute tracts and teach Sunday-schools; if they live within the rule of a High-Churchman, the ecclesiastical autocrat relieves them of the burden of their time, together with that of their conscience. He rules their lives for them; he portions their days

* Far below the class here spoken of, we find the same thing. Farmers' and tradesmen's daughters are as idle, and therefore suffer still more from *ennui* than the daughter of the peer, since they have not her resources of society. If the hands are not constrained to work, earnest head-work alone can save from living for pleasure.

and hours to certain exercises and forms of devotion; he sanctifies a frivolous occupation by allowing it to be devoted to the Church, and forth-
with the embroidering of altar-cloths takes a place among the serious
duties of life.   He forbids thought, and exacts obedience; there is no
room for doubt or hesitation about charities, or duties, or pursuits,—he
has regulated them all, and the sternness of the interference is softened by
the dignity of the office, which makes the man almost sacred.   The vague
suffering of the former condition cannot be more emphatically set forth
than by the fact that this abnegation of all self-guidance is a welcome
change.   Doubtless great worth and ability in many men belonging to the
class I am here speaking of have aided their power, but its great secret
lies in the predisposing influences of leisure and idleness over minds longing for occupation and excitement, without knowledge or mental power
for self-regulation.   The Church provides the occupation, and dispenses
with the labour of self-regulation,—the weak, the enthusiastic, and the
timid naturally fall under its dominion.

When we see the establishment of nunneries under a thin Protestant
disguise, daughters enticed away from home-duties and affections,—
women of property persuaded to renounce all the responsibilities of property, and to devote it blindly to objects over which they are to have no
control,—young minds broken down by ecclesiastical despotism, till they
renounce Protestant freedom of conscience as a burden too heavy to bear,
and feel happy only when their shackles are riveted by that power which
enjoys at least the prescription of centuries for destroying human liberty;
when, I repeat, we see these things going on around us, are they not
evident signs among many others how much is at fault in the mode of
existence which leaves some of life's dearest possessions at the mercy of
any strong impulse from without?

But not only do education and society do nothing to prepare young
women for a position which requires all the resources of well-disciplined
minds, but parents themselves do much to aggravate the evil by the needless dependence in which they keep their unmarried daughters.   There
can be no doubt that, in the great majority of cases, the utmost kindness
is intended; there is only an utter want of perception that the life which
was both fitting and pleasant at eighteen, is distasteful ten years later, and
to many almost unendurable ten years after that.   Perhaps they are not
expected to own to so many years; the farce of youth is enjoined upon
some, and played, alas! by many more; but characters, and tastes, and
spirits cannot be made to fall into the part,—a dreary discontent settles

upon the unoccupied mind, and society, to which they are no longer an ornament, laughs at what is supposed to be mere disappointment at not having married. It does not care to trace there the effects of a want of expansion in all that gives healthy energy to life, of the vain attempts of the full-grown creature to take exercise in a go-cart, or to find rest in the infant's crib !

I know all that can be said about care and protection, &c., and much of it is true, up to a certain age; but why set so high a price upon protection at an age when it is no longer wanted ? shackling a woman's movements in the name of a guardian care which she is more fit to exercise over those who protect her, than to be still the object of herself? Domestic arrangements, and all the detail of life, must necessarily be settled according to the parent's habits and wishes, and none could certainly desire to see that tender care, which sons engaged in professions cannot give, withheld by daughters ; but we might wish to see this lavish, unselfish devotion allowed more often to assume the form of a free-will offering.

It is common to see young women, and women no longer young, kept dependent in every movement, with a moderate allowance for dress, from which not unfrequently they hardly dare to economize for any other object. They are without the power of making a journey,—of asking a friend to stay with them,—of making acquaintance,—of engaging in any undertaking, unless it is to cost nothing beyond their own trouble, and to square exactly with the most trifling arrangements of the rest of the family,—without even a quiet room of their own in which they may if they choose enjoy solitude and their own pursuits.* If seclusion from society suit the taste of the elders, the younger must share it ; if, on the contrary, the taste for gay society survives, or if it is supposed that in that society is still to be found the best chance of accomplishing that one great object, an eligible match,—then, no matter what the daughter's own tastes may be, she must run the giddy round of pleasures that have ceased to please. In such cases many a one spends yearly in a court dress, sums

---

* One of the most common forms of petty domestic oppression is that of insisting that a whole family, whose tastes and occupations are different, shall spend the day in the same room, generally under pretence of the extravagance of burning many fires! In many wealthy houses, the daughters could no more venture to order a fire in their own apartment, to avoid the talk and interruptions of the drawing-room, than they could order from the bookseller a work from want of which some favourite study is arrested. Truly, economy of books and of peace to read them, go fitly together with the lavish expenditure on dress which is characteristic of the present day!

which would have purchased the indulgence of tastes she has no means of gratifying. If the parents' pursuits happen to be different, then she may indeed enjoy access to better things,—books, paintings, lectures, all means of acquiring knowledge may be at her disposal ; but I am contending for the one right of disposing of her own time according to her own tastes. In many cases, perhaps in most, parents could not afford to give their daughters more money than they actually give or at least spend upon them, according to their own views of what is suited to make them happy; but the same money spent really as we please ourselves, gives a very different amount of enjoyment. Fortunately, benevolent schemes have commended themselves under the name of piety, and thus have been allowed to pass in many instances when other pursuits equally innocent would not have been permitted to occupy time and attention ; and it would be curious to inquire from how many nervous complaints, from how much morbid feeling and mental suffering bordering more nearly on derangement than we like to allow, young women have been rescued by ragged-schools, district-visiting, Dorcas societies and the like ? But why, we may well ask, should the field of activity be limited to things of this nature ? why must the mind be forced in very weariness to seek relief in occupations for which it often has no natural bent ?

Looking calmly at that system which has added so needless a weight to the inevitable evils of the position of unmarried women, combined with the custom of making such miserable provision for daughters that they can scarcely, when left to their own resources, maintain themselves in respectable independence in the station to which they belong, how can we avoid the suspicion that, so far as it has any purpose at all, that purpose is to make them think that almost any husband who offers them a home of their own is preferable to remaining unmarried ? Mothers have indeed made the sad confession that they feared the influence of a happy home, of strong sisterly affection, even of the love given to themselves and so dear to them, in lessening the willingness to marry ; in other words, lessening the artificial inducements to embrace without affection a course of duties which, had affection spoken, would have had more than attraction enough. We may hope that such instances are rare ; but whether purposely designed or not, how many uncongenial marriages are owing to the mode of life we have been considering ?

The excitement of a flirtation is a perfect Godsend in that inactive colourless existence. Where there is no active life of thought, fancy and feeling are easily stirred, and mere novelty has an unspeakable charm.

When the probable result of this exciting pleasure is forced upon a girl's mind, when she sees it will soon rest with herself to fix her destiny for ever, or to fall back into the dreary nothingness that went before, an interval of painful hesitation ensues. In presence of such a reality she tries to reflect. She is quite aware that she knows nothing of the man's real character to make her trust to him for happiness, nothing of what he is, even as a companion, apart from the pleasant nonsense of flirtation, still less what he may be as a master, when the task of seeking to please has changed hands; but she believes in his love, and she has read in many a novel of woman's power to make what she pleases of the man who loves her. Does she love him? Perhaps she is really incapable of answering that question; at least she loves nothing better. The new language she has heard from him has stirred some feeling she knew not before, and the weary monotony of life is instinct with a new animation that looks like happiness. If she cannot even so far deceive herself, she tries to view the subject *rationally*, according to the world's notion of rational marriages. ' Love is not the first consideration in life,—she ought to marry, her parents expect her to do so,—an honourable useful life is thereby opened to her,—a woman cannot choose, she may never have an opportunity of making a marriage that would offer more chance of happiness,—if she refuses, there is only the same routine, so dreary before, more dreary now, to fall back upon,' &c., &c. ; and so she decides, and while the turmoil lasts, which seems to surround a wedding on purpose to drown thought, she may not again pause to ask whether she is not paying too high a price for escape from a life which, if devoid of interest and activity, was free from the perils she may be blindly encountering now.

It does not suit either the pride of women or the vanity of men to own how often the former marry with no stronger feeling than this, but let any who have had frequent opportunities of looking behind the scenes deny it if they can. And how should it be otherwise, when not only by the unavoidable conditions of life marriage is a girl's one hope of improving her position, of taking an honoured place in society, and having a course of active duties and interests before her; but when every artificial aid is given to enhance the desirableness of that position, and to depress the one in which she stands already? Truly it may create astonishment that so many marriages are even as happy as they are. The ideal of happiness, indeed, is not high, but there is more cheerfulness and content than might reasonably have been expected. Fortunately, the world occupies a man, and children engross a woman's mind, and thus very often neither has leisure to accuse the other of the disappointment of better hopes or higher views of life.

If we require further proof that fear of poverty, undue constraint, and the want of definite occupation and station in society, are what drive many women to look to marriage as their only resource, let us view the case of those who have independent fortunes in their own hands, and see how well contented they generally are with their position. No false inducements urge them to marry, and unless moved by real affection they remain single. In far less favourable circumstances the same thing may be seen. Some, on whom has devolved the charge of a brother's or sister's children, daughters placed by their mother's death at the head of their father's house, these show no dissatisfaction with their condition as single women, and adhere to it in cheerful activity. Yet they have, perhaps, a course of arduous duties which, at first sight, seem to stand in hard contrast to the lot of girls who are living in leisure and freedom from care under their parents' roof; the difference is in the definite position with its duties and responsibilities, and the consideration that attaches to it. To some natures, and perhaps the highest and most gifted with all the rich capacities of life, it is better to have thought, felt, and acted, ay, even to have struggled and suffered, than to feel the deadness of an existence sheltered from woe and care, but sheltered also from activity and joy.

But, however, parents may remove all needless restraint, the position of single women generally must remain a confined and inactive one; the remedy must come from within. Mental resources, and energy to use them without external stimulus, are the surest safeguard against the depressing influence of circumstances we cannot control. And next in importance to this would be the advantage gained if girls were educated to contemplate single life as the probable, marriage only as the possible, contingency. Under ordinary circumstances, every woman has certainly the power to marry at one time or another if she chooses; but since she has, and can have none but a negative choice, it is far from likely, if feelings, character, and tastes are to be considered, as well as mere worldly considerations, that she will have it in her power to make a really suitable marriage. It would, then, be far better if girls were brought up to look at this side of the question, and to feel that their lives must really be what they can make them themselves; useful or frivolous, cheerful or embittered with discontent, according as they have strength of mind to contend against narrowing influences, and to keep a high and independent bearing.

There is little fear that the young creature, full of warm affections, should form too bright an anticipation of a lonely life; but it is well that she should feel that no evils that life can bring can equal the humiliating misery of a wife's dependence without perfect esteem; or even,—with some natures at least,—the cares and sufferings of married life, without that earnest love in whose fulness is abnegation of self.

If mothers talk lightly of marriage before their daughters, if it be represented as an inevitable necessity in which, if one form of suffering be avoided another must be endured,—as a lottery in which no one can know what will fall to their lot,—as *made in Heaven*, by which phrase all earthly prudence is supposed to be rendered needless,—if these are the sentiments idly uttered, while novels fill up the picture, no wonder that the young are either worldly or rash. The higher the ideal of married life in a woman's mind, the safer she is from being swayed by any of the social considerations which give an undue importance to marriage, and tempt so many to barter their lives for station and independence.

A high ideal of married happiness involves a high standard of manly character. The low opinion of men so commonly expressed by women, combined with their servile submission to the faults they ridicule and condemn, are calculated to produce the worst moral effect on any young mind. If it were true and unavoidable that men must be ill-tempered, despotic, selfish, unjust to women's claims, that their wives must be content if no positive vice or unkindness makes their home wretched, then indeed there is little use in anything we can say or do; there is merely the alternative of the evils of loneliness and the sufferings of marriage. But since such a view is as false as it is mischievous, it is sad indeed that the errors of individuals, made worse by the insane flattery of women's submission, should be covered over with this assumed cloak of universal failing. Doubtless there are faults which education and position make very common, and which must therefore to some extent be made allowance for. For instance, from childhood a woman is trained to care for others, a man to struggle for himself and by himself; to her, then, there is self and *home*,—to him, self and the world. Thus while a selfish, like a hard woman, is one who sins against nature and her own position; some selfishness in a man only shows that he has been more affected than he ought to have been by the circumstances and temptations of his position. And so with a certain degree of sternness or despotism of temper. We cannot forget the rude schooling of men, the hard trials, the weary toil, the competition awakening fierce passions in some, gloomy despon-

SOME PECULIARITIES OF WOMAN'S SOCIAL POSITION.   271

dency in others, the mortifications and disappointments which lay low the hopes of years of honest ambition, the disgust at the world too apt to become hardness in the heart that has been homeless for years;—all these we, by our quiet fireside, with our gentle nurture and our home sympathies around us, must bear in mind when we estimate the characters of men, and remember that in the order of Providence the differences are intended to harmonize, and that while every woman who respects herself will shrink from the degradation of bowing down before faults that lower her esteem, because marriage offers her a better worldly position; yet that we owe no scanty measure of gentle forbearance, and sympathy, and high-souled cheering to those whose labour and power shelter us from the rude contests of life; and the tribute of earnest reverence to the noble qualities that come out unscathed from an ordeal we ourselves have never known.

Some of my readers may think such remarks wander far from the purpose of a work on Education, but I would remind them that right views on these subjects are part of the education for life, which, if a mother does not give to her daughter, she will get in most questionable forms from the experience of her own narrow circle of observation. And should this girl, in her complete ignorance of the realities of life and of the characters of men, marry early, she may be blind to the consequences of what is before her very eyes, neglect opportunities of good, aggravate evils, and seal her misery day by day through the course she takes when first her ignorant delusions begin to melt away. By senseless submission to what no human being should bear from another, or by no less senseless severity towards faults which her narrow code of morals exaggerates into vices, she may be hourly undermining every chance of future happiness.

There is one other subject of growing importance in the present day on which I think a careful mother would wish to influence her daughters' opinions; this is the subject of employments for women. It is a large and in many respects a painful one, and which could not be discussed here; I would only offer a few remarks on some views which appear to me erroneous, and deeply affecting the condition and the happiness of women.

After what I have said of the real difficulties that belong to the position of unmarried women, it seems almost needless to state how gladly I should welcome anything that opened a career of honourable activity to those who from circumstances must desire to better their condition, or who are mentally unfit to find cheerful enjoyment in intellectual pursuits.

But I own that at present the difficulties appear to be too great to be removed. Some fresh openings may perhaps be found for those who work for subsistence, especially for those who suffer under that dire form of calamity, genteel poverty; we can at any rate have no doubt that whatever overthrows an obstacle which mere custom or conventional notion had placed in their way, and leaves them free to exert their industry wherever they can find room for it, is an immense benefit. But for women who are above this necessity to find any career of activity analogous to men's professions, seems to me utterly chimerical, and of very questionable advantage could it be found. What society wants from women is not labour, but refinement, elevation of mind, knowledge, making its power felt through moral influence and sound opinions. It wants civilizers of men, and educators of the young. And society will suffer in proportion as women are either driven by necessity or tempted by seeming advantages to leave this their natural vocation, and to join the noisy throng in the busy markets of the world. It is true that the unmarried are to some extent thrust by circumstances out of their natural vocation; they cannot fulfil it as they should, and much of their power to do good remains undeveloped; but this is only one of many social evils to which as individuals we can but submit.

As society is constituted, I might perhaps say, as human nature is constituted, I see no relief from without to a condition which in many or even in the majority of cases is hard to bear; therefore it is that I think it wiser to bid women look for resources within, and learn to infuse the excitement and vigour of intellectual activity into their inactive lives, than to look beyond to one small opening or another, which is but like pulling out here and there a brick from the massive wall that hems them in. The favourite scheme of the present day which has been recommended by so much high-minded benevolence, namely, the unpaid labour to be given by educated women in hospitals and other institutions, appears to me as little productive of good as any other which the pressing feeling of the evil of too much leisure has suggested. That gifted woman who, in a moment of national depression and sorrow, stepped forward to set the example of noble self-devotion to a lofty purpose, must stand as an exception when we speak of those who, with the best and purest motives, wish to follow in her steps. She possesses all that is required in a leader,—in one who is to organize a system and enforce its execution; and I have no doubt that as superintendents the services of gentlewomen may often be most valuable; but I cannot think that in ordinary occasions it is desirable that women of education and refined habits should devote themselves to menial offices, however ennobled by charity.

It is not any degradation in the office of personal attendance that I would have them shrink from, where such attendance is called for in private life, in nursing the sick of any condition, who in one way or another are thrown upon their care; I would have them turn from no office that can give relief,—from no service which is required. We all know that in the illness of those who are dear to us, such service is a privilege we are jealous of relinquishing; nothing can weary or disgust, for

True affection scorneth nicer hands.

But when there is not this call of either feeling or duty, I cannot persuade myself that manual labour is the right field of occupation for an educated class. There is work enough for brain and hearts to do without working the hands that are not required to earn bread, and thus entering into cruel competition with those who do labour for subsistence. It is an ungracious task to search for mixed motives where the course is apparently noble and disinterested; but I must confess that I believe the weariness of a vacant, listless life, impels more young women to wish to follow the example of Miss Nightingale than any consideration of the superior value of unpaid labour, or any consciousness of possessing like her that decided vocation and power which marked her out from early youth as fitted for a wider sphere of action and influence than home life can afford. Doubtless others will rise up, and they also will find a work to accomplish, and in every such case we must wish them God-speed in the noble career they have strength and moral courage to open for themselves; but setting aside these exceptional cases, I repeat that there is yet much to do in developing the resources of ordinary home and social intercourse, and that I would earnestly desire to see these tried to the utmost before young women of refined and cultivated habits are persuaded that their own happiness and the good of society are best consulted by undertaking servile duties, while numbers to whom manual labour is their only resource are starving around them for want of employment.

With regard to other professional occupations for women who are able to live without them, the subject is full of practical difficulties which would make the hope of such occupation almost nugatory, even were all conventional obstacles and all doubts of women's capabilities removed. What parents, for instance, who can support their daughters in comfort and refinement at home, would willingly see their youth exposed unprotected to the chances of any public career?　And as regards them, we may apply the word public to whatever takes them among chance companions, and brings them into the rough contact of business.　It is said that such is not the time when the occupation is required, that it is not desired to see young girls engaging in that mode of life; then we must suppose a certain number of years to pass, and that at thirty, perhaps, young women are to begin their professional career; in other words, to give to men the advantage of ten or twelve years' experience in advance of them, added to all the other advantages they already possess.　What chance would they have in such competition? and yet this is what they must encounter, since in the present crowded state of every profession and form of business, men themselves find great difficulty in obtaining employment, and the additional labour that would thus be thrown into the market would only succeed in reducing the remuneration for head-work, already so ill paid.

But the tone so often adopted in the advocacy of woman's claims has been far more injurious than any such plans can be in themselves.　The boast of equal capacity supposed to be jealously kept in the background by unequal privileges would have been an ill-judged one to bring forward at any time, but is most ill-judged, because most ungracious now, when old prejudices have been abandoned, and the claims of women in so many ways are advocated by the ablest men in an unselfish, generous spirit.

And where are the proofs of this boasted equality?　No obstacles have sufficed to prevent men rising by their own untiring energy and gifts of intellect from obscurity and want, to fame and power; but where are the works of genius that should be the title-deeds of woman's claims?　Alas! why expose ourselves to hear this question asked in pride and derision? The dream of equality was, I believe, born of wild political theory, which would have founded government on a basis as unsound as that on which some women now seek to found social reform.　It is said that privileges and unjust laws alone create inequality; but until the weak are equal to the strong, till the soft and feeble are equal to the steadfast and energetic, and fools and ignorant men to the learned and the wise, how will that equality of rights be maintained for a month, yea, even for a week, among any score of human beings?　Truly there seem to be few facts written in more indisputable characters on the face of the universe, in all its aspects, moral, physical, and intellectual, than inequality.　As regards the competition between men and women in professions, one form of natural difference which none can deny, that of physical strength, would almost suffice to decide the question.   Supposing women on the average to have equal ability with the average of men, how many are physically capable of enduring the close application, the severe mental toil, which men undergo?   And if one person is strong enough to bear continued exertion for ten hours, while another endowed with equal mental power is tried to the utmost by eight hours, can they contend in any form of labour with equal chances of success?   Evidently not.

But supposing the contest to be to a certain extent successfully carried on,—suppose that many able, energetic women are able to make their way among a throng of competitors, many of whom are, undoubtedly, their inferiors, it will be well to consider at what cost the triumph is achieved. What will be the moral effect on society, what the influence on woman's happiness, when men have ceased to be protectors to become rivals, when the appeal to their generosity, to the loftier qualities of their nature is dropped, leaving only the eagerness and irritation of contest, coupled with probable contempt for oft-defeated competitors?   What hold will then be left to women save through those feelings which must always give them power for a time, but on which the pure and high-minded will never base their influence?

If we would try to read Nature instead of indulging in proud dreams or ambitious theories, we might discern in the best feelings of men and women towards each other the relation in which they were destined to stand, and see how they harmonize with the difference of both mental and physical power between them.   Is not man's affection in its noblest form, blended with the feeling of protection and sheltering care, due to her he loves?   Does he not eagerly brave toil and danger, and bear the heaviest burdens of life, sooner than the loved one should feel the ' breath of heaven visit her cheek too roughly ' ?   And what, on the other hand, is the character of woman's love?   Is it not a clinging, trusting tenderness?   Does it not live in the sunshine of an approving smile?   Is it not so engraven in her nature to seek a superior in the man to whom she gives her affection, that the commonest fiction of woman's love is to believe in that superiority where it never existed?   Does she not through her own pure thoughts and exalted feelings invest with ideal excellence the being whose love seems a privilege she scarce believes herself worthy to enjoy?   What woman ever truly loved, and did not rejoice to merge her will in that of him she has chosen, the playful empire of holiday hours forgotten in yielding tenderness when a sacrifice is required, or an act of devotion is to be accomplished? Do not the proud become humble, the gifted diffident? Do not the ambitious lose their ambition in dreams for another? And are not all these so many signs that woman's nature spontaneously looks to man as a superior, and when she does not find him so, their natural relations are disturbed, and out of harmony?

The character of the subjection is quite another question; and that which has been so prevalent in the world is perhaps no less opposed to nature's laws than the theories of equality and female emancipation. But these are individual questions, and each woman has her own fate in this respect in her own hands. Acquiescence in the superiority of man as a general law does not imply acknowledgment of superiority in particular instances. This or that woman, or a large number of women, may be as superior to an equal number of men as gifts of intellect and worth of character can raise them above sordid or homely natures and feeble minds; but the law remains the same, and each woman is free to avoid binding herself in willing subjection where she feels that the order of Nature is reversed.

The whole discussion of comparative claims, and powers, and rights, may well be dismissed as philosophically unsound, and practically vain and unwise. The different qualities of the two sexes do not stand in antagonism, but the one nature is the complement of the other; improvement in the one is not a conquest over the other, but rather reflects good upon it, and blends with the higher qualities it has tended to foster. So far as it is true that 'Nature is a stepmother to women,' it is of her that we must complain, or to her that we submit; but whatever improvement her unalterable laws do not prohibit we shall attain, not by angry clamour or proud contention, but by proving our own capacity; by rendering ourselves fit for higher social and domestic influence; by entering into the true spirit of that moral and intellectual vocation through whose power the very forms of thought, and feeling, and action in another generation wait in great measure to be moulded by the hands of women.

THE END.

London: Printed by Smith, Elder and Co., Little Green Arbour Court, Old Bailey, E.C.

Lightning Source UK Ltd.
Milton Keynes UK
UKHW012252121219
355304UK00001B/14/P